THE HOWARD GOSSAGE SHOW

OTHER WORKS BY THE AUTHORS:

STEVE HARRISON

How To Do Better Creative Work (2009)

Changing The World Is The Only Fit Work For A Grown Man (2012)

How To Write Better Copy (2016)

Um Conto De Duas Cidades [A Tale Of Two Cities] (2019)

Can't Sell, Won't Sell (2021)

DAVE DYE

Advertising Unplugged (2024)

THE HOWARD GOSSAGE SHOW

And what it can teach you about advertising,
fun, fame and manipulating the media

Steve Harrison and Dave Dye

A
STUFF
from the
LOFT
BOOK

ADWORLD
PRESS

First published in the United Kingdom in 2024 by
Adworld Press

ISBN 978-0-9571515-3-6

This book is dedicated to Alice Lowe
or "Big Al" as Howard Gossage affectionately
called his diminutive yet dynamic colleague.

She knew him when he was an out-of-work
copywriter in 1954 and was one of the last people
to see him before he died in July 1969.

She was the driving force behind
the agency and held its disparate parts - and its
sometimes dissolute chief - together.

For fifty years thereafter, she kept the
Gossage flame alive - first with the unpublished
biography, *The Wizard of Ads*, then with
her archive - which now resides in The Bancroft
Library at University of California, Berkeley.

I had the privilege of knowing her, the benefit of
her guidance and the pleasure of her friendship.

I hope that Dave and I have done justice to Alice
and her colleague and comrade, Howard.

WHY WE WROTE THIS BOOK
- AND WHY YOU SHOULD READ IT

In 2012, I wrote a biography of Howard Gossage: *Changing the world is the only fit work for a grown man.*

I thought I got a good handle on how influential and innovative he was. Not the least in how he pioneered the idea that advertising has a role to play in changing society. He set an excellent example: fighting the flooding of the Grand Canyon ... helping found Friends of the Earth ... and funding his own idealistic campaigns.

But maybe, as that book's title suggests, I gave too much emphasis to his cause-related work. His agency did ground-breaking charity and *pro bono* ads, but they were a fraction of those he created for his commercial clients.

And I don't think I did justice to that work - or his great talent.

I'd been working on a reappraisal but writing another book diverted my attention. Then, in the summer of 2022, Jeff Goodby asked me to curate Alice Lowe's Gossage Archive.

That wonderful woman had left box upon box of Howard's writing, correspondence, photos and ads with the request they be sorted and sent to the Bancroft Library at University of California, Berkeley. The days I spent working at this golden seam renewed my appreciation of Gossage's commitment to, genius for, and love/hate relationship with his craft.

When Dave Dye asked me to write a post on Gossage for his blog, "Stuff from the Loft", I got the chance to showcase Gossage's body of work - and what it can teach us today.

The first convert was Dave himself whose reaction was, "Some of this is better than Bernbach, it deserves to be a book".

And that's what it's become. But one that has been greatly enhanced by Dave's encyclopaedic knowledge and his forensic archival skill. For example, as part of his research, Dave has gone through every issue of Gossage's medium of choice, the *New Yorker* magazine, from 1955 - 1966. The overall result: Gossage ads that haven't seen the light of day for over 60 years.

We both believe it's time they were seen again. And urgently.

In recent years, creative agencies seem to have lost confidence and direction. And, as a result, their audience. Where once the public could recite the ads they saw and hum the ones they heard, the work is now unnoticed or avoided.

Which is why we all need Gossage.

Decades before digital, he understood the importance of interactive advertising - and the need to speak directly and intelligently to his audience. He also knew that the ad was just the first part of a media strategy and aimed to involve all other forms of media in amplifying his message.

He also grasped the importance of fame. *The Ad Contrarian*, Bob Hoffman, recently said that if he was a client his three word brief would be "Make us famous". As you'll see, Gossage did exactly that for his clients, his "gurus" and, most definitely, himself.

Finally, for an industry that has lost the ability to engage its audience, this book has one other vital message: we are in showbusiness. Gossage was a media-savvy entertainer who used humour, intrigue, outrage and flights of fancy to win his audience's attention, affection - and response. The result was highly effective advertising that people looked forward to seeing. Not only was it enjoyable - it enhanced their lives.

Imagine being able to do that nowadays. In your agency.

Well, Dave and I chose the title because *The Howard Gossage Show* reflects the respect he had for his audience and the talent, flair and exuberance he brought to the work he presented to them.

We hope you come away not only entertained but also enthused. And that maybe you'll want to go out and do to your industry what he set out to do to his. Because, as we hope you agree, changing the advertising world is fit work for grown-ups, too.

CONTENTS:
THE HOWARD GOSSAGE SHOW

BEING
YEARS
AHEAD

I was talking about Howard Gossage to Rory Sutherland - a big fan (and Vice-Chairman, Ogilvy).

When assessing Howard's legacy, Rory jumped straight to a showbiz analogy: "Howard Gossage was the Velvet Underground to David Ogilvy's Beatles and Bill Bernbach's Rolling Stones. Never a household name but to the *cognoscenti*, a lot more inspirational and influential."

Howard would, I imagine, have been delighted with the favourable comparison but appalled at the company Rory had him keeping.

A political liberal but culturally a conservative, he hated pop/rock music. While it's true that the epoch-defining San Francisco Trips Festival, headlined by The Grateful Dead, was organised in Howard's offices, the stage manager there was the much more radical Jerry Mander (who we'll be meeting shortly).

No, Howard was much happier at home, standing in front of his KLH sound system, conducting his favourite symphony or sonata.

Does that sound dull? Don't you believe it. He was, according to journalist turned novelist Tom Wolfe, a "mad impressario" - and one who orchestrated the most audacious and innovative campaigns from his podium in his Firehouse agency.

Indeed, as you're about to discover, Howard Gossage was as much an entertainer as he was an adman. And it was this combination that made him a star.

How big a star?

Well, let's hear what Rory's *cognoscenti* have to say.

Jeff Goodby is convinced "the best of Gossage is the best advertising ever done." It was Goodby who turned Dan Wieden on to Gossage. And he was equally impressed: "When I read what Gossage was doing, I felt Kennedy and I had found a kindred spirit. He was kicking over the apple cart and doing everything with a searing honesty. Yet he was doing it all fifty damn years ago!"

To complete the plaudits from three of the modern era's most successful creative agency chiefs, here's Alex Bogusky: "His ads were different from anything I'd seen in that they lived at a level just above advertising. They were conversations with an audience and often designed to let the audience speak back. As Crispin Porter's work moved online we used to sit around and wonder, 'What would Gossage do?'"

What Gossage did back in the 1950s was reject the repetitive, finger-in-the-chest school of advertising that characterised the industry's output in that decade. And in its place he pioneered ways of communicating that the rest of the industry didn't cotton on to for another 50 years.

To understand how and why, let's begin with his most famous aphorism: "People read what interests them, and sometimes it's an ad."

By that he meant it wasn't enough to try and do a better ad than those you were competing against for the reader's attention. Doing better advertising was easy because most of it was, in his words, "bad enough to rot the paper in which it appeared".

Gossage set out to say something that was as interesting or, better still, more interesting than the articles and features that surrounded the ad. So he strove to come up with ideas that had as much "stand out" as the most sensational, topical or trending news report.

How did he achieve this?

Well, it is true that David Ogilvy and Bill Bernbach shared his disdain for the dominant hectoring style. But, whereas they had a narrow focus on advertising's creative properties and possibilities, Gossage looked beyond the industry to harness the galvanising ideas of his age.

INTERACTIVE ADVERTISING SIXTY YEARS AGO

First up, MIT mathematician Norbert Wiener.

Norbert who? Well, just think of him next time you ask your client for "feedback" or get "in the loop" by logging on to Instagram, Facebook or TikTok.

Both terms are fundamental to Wiener's theory of cybernetics – the idea that both man and machine work best when immersed in flowing loops of information that give feedback on past performance and guidance on future direction.

Here is Gossage describing his feedback-driven approach: "We do one ad at a time. Literally, that's the way we do it. We do one advertisement and then we wait to see what happens, and then we do another advertisement. There's feedback in every ad."

To get that response, he put a coupon on his press ads: asking people to write in with a request for more information … a comment … to take part in a competition … to win some crazy prize (a kangaroo, perhaps) … or just to ask their opinion.

Gossage used information loops and feedback to create a whole new style of advertising. As his colleague, Jerry Mander, told me: "He had a term for it: he called it 'interactive'."

Gossage himself said in a 1961 lecture: "The key word is involvement. That is where we start. Whatever we do in the promotion of anything should be involving both of the people inside and the people outside … involvement is the essential concept. And it is an efficient one. Because if a concept is involving it gains a life of its own, it becomes social organism; it acts, reacts, and interacts through people: it produces activity and energy."

Every campaign was aimed at generating this involvement and energy. And, as you'll see, by asking people to participate, he was creating his own analogue communities.

The fact that his ads appeared almost exclusively in the *New Yorker* magazine helped reinforce the camaraderie. Or should we say Friend-ship. Jeff Goodby thinks so:

"He was friending people long before anyone friended anything … It's like he was communicating to the world through the *New Yorker* as your Facebook page."

THE MASTER OF THE "PSEUDO-EVENT"

In explaining this intimacy, Gossage said: "I can't write to everybody, just somebody." Yet, while he considered each ad to be one-to-one communication, he also knew how to use mass media to maximum effect.

To achieve this, he channelled the insights about mid-Century culture that made a best-seller of Daniel J. Boorstin's *The Image: A Guide to Pseudo-Events in America.*

According to Boorstin, these synthetic happenings were flooding the media and blurring the line between real news and what we now call marketing spin.

As he explained, the pseudo-event "is planted primarily (not always exclusively) for the immediate purpose of being reported or reproduced. Therefore its occurrence is arranged for the convenience of the reporting or reproducing media. Its success is measured by how widely it is reported".

Have another read of that: "Its success is measured by how widely it is reported".

In Gossage's mind, an advertisement was just the start of a media strategy that could include PR and every available form of unpaid for media. Indeed, for him, an ad's fundamental purpose was to generate publicity and get newspapers, radio, TV and other media to amplify its message.

Sound familiar? Of course. Because if you look at most big Cannes Lions Award winners of the past 15 years you'll see they are simply an expression of what Howard Gossage called his "ad platform technique". Think of all those award entry films with their "millions of likes and shares". All their epilepsy-inducing quick cut references to internet news feeds and TV coverage.

Hundreds of Cannes, D&AD and One Show winners have been emulating Howard Gossage and building their reputations on a creative strategy he perfected before they were born.

FAME

Gossage was ahead of the game in another way. By merging advertising with publicity, he was making his clients famous.

It was one of Gossage's contemporaries, Jeremy Bullmore, (they both started as copywriters in mid-'fifties) who alerted us to the pulling power of fame in his 2001 essay: *Posh Spice and Persil*. He said, "Just about the only thing that succesful brands have in common is a certain kind of fame … for most human beings, fame not only holds a powerful fascination but bestows an incalculable value on anything that enjoys it."

More recently it took another of the industry's wise men, Bob Hoffman, to remind us: "I believe the most probable driver of brand success - and the central principle of communication that we advertisers can control - is fame. Not brand meaning, or relationship building, or brand purpose or any of the other fantasies that the advertising and marketing industry has concocted … If I was the ceo of your company - or if I was your client - I'd call you into my office and give you a three-word brief: 'Make us famous'".

Of course, all advertisers strive to gain and retain the attention of their prospects and customers. But, as Jeremy explained, to be famous is to be talked about by people way beyond those who might be interested in buying the product or service. In other words, by the general public and not just the target market.

Gossage knew this. And, as you're going to discover, he got people who had never flown in their lives, talking about Qantas … who didn't have a driving licence, talking about both FINA petrol and Rover cars … who were baffled by anything more complex than a cigarette lighter, talking about *Scientific American* … and who were teetotallers, talking about Rainier beer, Paul Masson wine and Irish whiskey.

And it wasn't just products and services that Gossage brought to the general public's attention.

In Part 2 of the book you'll see how he made a "53 year-old Canadian English teacher, grey as a park pigeon [into] an international celebrity and the most famous man his country ever produced."

Then, in Part 3, there's our grand finale as Gossage turns the spotlight on to perhaps the most brilliant of his creations: the manufacturing of his personal brand - again thirty years before such a concept gained common currency.

FUN

But if Gossage's pursuit of fame was forward thinking, his *modus operandi* was rooted in the past. In fact, way back to advertising's early days when, in the words of the doyen of Account Planning Paul Feldwick, "the pedlar sang."

It's Feldwick's contention that advertising's roots lie with the hucksters, hawkers and barkers who pulled the punters and pushed their wares by being entertaining. It was their shtick that made them stand out from the crowd and their message memorable. In a riposte to today's proponents of Social Purpose and their po-faced propaganda, Paul tells us that advertising works best when it is fun.

Gossage was a throwback to those days. As we'll see, he came from a long line of vaudevillians - show people who worked the same side of the street as the back-of-the-wagon salesmen Feldwick has in mind.

This chimed with Gossage's own background in Sales Promotion - which, I hope its practitioners won't be offended when I say, has been largely concerned with the grabbing of the public's attention by fair means or foul.

As such, he never subscribed to the dominant styles of advertising, and particularly hated Rosser Reeves's repetitious hard sell. Nor did he share David Ogilvy's faith in research and rules. He even dared to doubt Bill Bernbach's genius, describing him as "a very dogmatic sort of man, firmly convinced that his way is the only way."

Randall Rotherberg compared Gossage to the others in *Where the Suckers Moon* and concluded that for him "Success in advertising depended not on expertise in consumer manipulation, but in media manipulation. It required self-promotion, daring, a flair for hype and, equally important, a venue."

For Gossage, that "venue" was his medium of choice, the *New Yorker* magazine, and its readers - not his clients - were his priority.

As he said, "The buying of time or space is not the taking out of a hunting license on someone else's private preserve but is the renting of a stage on which we may perform."

And that's what Gossage was, a performer. In his hands, John E. Kennedy's "Salesmanship in print" became "Showmanship in print."

Not that he was against selling. As his partner Jerry Mander explained: "It always had a commercial intent. That is to say the idea had to acquaint the reader with something about the product or, at the very least, the point of view of the advertiser."

But he did it in such a way that the reader never knew where the ad was taking them. They were enjoying the ride too much to notice.

So that's the drum roll: interacting with the reader ... being newsworthy ... making his clients famous ... and keeping everyone entertained. You will find elements of all four in every ad in this book.

But let's not lose sight of the fact that you'll also be seeing the work of one of the finest and most prolific copywriters of all time.

KEEPING THE AUDIENCE INVOLVED AND ENTERTAINED

If you've any knowledge of Gossage's work, "prolific" may be news to you.

You might be familiar with the handful of Eagle Shirts, Whiskey Distillers of Ireland, FINA and Sierra Club ads for which he's famous.

But in his exhaustive search through contemporary newspapers and magazines, Dave has discovered hundreds for those clients and others like Aalborg Akvavit, NUCOA, Paul Masson, Rover Cars, Rainer Ale and Blitz-Weinhard.

Then there are campaigns that will be new to even Gossage's biggest fans: The San Francisco Redevelopment Agency for instance, and his work for Salada Tea.

As you're about to see, the vast majority are elegant and eloquent long copy ads that would take the most gifted of copywriters several days to fashion and finesse.

But then again no one before - or since - has written ads like Howard Gossage. With his rhetorical questions, digressions, asides, colloquialisms and quips, Gossage mastered a naturalistic, conversational approach to copywriting. His ads aren't ads, they read like personal letters to a target audience of one.

In an ad industry that took itself - and its output - very seriously, he was defiantly irreverent. And unconventional. From his first ad (the first humorous bank ad) to his last (with an 168 word headline) he and his brilliant art director, Marget Larsen, experimented with tone, type, pagination and layout.

The man himself reckoned it took him 48 hours to have the idea and complete the copy for one of his ads (that was six days at 8 hours a day). He also said that he didn't trust other writers and, until Jerry Mander joined in 1966, Gossage wrote pretty much all the agency's output.

This vast catalog of work casts new light on Gossage's decision to get out of advertising after 1966. The conventional wisdom is that he grew to despise the industry and its primary role in a materialistic, consumer society. I've come to think there's a simpler reason.

The guy was exhausted.

We'll get to that later. For now, pour yourself a Paddy (his favourite whiskey) and prepare to be entertained. The Howard Gossage Show is about to start.

Gossage was 30 when he began his advertising career, selling air-time for Oakland radio station, *KLX*. While there he went to night school to learn copywriting under Herb Reynolds the master of the "soft sell". He put this to good use when he moved to Charles R. Stewart Advertising whose main account was the Bank of America. His first brief was for a series of half-column ads for the front page of the *San Francisco Chronicle*. Today they look pretty tame. But they were probably the first whimsical bank ads ever (it's still a small field).

He started with "A" and got as far as "L" when a bank stockholder complained about the frivolous tone. The advertising was canned. Only for more letters to come in asking "whatever happened to 'M'?" So the campaign survived. Alas, Gossage did not. He was fired soon thereafter. Incidentally, the illustrations were done by a kid called Lowell Herrero. He'd done Gossage's caricature in a San Francisco nite club. So Gossage hired him for the campaign. Not for the last time, Gossage had discovered someone who went on to much greater things. (Google the chap.)

His next job was as Sales Promotion Manager at another radio station: *KCBS*. The truth is, most of Howard's successes were not conventional ad ideas but sales promotional. Like the one you're about to see that made his name.

In 1955 he was working as a junior writer at Brisacher, Wheeler & Staff when he asked his boss: "You got some account that's a real dog … that no one wants and that doesn't amount to a damn?" He was given Qantas airline and quickly came up with a dozen or so whimsical trade press ads.

Then came the brief that changed his world. At the time, TWA airlines was spending $1.5 million on full colour ads publicising their new jet aircraft, the Super-G Constellation. Qantas had the same big plane but a tiny budget.

So, to counter the opposition's corporate chest-beating, Gossage suggested a competition inviting people in the travel industry to come up with a name for the new Qantas plane. Here's the ad to your right:

I've said that Gossage's ideas were very sales promotional - and this is no exception. Indeed it is typical Gossage: inviting the reader to join the fun and thereby making Qantas memorable. But there's a clever bit of positioning here, too. As he later

TWA SUPER-**G** *Constellation*   QANTAS SUPER-**?** *Constellation*

BE THE FIRST ONE IN YOUR BLOCK TO WIN A KANGAROO!

WE ARE pleased as Punch with TWA, and we are sure that Henry Dreyfuss is, too. For TWA have chosen for their domestic service the same splendid *super* Super Constellation that Qantas flies across the world to 26 countries on 5 continents. Dreyfuss designed interior and all.

And we admire the special name TWA have chosen for their version of this ultra Super Constellation. Super-G just, well, *fits* as a designation. We wouldn't mind using it ourselves, seeing they've done such a bang-up job of advertising it, but would that be playing the game?

What we really want is a name of our *own*, neat, evocative, alluring; a name calculated to send hordes of tourists to their Travel Agents. Tourists brandishing fistfuls of large notes and demanding to be sent via Qantas Super Constellation to Sydney, London, Johannesburg, Tokyo, or wherever. Wallowing in Henry Dreyfuss luxury at several hundred miles an hour. We need a name, and *your help*.

So we will be much obliged if you will fill out the attached entry blank and send it to us. Neatness and legibility will count for next to nothing, but please try to spell Qantas without a "u". You pronounce it* but you don't write it.

First prize is a real, live Kangaroo; second prize is a stuffed Koala Bear (*live* koala bears are very picky eaters—you wouldn't want one); and 98 prizes of one boomerang each. In addition, *every entrant* will receive, absolutely free, an explanation of why there is no "u" in Qantas. All set?

NEXT WEEK . . . *an idyllic domestic scene!*

*As in Qality.

explained: "One thing I did try to do was give a warm and distinctive personality to the line; something we hoped would be interpreted as peculiarly Australian in its candor, forthrightness and hospitality."

It all worked so well, they decided to run a few ads in the *New Yorker*. I imagine they thought it might look more suited to the magazine's style if they used an artful illustration.

You'll notice that the above ad finished with the promise of something for "Music Lovers!". It came in the shape of:

All this and didjireedoo!

5 FEET

BLOW HERE

This is a didjireedoo

What has happened till now: Qantas, the world's fifth longest airline and a real sweetheart of an outfit, is somewhat panicky because while they fly to five continents in the same splendid planes TWA uses in domestic service they don't have as grand a name as Super-G Constellation. They need help.

III.

Those of you who are music lovers will be delighted to know that second prize in our sensational Super Constellation naming contest has been changed from a stuffed koala bear, which makes virtually no sound at all, to a didjireedoo, which sounds terrible even when played by a virtuoso. There are no didjireedoo virtuosi on this continent. To remedy this, we have arranged with a Sydney music teacher for a correspondence course. After a few lessons it would be awfully nice if you invited the first prize winner and his kangaroo over for a recital. The kangaroo may like it.

Some of you may not know what a didjireedoo

is. It is probably the world's oldest musical instrument (Qantas itself is very old—the oldest airline in the English speaking world. But wiry).

It is played by the Australian aborigines at their Corroborees, or hoe-downs, and reportedly adds a great deal to these occasions, though it is hard to see why.

Now, here's the way the prizes stand: First Prize is a real, live kangaroo; Second Prize is a didjireedoo; Third Prize is a stuffed koala bear; Fourth through 28th Prizes are Qantas old school ties; 29th through 100th Prizes are boomerangs with instructions for oiling.*

While we don't like to be always complaining, it has come to our attention that some of you are not pulling your weight in this contest. Certain people—we mention no names, *but we know who you are*—have not sent in their entries. This is absolutely your last warning. DO YOU UNDERSTAND? MAIL THIS COUPON TODAY!

*and everybody gets an explanation (suitable for framing) of why there is no U in Qantas. Incidentally, you pronounce the Q as though there *were* a U—as in Qality.

QANTAS

AUSTRALIA'S OVERSEAS AIRLINE

OFFICIAL ENTRY BLANK—LAST CHANCE!

QANTAS
Union Square, San Francisco, California

FOLKS!!!!

I don't know what to say except that I feel terrible about not having been more prompt. You know how I am about writing anyway. Well, I don't know whether you really care any more but here is what I think you ought to call those swell Super Constellations of yours:

_____

NAME_____

ADDRESS_____

All entries must be postmarked before midnight October 1, 1955

Gossage used the tried and tested techniques of classic direct response and mail order ads. But he also parodied them. For example, take a look at the last paragraph of the above ad. That's some call to action!

Then came the ad announcing the winner. Even as the campaign closed, Gossage was striving for a response (and a smile - see the spelling in the return address.)

NEW YORK CHILD WINS KANGAROO, HER FIRST!

THE gigantic Qantas Super Constellation naming contest is history and things just couldn't have worked out better, about the winning name we mean. It's got everything: class, verve, brevity! Especially brevity and class. And when you come right down to it, there's too much verve in the world today anyway, we say.

We won't keep you on tenterhooks any longer, the name is SAM! Not "Super Sam Constellation," just plain old Sam. And don't try to read any hidden meaning into the letters S-A-M, for it's no use. Sam. Oh, there's consternation at TWA tonight you can wager.

Of course there *may* be a little difficulty working this gracefully into our advertising. (Fly Qantas to the South Seas, Australia, the Far East, South Africa; or conversely from London to Rome, Cairo, Singapore, and around that way. All by Sam, splendid, speedy, Henry Dreyfuss-decorated Sam.) We'll think of something. If you think of something first please feel free to write. We insist on it, if it comes to that.

So, to you, Dena Walker Seibert, small daughter of Mr. and Mrs. Wilson Seibert, 17 Stuyvesant Oval, New York 9, N. Y., our Grand Prize Kangaroo and gratitude. Good show.

Now, in the travel trade category Norma Davis of the San Jose (Calif.) Travel Service wins a kangaroo as well. There'll be hopping in the streets of San Jose, one feels sure. And a kangaroo to Mr. Warren Lee Pearson, Chairman of the Board of TWA, so they can start their own contest. We personally feel that they're stuck with "Super G," though. After we started our contest, they were nice enough to say we could use "Super G" if we wanted to. Well, maybe we will from time to time, if it just happens to fit. And they can use Sam.

If you're wondering why all the kangaroos, the fact is we got carried away. And after all, it's that first kangaroo that's tough; the ones after that come easy. Winners of didjireedoos, stuffed koala bears, Qantas ties, and boomerangs will be told by mail. Congratulations, all!

Well, there are probably some die-hards around who think that Sam is an absolutely terrible name. Although we're a big corporation (ltd., but not very) we're willing to listen. We're not querulous*, so if you want to toss in your two bob's worth, pro or con, even at this late date, go on ahead. A simple "Sam!" or "Sam?" scrawled on a post card will do nicely. Qantas, Union Square, Sam Francisco.

Pronounce the Q as in Qantas.

QANTAS

AUSTRALIA'S OVERSEAS AIRLINE

There was then a follow-up campaign aimed at communicating Qantas's range of destinations across five continents. It has all the hallmarks of Howard Gossage. But it does seem like a flight of fancy too far. If you can work it out then you deserve a kangaroo or, at the very least, a didjireedoo.

ARCHDUKE! COMMUTE TO THE NEW JOB BY SUPER-G CONSTELLATION!

[What has happened ere now] Qantas, in a flight of Graustarkian derring-do, changed the name of the South Pacific to the Archduchy of Qantasylvania. This stroke has not set too well with our competitors; they thirst for revenge. Unless we act with all speed the rascals will, we feel sure, impose their own names on the five continents that Qantas serves; viz., North America, Europe, Asia, Africa, and Australia. You wouldn't want that, would you? Of course not. What we've got to do, then, is scoop them and rename the continents ourselves. We need your help.

Meanwhile, back at the Archduchy . . .

II.

High jinks at the castle! Village girls are strewing the courtyard with hibiscus and the Qantasylvanian Silver Cornet Band—actually a pickup group of beach boys who grouse continually about the high collars and puttees—is practicing up on "To Thee, Qantasylvania," "Hail, All Hail, Vernon VI" (you), and "There'll Be A Hot Time On The Old Atoll Tonight." Your subjects await.

The winner in our Rename the Continents Contest becomes hereditary Archduke (Archduchess) of Qantasylvania and receives a magnificent, emblazoned coat of arms and a family tree going back 22 generations. Plus a stuffed koala bear 5 feet high. Wow! You will, in addition, be empowered to dispense sinecures to relatives, appoint dignitaries and purveyors, and fill vital government posts with fawning friends. Just the other day we interrupted a protocol discussion (whether your mother-in-law, the Dowager Countess, outranks Commander Whitehead) between the Court Chamberlain and the Grand Vizier to tell them to start cleaning out their desks.

Second prize is a Fijian kava bowl, just the thing for convivial occasions, and not unattractive. Third prize is a stuffed 14-pound New Zealand Rainbow Trout; we're sorry we couldn't get a large one for you, but that's the breaks. Fourth through 100th prizes are smallish koala bears and Qantas old school ties, one of each. *All* entrants will receive Certificates of Citizenship in Qantasylvania suitable for framing.

OFFICIAL ENTRY BLANK — *Deadline December 1, 1956!!!!!*   *Qantas, Union Square, San Francisco*

Gentle Lieges: Look, we hardly have room in the Great Hall to feed the heirs apparent and the Dowager Countess much less a lot of serfs, vassals, and old family retainers. Still, it's not every day one becomes an Archduke (Archduchess). I think the continents should be renamed:

NORTH AMERICA:_____ AUSTRALIA:_____

AFRICA:_____ ASIA:_____ EUROPE:_____

Australia's Overseas Airline   **QANTAS**

NAME:_____

ADDRESS:_____

CITY:_____ STATE:_____

P.S. Say, I hear the Pacific Area Travel Association is giving away an island. Could you send me one of their contest blanks?

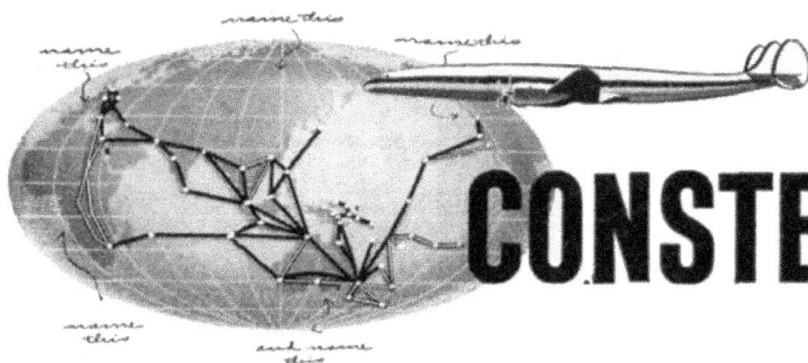

NOW, BECOME AN HEREDITARY ARCHDUKE!

Daydream no longer, thanks to Qantas

Much as we hate to panic the Rand McNally people, we have decided to change the name of the whole South Pacific to the Archduchy of Qantasylvania!

As might be imagined, this brilliant maneuver has stunned the competition. No need to tell of their office lights burning far into the night. We fear reprisals, for, in addition to superb Super-G Constellation coverage of Qantasylvania, Qantas global air routes also serve 5 continents. And we just know that unless we beat them to it, some other airline is going to rename North America, Africa, Europe, Asia, and Australia on us. We need splendid new names for these continents, too, and fast.

I.

Imagine the thrill of being the hereditary Archduke (or Archduchess) of Qantasylvania! All you have to do in this latest, greatest, Qantas contest is "Rename the Continents" and win glory *in perpetuo* for generation after titled generation of your family. You and the wife will while away many happy hours poring over the *Almanach de Gotha* and the Philadelphia Telephone Book selecting suitable mates for the kids.

Yes, for family fun an archduchy beats TV a mile. And think of the intrigue! Why, your brother-in-law, hereafter known as Count Rudolf the Ruthless, will be forever hatching plots. He's already acting a bit strange, we'll wager. So keep in solid with the Minister of Police, the Captain-General of Dragoons, and the old Gypsy fortune teller is what we say.

The prizes then: The one who submits the best new names for the continents succeeds to the archdukedom and receives certain magnificent gifts and perquisites which we shall enumerate shortly along with the 99 other mouth-watering prizes. *All* entrants will be given a handsome certificate of citizenship in Qantasylvania, suitable for framing. Do not delay, enter now and often!

OFFICIAL ENTRY BLANK !!   Qantas, Union Square, San Francisco, California

Sires: Another crisis, eh? Very well, here's what I would name the continents if they were mine:

EUROPE:_____ AUSTRALIA:_____ NORTH AMERICA:_____

ASIA:_____ AFRICA:_____

NAME:_____

ADDRESS:_____

CITY:_____ STATE:_____

QANTAS
AUSTRALIA'S OVERSEAS AIRLINE

P.S. Can't we please arrange to get Rudolf exiled?

And at the end of all these fun and games came:

J. DUNLAP McNAIR EMERGES VICTORIOUS

Our Judges: Mr. Stan Freberg; The Rev. Bob Richards; Parky the Tidy Kangaroo*; Miss Anna May Wong; Mr. Stanley Slotkin, Pres., Abbey Rents

The latest, and very likely the last, Qantas contest is history. Its purpose, you may recall, was to secure new and fitting names for the 5 continents served by Qantas Super-G Constellations; new names as appropriate as Qantasylvania is to the Pacific area.

After much soul searching, the judges awarded First Prize to Mr. J. Dunlap McNair of 512 South Talley Avenue, Muncie, Indiana for his entry: Natasq (North America); Antsaq (Australia); Sqanta (Africa); Asqant (Asia); and Tanqas (Europe). The panel felt that these names, while a trifle odd, had each the virtue of containing the same letters as the name of a prominent global airline. The next move is up to Rand McNally.

Many promising entries were discarded because of certain confusion factors; i.e., naming all the continents Texas, or Boston, or Zimmerman.

Thus Mr. McNair becomes Vernon VI, Hereditary Archduke of Qantasylvania and, in addition, wins permanent custody of a 5-foot stuffed koala bear, a lovable but bulky creature weighing 7 stone 5 (103 lbs.). Chief Judge Freberg has volunteered to deliver it in person. Good on him, we say.

In his coronation statement Vernon VI, a metallurgist for the Indiana Steel & Wire Co., Inc. and a family man, said "There are indeed few Archdukes in Muncie."

The other 99 winners will be notified by mail. Congratulations, all!

*Parky hops around Griffith Park Zoo, Los Angeles, picking up paper and stuffing it in her pouch. An example for us all. While not actually a judge, Parky performed yeoman duty collecting the ballots.

QANTAS *Australia's Overseas Airline*

Thereafter, client and agency opted for a more straightforward approach to promoting the five continents and destinations.

Here's one Gossage created alongside graphic design genius Saul Bass.
Bass also designed the "I DID IT" badge Gossage promised to his respondents.

DESIGNED BY SAUL BASS

*To fly around the world is a shining personal achievement; the greatest inner space travel experience.
The Qantas route takes you clear around—no shortcuts; to Europe, Africa, Asia, Australia, New Zealand,
the South Seas (and America, too)—and in exceptional comfort. The fare for this Everest of grand tours
may surprise you considering what even ordinary shining achievements cost. If you will write
"Grand Tour" on a card to us, we'll send you some splendid folders that tell all. If you can't wait
that long ask your travel agent (if you don't have a travel agent we can recommend some near you).
Write Qantas, Union Square, San Francisco, California.*   **AUSTRALIA'S OVERSEAS AIRLINE**

QANTAS

...uh, would you like an "I Did It" badge to commemorate some other shining personal achievement?

After Qantas, Gossage moved on to writing zany radio spots with actor/comedian Stan Freberg. First for Contadina Tomato Paste and then Pictsweet Frozen Foods.

Here's Howard writing about his favourite script and how he met Freberg:

```
Gossage, Chap. 17: 3


of a friend, and I found a radio commercial Freberg and I did once,

but never produced, as I recall. I guess I like it best of anything

we did:

First Man: Hey, I got that jingle worked out for Pictsweet Frozen

Foods.

Second Man: Good.

First Man: Do you want to hear it?

Second Man: Sure.

First Man (sings): Pictsweet, Pictsweet, something something something

                   something, something

                   Pictsweet, Pictsweet, something something something

                   something, something

                   Lah dah dah dah dah dah dah dah you and me

                   Lah dah dah dah dah dah dah dah quality too

                   Pictsweet, Pictsweet, where the mountains meet the

                   sea.

First Man: Well, how did you like it?

Second Man: Fine, but I'd tighten up those lyrics a little.

     I met Freberg when I was trying to get somebody to do a jingle in

a simple, direct, child-like fashion. It's very hard to find that

sort of thinking. I remember running through all the first returns in

Qantas contest to name a Super-Constellation, and desparing of find-

ing a decent entry; you'll see in a moment what happened.

     Well, then we started Weiner & Gossage. In 1963 I bought Joe out,

and Robert Freeman, an art director I've known since the end of

the war, went on the masthead.

     Our agency opened up in a second-hand firehouse, where it still is.

     People in the business probably feel we haven't made much progress

in all that time; we started with ten people, and in ten years we've
```

While that Pictsweet spot was Gossage's favourite, he and Freberg had their biggest success with their Contadina Tomato Paste radio commercials - which are widely regarded as the first ever intentionally funny radio spots.

As you'll see over the coming pages, both men refused to take the industry seriously. And you could interpret much of Gossage's work as a parody of advertising's conventions. He knew the formulae but he also knew that the audience knew the formulae, too. And he happily sent up the standard techniques whilst always capitalising on their effectiveness.

Indeed part of the appeal of Gossage's ads lay in the high jinx that ran counter to the high seriousness that characterised much of the advertising of the day.

In the mid-'fifties, the same impudent, iconoclastic humour was to be found in MAD magazine. It, too, regularly spoofed Madison Avenue's output.

This send up of the Contadina campaign - featuring Freberg - is taken from its pages. As a beacon of irreverence in a conservative media landscape, it's not surprising that Freberg contributed articles and Gossage was himself a MAD reader.

I'm the guy who puts eight great tomatoes in that little bitty can!!

All day long – squashing, squooshing, slamming, splattering . . . Yeccch, what a mess! Thank goodness it's my last week at this gooky job! Next week my company starts using a new-type can, and I'll be able to stuff those eight great tomatoes in that little bitty can without ending up looking like I've been attacked with a meat cleaver. Mainly because our new "little bitty can" expands into a "biggy wiggy can" like an accordion.

Concertina EXPANDING CAN

Gossage also turned his hand to another of the agency's smaller and, one assumes, otherwise neglected accounts: Aalborg Akvavit. The idea here involves inviting readers to apply for a permit to add ice to their Aalborg (the Danes would never drink it that way). Have a read and you'll see a portent of what was to come a year or so later with his work for the Whiskey Distillers of Ireland.

I saw it with my own eyes
I heard it with my own ears
and a piece of it *fell in my Aalborg*

Before we get into the hard sell, may we remind you that Aalborg Akvavit is a dry, delicious, 90 proof, crystal-clear schnapps, made in Denmark from 100% potato neutral spirits and has delightful overtones of caraway. Aalborg Akvavit should be tossed off neat and ice cold (keep the bottle in the refrigerator). Unfortunately, Aalborg is very mixable and an alarming number of people are adulterating it with other things like vermouth, tomato juice, tonic, and/or ice cubes. In the face of what may well be the end of akvavit-as-we-know-it, we are trying to keep a sense of proportion (4 to 1 in the case of Danish Martinis). We don't want to be like Chicken Licken, the nursery story prophet of doom.

Chicken Licken, while standing under an oak one day, was smote on his tail by an acorn. He panicked. "The sky is falling down!", he blubbered. "I saw it with my own eyes, I heard it with my own ears, and a piece of it fell on my tail". But we digress. If you are curious to know how Chicken Licken made out, we'll send you the unexpurgated Chicken Licken in a plain wrapper.

The point here is that we may be making an iceberg out of an ice cube. It's not as though we were going to call the law on you if you want to drink akvavit and tonic or Aalborg-on-the-bergs. Good gracious, no. We're grateful if you just hustle out and buy a bottle. We don't care what you do with it. Buy two and use them for book ends. But somewhere along the line we'd like you to try akvavit our way, frigid and straight, eating a little smorrebrod or other light snacks as you go. We'll not give up on this; the last word has not been heard.

Although we have instructed all bartenders to give you Aalborg any old way your heart desires, there may be a few isolated die-hard purists. Play safe and carry your Aalborg Ice Cube Permit wherever you go. Protect yourself.

33

In those ads he's starting a community by asking people to send for their "Ice Cube Permit". Later we'll see much the same thing with the "Pride" and "Profit" badges for Irish whiskey drinkers. In the next series, you see Gossage experimenting with another idea: the editorial style Q&A format - which he later used to good effect in his FINA campaign.

Some thought-provoking enquiries about Aalborg Akvavit

Dear Aalborg:

I am an earnest seeker after truth. I note in your last advertisement that dry, delicious, crystal-clear, 90 proof Aalborg Akvavit is made in Denmark of 100% neutral spirits distilled from potatoes, and that it has a marvelous flavor of caraway. This is fine but I need more assurance before I go down to the store and buy a bottle. Is Aalborg Akvavit really all that good? Is it simply great? I've got to know.

CONSTANT READER

What do you mean "simply"?

Dear Aalborg:

Does one pronounce Akvavit the same as aquavit?

IN THE PUBLIC WEAL

More or less. Akvavit is the Danish spelling of aquavit. Aquavit is from the Latin aqua vitae, which means "water of life." Yes, indeed.

Dear Aalborg:

I have heard about certain spirits that apparently have no flavor, where the only way you know you've had one is when the waiter gives you a check. Is akvavit like this?

ANXIOUS

No, but don't believe everything you hear. What have you heard?

Dear Aalborg:

How do you make a Danish Martini?

EARNEST-SEEKER-AFTER-TRUTH

Actually, we'd rather you didn't. You know what we say: buy a bottle of Aalborg —put it in the refrigerator— and forget about it until it gets ice cold. Then drink it straight, eating smorrebrod (see below). Some fun. If you're serious about Akvavit Martinis, the best mixture is 4 akvavit to 1 dry vermouth, a ratio which makes the vermouth people very happy. Instead of an olive or an onion, you just shout "Skaal" Pronounced Skoal.

Dear Aalborg:

Me, I love to experiment. However, is it true that no Dane deigns to dilute akvavit with ice cubes or anything else?

WELL-WISHER

Almost. When he does it's a great deign. Have you tried a Bloody Dane (tomato juice & Aalborg)? Or a Danish Screwdriver (orange juice & Aalborg)? Or Aalborg and Tonic? Or a Biørn Collins?

IT'S NOT TOO LATE TO GET YOUR AALBORG ICE CUBE PERMIT

While as you know we totally disapprove of diluting akvavit with ice cubes, we recognize that you in the New World have strange and bizarre tastes. If you must drink it on-the-rocks, or in Martinis, etc., it's better that you have our permission than go sneaking around behind the barn. With the Permit, any bartender will issue you ice cubes for your drink with no questions and at no charge.

Aalborg Akvavit

P. O. Box 240, New York 46, New York

Please send me my Aalborg Ice Cube Permit. Also, have you any of those booklets on smorrebrod left? I don't want life to pass me by.

NAME ....

STREET......................................

CITY......................................

STATE......................................

90 proof · 100% potato neutral spirits
Briones & Company, New York 4, New York

Questions and Answers about Aalborg Akvavit... a public service feature

Dear Aalborg:
Let me understand you. A Danish Boilermaker is a shot of ice cold Akvavit taken neat, in one quick movement, and followed by a leisurely beer, right? What do you do when the bar does not keep a bottle of Aalborg on ice? You follow me.
PURIST

A knotty but not insoluble problem. Do this: order an Aalborg on the rocks, twirl the ice around for a minute and then toss it off, meanwhile keeping your beer at the ready. This is not absolutely ideal but you won't miss the 5:38 while waiting for the bottle to freeze, either. Life is full of compromises; if only all of them were as tasty as this one.

Dear Aalborg:
Is Aalborg Akvavit a crystal clear, dry 90 proof schnapps with delightful overtones of caraway? Just thought I'd ask. It is dry, isn't it?
PARCHED

Dry! If Aalborg Akvavit were any drier it would be brittle.

Dear Aalborg:
While browsing in a liquor store recently, I noticed that the management had mistakenly placed Aalborg Akvavit in the liqueur section instead of over with the gins and vodkas where it belongs. Shall I organize a Citizen's Protest League?
FRIEND OF AKVAVIT
(pronounced Ah-kwah-veet)

No. It is far more in keeping with our genial traditions that you point out the error in quiet but firm tones. Also buy a bottle so they won't think you're just a do-gooder.

Dear Aalborg:
One of your ads recommends 3 to one as the proper proportions for a Danish Martini, another suggests 4 to one. And in one place you call Aalborg Akvavit and tomato juice (which I have tried and find supremely delicious) a Bloody Hildegarde, while a later advertisement refers to a Bloody Dane. I'll grant that you haven't wavered on akvavit and tonic yet. Still, such indecision is disconcerting.
PUZZLED

Isn't it though?

AALBORG AKVAVIT
P. O. Box 240, New York 46, New York

Please send me my Ice Cube Permit and the free recipe folder.

NAME:

ADDRESS:

CITY: STATE:

90 PROOF • 100 PER CENT POTATO NEUTRAL SPIRITS
BRIONES & CO . INC . NEW YORK 4. NEW YORK

AALBORG AKVAVIT WITH A BEER CHASER IS UPTOWN IN DENMARK
But they don't call it a boilermaker

It's hard to know where to begin. We've spent so much time telling you how we'd rather you didn't drink Aalborg Akvavit in Danish Martinis, on the rocks, or as Bloody Hildegardes, etc., that now, when we want to get down to cases (though we'll be very happy if you just buy one bottle to start), it's not easy.

For one thing, the Danish way of drinking akvavit has a marked resemblance to what you term a "Boilermaker". This, our informants tell us, is not regarded in the New World as a particularly high-toned refreshment, but we refuse to pussy foot. If what we are drinking is a Boilermaker, so be it. A Danish Boilermaker.

Why you should drink Danish Boilermakers

As you know, akvavit, pronounced (ah-kwah-veet) should be taken neat, ice cold, and in one quick toss. With a shout of "Skaal!", pronounced Skoal.

If you don't have a nice glass of beer alongside you will find yourself either, A) twiddling with your watch chain while waiting for the other fellows to order another round or, B) not waiting for the other fellows, which may or may not be a good idea.

Beer tastes wonderful with Aalborg. Everybody says so.

Also, when you order a Danish Boilermaker, do it in a clear, resonant voice. Don't mutter. Everyone will look around and, if you are reasonably well groomed, immediately assume you to be a connoisseur. Social success and prestige lie in this direction. Your whole life may be different thereafter. If this happens, please write to us and tell us all the details.

Notice for die hards

For those who still wish to drink akvavit as they would gin or vodka, the Aalborg Ice Cube Permit is now in its seventh printing. We will send you one if you insist.

Aalborg Akvavit
P.O. Box 240, New York 46, New York

I want to think about the Danish Boilermaker. Meanwhile send me my Ice Cube Permit, Chicken Licken Confidential (and mixed drink folder).

Name

Address

City State

BRIONES & CO . INC . NEW YORK 4 . NEW YORK 90 PROOF • 100 PER CENT POTATO NEUTRAL SPIRITS

By the late 1950s, Gossage had mastered his discursive, conversational style of writing and his ability to generate response and publicity. He'd also set his stall at entertaining his readers. But this unconventional approach made him virtually unemployable. When he left Brisacher (or Cunningham & Walsh as they'd become) in early 1957, he got a job as, not a writer, but an account executive tasked with generating awareness of the NUCOA margarine brandname.

Gossage was again working with Freberg and the gag here revolved around hiring a novice pilot (Dudley) to write NUCOA in the skies above Manhattan.

For four days he mispelt the name as NOCUA ... NAUCO ... NOCAO until eventually getting it right: NUCOA on Friday afternoon. All of which was covered in the daily radio ads. Here's the launch ad - in advertorial style. Note Gossage doesn't mention the brand name at all in the ad.

NEW YORK'S PRAYERS GO WITH YOU, DUDLEY!

Victor A. Dudley accepts best wishes from coach and handler Stan Freberg on eve of skywriting record attempt.

As millions of Gothamites anxiously scan the skies next Monday at High Noon, a pioneer, alone but for his frail airplane, will attempt what no man has done before. Victor A. Dudley, the unassuming sign painter from North Hollywood, California, will make his assault on the orthographic barrier by skywriting a five-letter Anglo-Saxon word over New York.

"I'm skywriting to win," says the intrepid Coast birdman, "I intend to wrest victory from 'The Lady in Blue,' as we say, and I sure hope one and all are gazing upwards as I spell the word right."

A self-admitted amateur, Dudley has never previously indulged his hobby at a height greater than 25 feet. "I got all my theory from a correspondence course and my field work with a crop duster friend on weekends. I traded him signs for lessons. This is the first time I've worked with smoke but I guess it can't be too different from DDT."

"Besides," he adds, "if I don't skin it the first time I'll try again at Noon the next day, and so forth. I don't have to be back at the drawing board till a week from Monday."

Cautioning against overconfidence is Dudley's coach and trainer, Stan Freberg. "One word doesn't seem like much to a sign painter," he states. "I only hope he doesn't overwrite, that's all. Bear in mind that except for 'GOOD EATS' and '50—GIRLS—50,' my boy has never written anything shorter than 'EVERYTHING MUST GO!,' 'PRICES SLASHED!,' or, 'IF YOU LIKE US TELL YOUR FRIENDS IF NOT TELL US'."

Up-to-the-minute pre-takeoff reports on the Dudley Trials will be heard on most New York radio stations throughout the morning beginning next Monday, July 29. They will continue until Dudley either joins the ranks of such aviation immortals as Dr. Hugo Eckener, Wiley Post and the Wright Brothers . . . or retreats homeward to his brushes lonely and discredited.

Well-wishers may send cards, letters, floral offerings, toast, and baked potatoes to Dudley Headquarters, The Best Foods Inc., 1 East 43rd Street, New York.

Godspeed, Dudley!

(Advertisement)

The week-long campaign was a hit, except with the NUCOA management who objected to someone so publicly messing with their precious brand name.

Once again, Gossage was fired. And, in October 1957, he was left with no alternative but to start his own agency: Weiner & Gossage.

Weiner & Gossage had a couple of beer accounts amongst their first clients. They were small local breweries with small budgets but Gossage aimed to get them national fame (or in Rainier Ale's case, notoriety).

First, Blitz-Weinhard Beer. It was brewed in Oregon - otherwise the home of pine forests and, erm, pine forests. To celebrate the 1959 Oregon Centennial, Gossage launched a campaign to plant a little bit of Oregon in the centre of Manhattan.

As *TIME* magazine reported: "It had nothing to do with beer, but thousands of readers blitzed Blitz with pleas for trees giving the company a word-of-mouth circulation far beyond the cost of the ad".

You'll find the ad overleaf but first, look at this Gossage and Freberg spectacular. In 1959, they created a 25 minute stage show, *Oregon! Oregon!* Gossage wrote the text and dialogue while Freberg hired Billy May - who usually worked with the likes of Frank Sinatra, Ella Fitzgerald and Nat King Cole - to arrange and conduct the music. There was also an LP, recorded in Hollywood (of course).

Not surprisingly, it came in three times over budget - and the client walked soon thereafter.

OREGON! OREGON!

A CENTENNIAL FABLE IN THREE ACTS.

STARRING

STAN FREBERG

BOOK, MUSIC, AND LYRICS BY STAN FREBERG
ADDITIONAL DIALOGUE AND LYRICS BY HOWARD GOSSAGE
STORY FROM AN ORIGINAL PLOT BY M. GOOSE
MUSIC ARRANGED AND CONDUCTED BY BILLY MAY
FEATURING JUD CONLON'S RHYTHMAIRES

CAST
IN ORDER OF APPEARANCE

HARRY . . . . George Spelvin
DAVID . . . . Stan Freberg
WITCH . . . . Helen Kleeb
CALIFORNIA FRUIT INSPECTOR . Byron Kane
TRUCK DRIVER . . . . John Frank
RALPH . . . . Stan Freberg
CINDY . . . . Barbara Ford
GOVERNOR . . . . Lou Merrill

Sound Effects: JAMES MACDONALD   Jacket Design: LOWELL HERRERO
Bottle Courtesy: BLITZ WEINHARD CO

KEEP TIMES SQUARE GREEN!

(A MODEST REFORESTATION PROPOSAL FROM OREGON'S LARGEST & ONLY BREWERY AS A FITTING PRELUDE TO OREGON'S GLORIOUS 1959 CENTENNIAL CELEBRATION)

Just picture what reforestation will do for Times Square! Cool and green, teeming with game, salmon swimming up-Pepsi Cola sign to spawn. Why, it'll be a little corner of Oregon! But let's start at the beginning...

The name of our Beer is Blitz. Perhaps we'd better spell it out for you so you won't claim later that you got us confused with some other beer because we mumbled. Please pay attention now: B-L-I-T-Z. "Beer" is spelled just the way it sounds.

It's hard to say what good this priceless knowledge will do you because you haven't a prayer of getting Blitz in New York or wherever it is you live; unless you live in the Northwest, which we doubt. Especially we like to think of you as living in New York, probably because we've always wanted to get ourselves a nice, old city with marvelous possibilities and do things with it. One thing we won't do is sell you our magnificent Beer of the Bright Cascades (as we say) although it'd very likely be the making of you.

You couldn't afford it. Supposing you rationed yourself to one bottle a day; the airmail alone would stagger reason. For that kind of money you could move to Oregon and enjoy Blitz postage-free for the rest of your life. And some life! You'd love it. Oh, yes you would, too.

We realize that some of you may not be able to come to Oregon right this minute. To you stranded unfortunates—wherever you are—we will send, absolutely free, an Oregon Do-It-Yourself Kit: an Oregon Fir tree and directions for planting. If you don't have a yard or a window box you might set them out in pots on the street*, though not under marquees; they grow to be a couple of hundred feet tall. Please let us know where you decide.

Like in front of Lindy's; a delicatessen that may in summer wear a nest of robins in its hair.

SEND FOR YOUR FREE TREE TODAY!

Blitz-Weinhard Company
1133 W Burnside Street, Portland 9, Oregon

Dear Blitz:
I'd love an Oregon Fir, please send one. I'll let you know where I plant it and how it's doing. Give my very best to the gang. Sincerely,

Name_____

Address_____

City_____State_____

P.S. You understand why I can't come to Oregon right now—I can't get out of that thing on Thursday. I'll be there for the '59 Centennial you can bet.

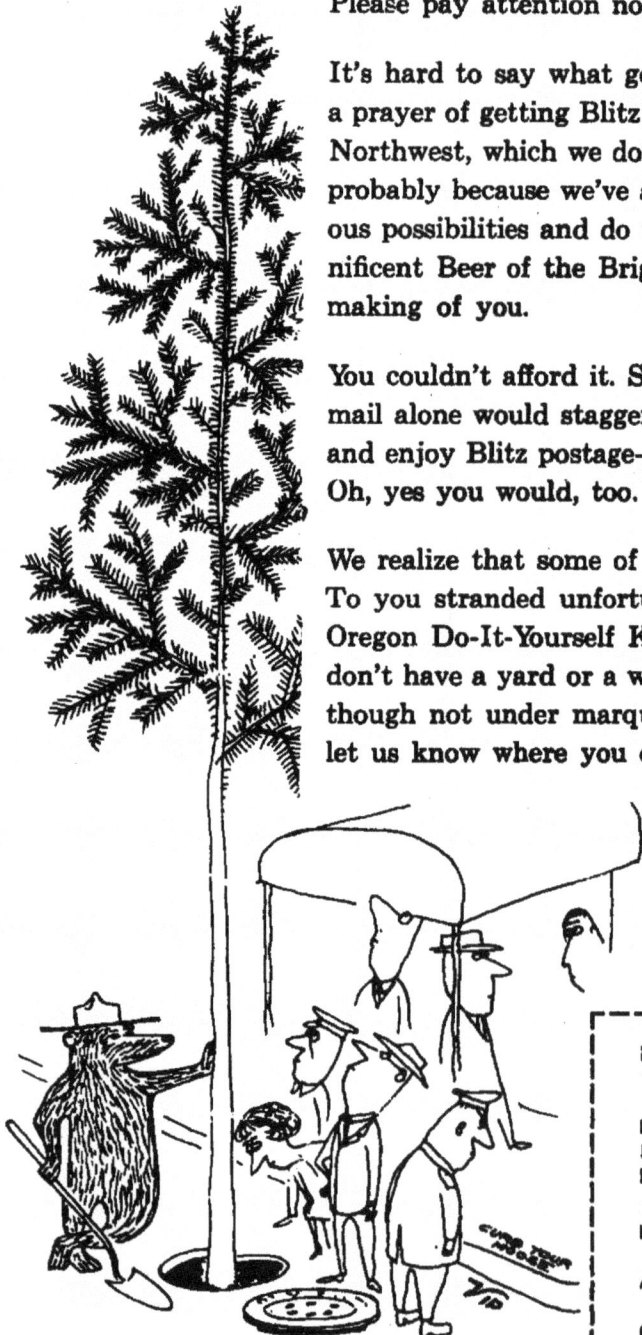

Next up is the Gossage campaign you're most likely to have seen before. It was for the agency's biggest account: American Petrofina.

FINA was owned by the Belgian government and a newcomer to the US market. As Gossage's art director colleague, Bob Freeman, recalled: The client "wanted an identity for the company: to project its vigour, size, diversification without being stuffy and hammering away at it in the usual advertising style."

Gossage delivered on that brief. In the following ads, you'll see he ticks off "vigour and size" with various references to FINA's refineries, pipelines, fleet of trucks and thousands of gas stations etc.

The "Free Asphalt" ads are a nod towards diversification. And the "Free Pink Valve Caps" are his way of introducing you to FINA's TBAs (Tyres, Batteries and Accessories).

In a couple of others ads you'll also see him cross-selling the FINA credit card.

But none of the above is ever a hard sell. He lures you in by being interesting - and likeable.

Advertising mavens amongst you will also note the reference to FINA painting their vast fleet of trucks bright pink. That was four years before Mary Wells, at Wells, Rich, Greene effected "the most dramatic image overhaul in the history of commercial aviation" by painting Braniff's aeroplanes bright colours.

Throughout all this, Gossage's aim was to differentiate FINA's advertising from the high octane hyperbole of other players in the market. And to lampoon the claims they were making about their gas.

See specifically "Q: Is it True that all Brands of Gasoline are Pretty Much Alike?" which may well be the most honest piece of copy ever written about a product. That was the last ad in the series.

But back to the beginning, and Gossage set up the campaign and sent up the whole category by introducing FINA's "additive of the future".

PINK AIR!

The following news item appeared in the San Francisco *Daily Commercial News* for March 21st, 1961:

Gasoline service stations will be filling your tires with tinted or brightly colored air in the foreseeable future, according to R. G. Lund, marketing consultant.

Detecting a strong trend in the industry, Lund said, "The oil companies are already adding additives to additives in their efforts to win motorists' favor in this highly competitive field. They have added extra ingredients to everything connected with an automobile except the air that goes in the tires. An additive for air will definitely be the next major advance."

It will take ten years, the Portland, Oregon marketer estimates, before the research and manufacturing problems are solved. Existing facilities will have to be converted to meet the public's demand for more colorful presentation of products. "But then," he concludes, "stations will feature air in decorator shades of green, blue, purple and even pink."

A word to the wise if we ever saw one. Fina's not the kind of company that has to be told twice. Pink sounds like as good a color as any and besides it's short and catchy. This is to serve notice we have settled on Pink Air.

Not only that, but as of right now we are starting a crash program: the Fina Five Year Plan. If it is going to take everybody else ten years we'll do it in half the time.

So look for Pink Air at the thousands of Fina stations on May 12th, 1966! Give or take a few days.

The reason we're in such a rush is, as the man says, if you want to stay on top you've got to have a little something new from time to time.

But Fina's gas, oil, and accessories are already just exactly as good as the best. We wouldn't want to add more things to them just so we could say we did. (Oh, we've got additives, all right, we just can't think of any good names or numbers for them.)

And that's why we're so pleased to have a brand new additive of our very own: Pink Air. If you see anybody else claiming it, just let us know and we will deal with them for sure. Keep your eyes open.

Meanwhile we'd like to be able to give you a better idea of what the air in your tires will look like on P.A. Day, May 12th, 1966. And right now we're trying to make up a few experimental batches of Pink Air. By the time our next ad comes out we'll be able to mail you a sample if we can just figure how to keep it from leaking out of the envelope.

Now, before we go here is a picture of our Fina emblem:

[**FINA**] . . . so the next time you see a Fina station you'll recognize it. And if it's on your side so you don't have to make a U-turn and there aren't six cars waiting and you need gas or something, please stop in.

SEND FOR YOUR FREE SAMPLE OF PINK AIR!

(As we know, there is a strong trend in the gasoline station industry toward adding a coloring ingredient to the air which goes into your tires. Like blue, purple, green, crimson, and others. The reason is: additives have been added to everything else connected with your car. Now it is air's turn. But authorities estimate that it will be ten years before the switchover from ordinary air is completed and colored air is in the hoses.

Meanwhile Fina, an alert young oil company, has staked out Pink Air.° And has started a crash program so they can beat everybody else by five years: the Fina Five Year Plan.)

WE are happy to report some progress. Our Pink Air Research Laboratory at Mount Pleasant, Texas is hard at work on the secret ingredient which will turn air pink. We are still confident that we will be able to get it to our more than 2,000 Fina stations by May 12, 1966. About 4:30 P.M., we figure; some of our trucks don't get around until late in the afternoon.

We will keep you posted.

However, a technical question has been brought to our attention: "How is anybody going to know what Pink Air looks like when it's inside a tire?"

That is a good question and to answer it we will send you a sample as we promised in our last ad. A Free sample.

Naturally, for security reasons* we won't be able to send you any *real* Pink Air. Besides, what would we mail it in? No, the best answer is a pink balloon,** so when you blow it up Regular air will look like Premium Pink.

And there'll be a Fina emblem on it so the next time you're driving down the road and you see it and the station is on your side so you don't have to make a U-turn and there aren't six cars waiting and you need gas or something, please stop in. And see for yourself that our products are just exactly as good as the best.

And when you're through looking at the Pink Air give it to the kids, they'll like it. How many children do you have?

It might float into the wrong hands. Enough said.
**Actually, TWO balloons, one inside the other. Don't worry, we'll send directions.*

- -

Fina Pink Air Development Division
American Petrofina
Dallas, Texas

Dear Fina:

I would like to see what Pink Air looks like. I have_____children.

Name_____ Address_____

City_____ State_____

[FREE PINK AIR COUPON]

PINK VALVE CAP SHOWN HERE IS
APPROXIMATELY 4¹¹/₁₂ TIMES BIGGER
THAN ACTUAL LIFE SIZE

FINA ANNOUNCES: FREE PINK VALVE CAPS!

EVEN if everything goes slick as axle grease you won't be able to get your tires filled with Pink Air, Fina's Additive of the Future, until May 12, 1966. Since that's a long time to wait for anything – even a pretty additive like Pink Air – we'd like to do something to tide you over.

So if you'll fill out the coupon below we'll send you a free pink valve cap that you can put on right now; to sort of give you the *feeling* that your tires are filled with Premium Pink even though you're still riding around on Regular air. In one way a pink valve cap is better than Pink Air (or any other additive) because you can at least see it.

At any rate, a pink valve cap will remind you that we are thinking about you. And also that Fina stations sell a lot of other things besides gas and oil, hundreds of items actually, all first rate; in tires, for instance, Goodyear and Firestone both. We even have a special division called TBA (for Tires/Batteries/Accessories) to handle them.

We'd spend more time here trying to sell you TBA except we know that usually the only time you are interested in buying windshield wipers, fan belts, spark plugs, and such is when the old ones wear out. At which point you drive in and we fix you up with new ones. So, outside of keeping as good a stock of TBA items as the size of the station permits – and standing staunchly behind their quality – the best thing we can do to sell TBA is wait for you to show up.*

Which is why we say: if you're driving down the road and you see a Fina station and it's on your side so you don't have to make a U-turn through traffic and there aren't six cars waiting and you need gas or something,** please stop in.

Before we forget it, one TBA item will be *free*: Pink valve caps; just as soon as we can get them out to the stations. Meanwhile, why wait? Be the first one on your block! You're probably missing a valve cap anyway, so fill out the coupon and send it in. We have also, at popular request (no kidding), included a box to be checked by those who wish to apply for a Fina Credit card.*** Thank you.

*So please forget we mentioned TBA.
**Like TBA.
***By the way, with a Fina Credit Card you can buy any TBA item no money down and six months to pay.

[FREE PINK VALVE CAP COUPON]

Pink Valve Cap Dept. B32
American Petrofina
Dallas, Texas

Dear Fina:

Please send me my free Pink Valve Cap. ☐ Please send me a Fina Credit Card Application, too.

Very truly yours,

Name_____ Address_____

City_____ Zone____State_____

© 1961, AMERICAN PETROFINA, DALLAS, TEXAS

A FINA ATTENDANT IS TRUSTWORTHY, LOYAL, HELPFUL, FRIENDLY, COURTEOUS, KIND, OBEDIENT, CHEERFUL, THRIFTY, BRAVE, CLEAN, AND BOY, CAN HE PUMP GAS!

What has happened up till now:

Fina, an alert young oil company, is going all-out to pioneer the additive of the future, the secret ingredient which will color the air in your tires. Everything else connected with your car is chock-full of additives already: only tire air remains; it is the last frontier, the additive Cimarron.

Hence, our crash program, The Fina Five Year Plan. If all goes well we should be able to crack the additive barrier on May 12, 1966, give or take a few days, and offer you Pink Air* (pink is Fina's, the other companies will have to settle for orange, chartreuse, purple, etc.).*

Mind you, we are not going to promise miracles of performance. All we can guarantee for Pink Air at this time is (a) it will make the inside of your tires prettier; and (b) it will be an additive, and after all that is the important thing, isn't it?

Now, in our last ad we offered to send you a free sample of what Pink Air will look like; actually a pink balloon, but when you blow it up regular air looks like Premium Pink. Several people wrote in.

Now go on with the story:

EVER since then people, especially little people, have been asking at Fina stations for pink balloons. Our stations don't give away balloons because:

1. Parents get enough pressure from kids already without us adding to it. We want you to drive into a Fina station of your own free will; not because a child is fussing for a pink balloon.

2. It just might interfere with our real job: taking care of your car. You know, if you asked us for a balloon we'd go back into the station and get it and in the process we might forget to check the tires. Not that we always remember anyway; everybody has his days.

Speaking of service, the reason you get so much more of it free at a gas station than at any other kind of store is very simple: Getting your car gassed is about as much fun as getting your pants pressed while you wait. In view of this you might wonder why you pay higher taxes on gasoline than you do on entertainment. Or luxuries; the tax on gasoline is steeper than the tax on diamonds. But we digress.

The sad truth is nobody *wants* to go to a service station; they go because they *have* to.

So we give you service to make you feel more kindly toward us. As a matter of fact, most of our stock in trade is free, too: road maps, water, windshield wipes, air, how far is it to the next town, battery water, rest rooms, & etc., etc. Just ask the man.

For anything but pink balloons.

However, we'll be happy to mail you one. The balloon** will have a Fina emblem on it so the next time you see a Fina station you'll recognize it. And if it's on your side of the road so you don't have to make a U-turn through traffic and there aren't six cars waiting and you need gas or something, please stop in. Our products are exactly as good as the best.

*We're sort of curious about which of our competitors is going to use purple. The next time you're in another station – don't make a special trip – you might ask them "Is your air going to be purple?". When you find out please let us know. Thank you.

**Actually it's two balloons, one inside the other. It sounds complicated but we'll send instructions, never fear. The kids will love it.

● 1961, AMERICAN PETROFINA, DALLAS, TEXAS

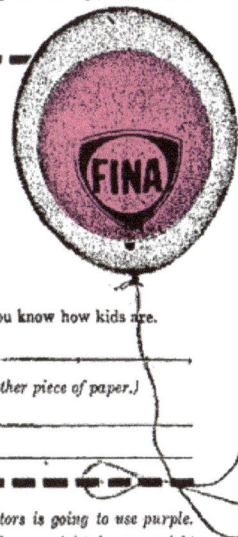

Sorry to interrupt the flow but take a look at the para beginning: "The sad truth..." and the one that follows. Brutal honesty followed by the soft sell.

YOUR CHANCE TO WIN 15 YARDS OF PINK ASPHALT

PINK ASPHALT?

Why not? *As you may remember Pink Air, Fina's Additive of the Future, was invented to make the insides of your tires look prettier because everything else that goes into your car already has all the extra additives it needs; sometimes more. And we started our Five Year Crash Program so as to be sure of getting it to all of our thousands of big and little Fina stations by Pink Air Day, May 12, 1966.*

WELL you know how it is in a company when one department gets something special; it's like with kids. Right away the TBA* Department wanted a Pink Program too. So the Pink Valve Cap ("the accessory to help you through the difficult withdrawal period from Regular Air to Premium Pink") was invented.

Then somebody in Trucking said: "How about painting a few of our trucks pink so people will know we're ready to transport the Pink Air from our Fina refineries in case the Pink Air Pipeline** isn't completed by P.A. Day?" And so we did.

Meanwhile back in the Asphalt Department people were feeling Left Out. It isn't an ordinary little old stick-in-the-tar asphalt department, either; we are one of the country's big manufacturers of asphalt. And it is good stuff, sort of an asphalt man's asphalt. But only in basic black – until our boys made some revolutionary experiments.

Which is why we now have 15 yards of very high-quality Pink Asphalt to give away to the one who can think up the best way to use it. (15 yards is a whole heap of asphalt; pink or otherwise it weighs about 30 tons and, if you win it, it'll take us two double-dual wheel dump trucks or semi-trailers to haul it to your house.) After we roll it out for you, it'll cover around 270 square yards which is enough to pave a pink driveway plus a pink badminton court plus a pink patio. Or about ⅞ths of a doubles tennis court; O.K., O.K., we'll pave the whole court.

Although nobody here knows how cows might feel about having their barn floor redone in wall-to-wall pink, we do know that asphalt is gentle on their feet; and neat. We suppose it would also be swell for paving sundecks on roofs; if only we can figure out how to get the steamroller up there. So if you happen to have anything you'd like paved for free with Premium Pink Asphalt just fill out part one of the coupon below and tell us what you want it for, and why. The best answer wins.

Meanwhile if you're driving down the road and you see a Fina station and it's on your side so you don't have to make a U-turn through traffic and there aren't six cars waiting and you need gas or something, please stop in.

* *For Tires Batteries Accessories; Fina stations sell several things besides gas and oil; hundreds.*
** *This is so complicated it took us a whole ad to explain it last time; but if you'd really like to know, just drop us a note and we'll be glad to send you a copy.*

- - - - - - - - - - - - - - - - - - - -

MOTHER OF FIVE WINS 15 YARDS OF PINK ASPHALT

CONSOLATION PRIZE

FINA

GRAND PRIZE

FINA

SPECIAL PINK PRIZE

FINA

THE great Fina Pink Asphalt contest has ended in an unexpected three-way tie. We didn't say anything about what we do in case of ties so all three of the winners will each receive the Grand Prize, 15 yards of Pink Asphalt laid down where they want it. (This, you recall, is what the contest was about; to find the most interesting use for a batch of Pink Asphalt our asphalt division whipped up to match Pink Air — Fina's additive of the future coming May 12, 1966 — as well as our pink gas trucks, pink valve caps, etc.) The entries were so stimulating that the judges couldn't make up their minds, so we have had to scrape up an additional 30 yards to cover the other two winners.

GRAND PRIZE goes to Mrs. Bernie Rohling of 3407 Belmont Blvd., Nashville, Tennessee. This poses some problems, being outside our marketing area; we may have to smuggle the stuff to her. She says "For years I have been tying pink ribbons on bassinets, all to no avail, — I have five sons. Your contest has brought new hope into my life. How could old man stork miss leaving the right bundle if our house was plainly marked with 15 yards of beautiful pink asphalt driveway?" And she concludes, "Here's hoping, or should I say expecting?" Good luck, Mrs. Rohling!

Consolation Prize goes to Valley Center High School, Valley Center, Kansas — a new suburb of Wichita — 86 of whose students wrote rousing letters. Several wanted a pink tennis court. "Which we badly need," says one, "since there isn't a tennis court, or swimming pool, or park even in the whole town — yet." Another states: "We have done so poorly at football this year there must be *something* we can excel in; maybe it is tennis." Still another: "The old school spirit at V.C.H.S. (established 1958) can't be beat. But we haven't ever done anything anybody has heard about. It is hard to brag under such conditions. A pink tennis court would make us famous. Also it would match the trim of our building, which is pink. Maybe we will even change the school colors from purple and gold to purple and pink." Four of the 86 thought they needed a pink drag strip more, however. Well, fight it out among yourselves and congratulations all!

A Special Pink Prize goes to Mr. W. H. Moseley of 3901 Sockwell Blvd., Greenville, Texas. We found Mr. Moseley's entry especially noteworthy since he happens to be a Fina dealer; the first known instance of a company man winning a contest; we forgot to make a rule against it. You may remember that one time we mentioned in an ad that not all Fina stations were big super-stations? That some Fina stations were more modest? Mr. Moseley's is one of them, but he is anxious to improve himself. He was about to repave his driveway when he heard of our contest. He has stalled off in the hopes that his could be the first Fina station paved pink; with the result that the drive is beginning to collect a bit of water in the wet weather while he waits to find out whether to go to pink or black. He ends on a somewhat familiar note, "Meanwhile if you are driving down the road and you see this station and it is on your side and there aren't six cars (or rowboats, if you don't hurry) waiting please stop by." So, congratulations to you, Mr. Moseley, and best wishes for a dry, Pink 1962!

Our sincere thanks to all of you who wrote in; we enjoyed the fun and we hope you did, too; and that we will hear from you again sometime.

[*OUR MOTTO*]*

"IF YOU'RE DRIVING DOWN THE ROAD AND YOU SEE A FINA STATION AND IT'S ON YOUR SIDE SO YOU DON'T HAVE TO MAKE A U-TURN THROUGH TRAFFIC AND THERE AREN'T SIX CARS WAITING AND YOU NEED GAS OR SOMETHING** PLEASE STOP IN."***

* We know it isn't very pushy as mottos go, but it's realistic and Fina doesn't expect you to do anything that isn't reasonable or convenient.

** Like oil. And 1503 other items your car might need.

*** Meanwhile, if you're missing a valve cap (and you probably are) and would like a pink one we will be happy to send you one free and post paid. Just fill out the coupon. If you'd also like a Fina credit card application just put an X in the right box.

------------------| COUPON |------------------
American Petrofina, Dallas, Texas
Dear Fina:
☐ Please send me a Pink Valve Cap.
☐ Please send me a Fina Credit Card Application.
Name_____ Address_____
City_____ State_____

🛡 **FINA**

© 1962, AMERICAN PETROFINA, DALLAS, TEXAS

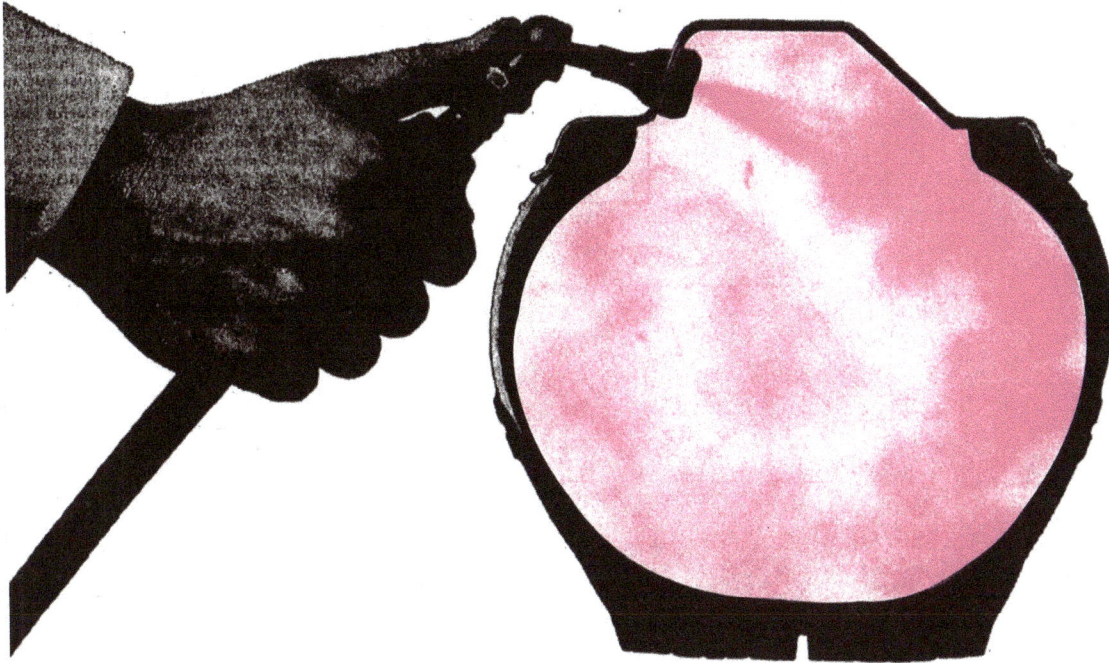

THE PINK INCH?

The question has come up: How are we going to get Pink Air* to the more than 2,000 Fina stations by May 12th, 1966?

(Pink Air, if you recall, is Fina's additive of the future; the secret ingredient which will color the air in your tires. It is the only possible additive left; everything else in your car has already been taken care of. So Fina can be first, we have started a crash program, The Fina Five Year Plan.)

There are two answers:

1. *That we transport Pink Air the same way we do our gasoline:* from our refineries in Mount Pleasant, Wichita Falls, and El Dorado to distribution points where our trucks would pick it up and deliver it to Fina stations who would then put it in your tires. This is impractical because the pink air might mingle with and color the gasoline. Our gas doesn't need any more additives; it is already as good as the best and we wouldn't want to gild the lily — not even pink.

2. *That we build a special pipe line for Pink Air:* The Pink Inch. (See map above.) This isn't as easy as it sounds; it would be a lot of hard work and would probably cost a pretty penny. You know, you don't just get out there and lay pipe across the countryside. You've got to ask people's permission and pay them something to boot. Still, if we have to do it we have to do it.

Maybe the easiest thing would be to make it a *hose* line, out of air hoses like we use in our stations, only thousands of miles long. And a little bigger: The Pink Inch Hose Line. We don't suppose people would mind so much having a hose strung across their front yards except they might trip over it.

The real advantage to the proposed Pink Inch Hose Line is that it would be fair. It would make Pink Air available at the big Fina stations and the little Fina stations at one and the same time, without fear or favor.

[BIG FINA STATION]

A big Fina station has, in addition to lots of pumps you can see, lots of underground storage tanks; and lots of attendants to keep check on them. So taking care of Pink Air would be no problem at all to them.

[LITTLE FINA STATION]

But a little Fina station might be just two pumps in front of a general store and the proprietor not only has no extra storage space but is plenty busy as it is, what with slicing bacon and all. You might have to honk twice, not that he doesn't give you good service once he knows you're there. So you can see that a direct hose from the refinery would be a real help to him.

There are still a few details to be worked out in laying that much hose; such as how to get it across highways. Maybe when we come to a road we could string it between poles. If the telephone company people will cooperate. Well, we have five years to iron out the kinks and we'll probably need every minute of it.

Meanwhile, if you are driving down the road and you see a Fina station and it's on your side so you don't have to make a U-turn through traffic and there aren't six cars waiting and you need gas or something, please stop in.

(We've said this so often now that it's gotten to be sort of the Fina motto. It isn't very pushy as mottos go but it's realistic. We don't expect you to do anything that isn't reasonable or convenient.)

PINK AIR: A MAJOR SCIENTIFIC BREAK-THROUGH IN AUTOMOTIVE KNOW-HOW?

In response to many enquiries about the progress of the Fina Five Year Plan to bring Pink Air to you and your tires at the thousands of Fina stations in the Midwest and Southwest on or about May 12, 1966, we present our second exclusive interview on the subject:

Q. *Let's see, it's been almost two years since you launched your crash program to produce Pink Air...*

FINA. That's right, the Additive Of The Future.

Q. *Then would you describe this additive as "The Coming Scientific Break-through In Automotive Know-how"?*

FINA. No.

Q. *Then how would you describe it?*

FINA. Pink.

Q. *It is fair to say, then, that you are developing Pink Air because yours is a very competitive field and you can't think of anything else to add additives to except tire air?*

FINA. Very well put.

Q. *How about your gasoline?*

FINA. Our gas is already as good as the very best and has all the additives your car can use. We don't see much point in giving them fancy names or numbers just so we can advertise them. Besides, we doubt that people are much impressed by additive claims anymore.

Q. *In that case, do you think they'll be impressed by Pink Air?*

FINA. No-o-o-o-o-o, but it's free.

Q. *Is that the only difference?*

FINA. Also, it's prettier. Much prettier, for instance, than XK-193, Zoomtane, Marlo, Brandon, or names like that...

Q. *Yes it is. Now, what progress do you have to report on the development of Pink Air?*

FINA. Well, our work on the secret ingredient is secret, of course...

Q. *Of course, but...*

FINA. But to keep our customers in touch — visual-wise, at least — we've done a good deal of work with the color pink itself.

Q. *Could you mention a few examples?*

FINA. Certainly. For one thing, we are painting our gas trucks pink. And you may recall that last year we offered Pink Valve Caps?

Q. *I recall that.*

FINA. As a matter of fact, if anyone would still like one, just drop a note to: Pink Valve Caps, American Petrofina, Dallas, Texas. I think we may have a few left and...

Q. *How many?*

FINA. 1,322,874.

Q. *I see. Do you plan to use that slogan?*

FINA. 1,322,874?

Q. *No, the one you mentioned earlier: "It's Prettier."*

FINA. You like it?

Q. *Yes.*

FINA. Do you think it's as catchy as: "If you're driving down the road and you see a Fina station and it's on your side so you don't have to make a U-turn through traffic and there aren't six cars waiting...*

Q. *Well, you can't go by me...*

FINA. Wait a minute! You spoiled the best part, the hard sell...

Q. *Which is?*

FINA. ... and you need gas or something, please stop in."

Q. *I'm sorry. Now, how does Fina plan to handle Pink Air at the station level?*

FINA. Glad you asked th...

Q. *Oh, excuse me, our space is up. So until next time, thank you.*

FINA. Thank you.

49

Q:
"IS IT TRUE THAT ALL BRANDS OF GASOLINE ARE PRETTY MUCH ALIKE?"

Today, instead of our customary tire-side chat on Pink Air, Fina's additive of the future, we would like to talk about gasoline. The interviewer, being an obliging fellow, has kindly agreed to ask some questions that may have popped into your mind, too:

Q. *Let's see, I'm afraid that some of the questions may get sort of blunt.*

FINA. Will that stop you from asking them?

Q. *No.*

FINA. In that case you might as well get on with it.

Q. *All right. First, in spite of all the advertising of special claims, I think most people believe that all reputable brands of gasoline are pretty much alike. Is that so?*

FINA. Certainly. With minor variations, all first-class gasolines are literally interchangable as to quality and ingredients.

Q. *You mean you could mix them together?*

FINA. Sure. Actually, that's exactly what you do whenever you add half a tank of a different brand to the gas that's already in your car, isn't it?

Q. *Yes, but ...*

FINA. Of course they both have to be top quality and the same grade.

Q. *There are quite a few grades of gas, aren't there?*

FINA. Only two that matter, we think: Regular and Premium. We can't recommend the others.

Q. *How about super-premiums; aren't they better?*

FINA. Well, they're more *expensive*. But the catch is that your car either doesn't *need* gas of that grade, or can't properly use it any more than it could use rocket fuel.

Q. *How about sub-regulars, at the other end of the scale?*

FINA. They are cheaper, of course, but the catch *there*, is that your car doesn't run as well or as efficiently with them.

Q. *So ...*

FINA. So, your best bet is to buy a Regular or Premium of one of the many well-made gasolines.

Q. *That means there are poorly-made gasolines?*

FINA. Oh yes; gas can be made to *any* specifications. If you're interested in antiques, there are some cut-rate grades that are quite inadequate for today's cars: 1913 model gas.

Q. *How do you tell the difference? Mostly a matter of price?*

FINA. Mostly, but it helps if you've heard of the brand, of course. A larger, well-promoted brand *has* to keep up its quality, if for no other reason than to protect its investment.

Q. *Then bigness has something to do with whether a brand of gas is good or reputable?*

FINA. Not altogether, but you have to be a *certain* size just to operate efficiently in an industry as huge as the oil business; that is if you're a diversified company.

Q. *Which Fina is?*

FINA. Oh yes; in addition to thousands of stations down the middle of the country, we have pipe lines, oil fields, five refineries, large petrochemical facilities, and we've done it all in six years. Say, does it sound like we're bragging?

Q. *As a matter-of-fact, yes. But look, do you have to have all those things to sell good gasoline? Couldn't a station, or a string of stations, simply buy its gas from somebody else's refinery and sell it?*

FINA. Yes. Many outfits, including some quite large companies, operate that way. Some of them sell old-fashioned, "Early American" gas and some sell the modern stuff. And some have pumps for every period: regular drive-in museums, they are.

Q. *But would you say that it's safer as a rule not to buy gas from smaller outfits?*

FINA. No, that wouldn't be fair. There are a number of small operators who sell good gas. As long as you know who you're doing business with, you're all right. Just keep your eyes open. Is all this clear?

Q. *Yeah, except if you have to think that much about it, why not pull into a Fina Station in the first place?*

FINA. Well, if you're driving down the road and you see a Fina Station and it's on your side so you don't have to make a U-turn through traffic and there aren't six cars waiting and you need gas or something, please stop in.

Q. *Do you ever wish that your history was as long as your motto?*

FINA. Youth is a wonderful thing, Mr. Q.

If FINA was the agency's biggest account, The Whiskey Distillers of Ireland won the most acclaim. When 100 creative directors were polled, it received an "honourable mention" as one of the campaigns of the 1950s.

To prepare for the task, Gossage took a 12 month lease on *Rathsalla* - a fabulous estate in County Wicklow - and told Bob Freeman "he was going to write the ads as though he knew nothing about advertising".

Instead he took on the guise of a raconteur seated in a Dublin pub sipping a whiskey, and drew on the ruminative rhythms of a literary tradition that stretched from James Joyce back to Jonathan Swift.

Initially, Gossage wrote a series of 13 ads that appeared in the *New Yorker*.

Coming up are the first four. They share with the reader the Distillers' dilemma: very few people were drinking Irish whiskey (preferring instead the Scotch variety). Those who were, were doing so as Irish Coffee (a sickly cocktail of black coffee, whiskey and double cream).

So, should the Distillers continue to profit by encouraging this practise? Or should they take pride in the quality of their whisky and promote it as a superior straight tipple?

The initial four ads appeared between 13th Sept, 1958 and 4th Oct, 1958. And, as you'll see, the first three end halfway through a sentence which then begins the next ad. The last of the four ads finally ends with a full stop. But only because the type grows progressively smaller in order to fit the copy to the page.

Has any copywriter ever had such audacity? Or faith in their own ability to engage and involve the reader?

Incidentally, as with the NUCOA ad above, Gossage was making his ads look like feature stories. He knew he was competing with the news - and was determined to command the same attention and respect. The *New Yorker*, however, insisted he flag it up as advertising. Have a look at his defiant response at the bottom of the ads.

HAS IRELAND BEEN LED FALSE
BY A BAKED BRAZILIAN BERRY?

[NUMBER I]

We'll not pretend that we 〖The Whiskey Distillers of Ireland〗 weren't the pleased ones when Irish Coffee became the darling of the Western World. We still are. There are few things more enjoyable than standing on the quay seeing the great ships off to America with golden cargoes of matchless Irish Whiskey. And yet, have we sold our birthright for a mess of coffee pottage? And money? It may well be. For while Irish Coffee is admittedly a luscious drink the fact remains that the Whiskey is somewhat *obscured* by the coffee, frothy cream, and the sugar cube. ☒ Do you begin to see the shape of this bittersweet quandary? There's much, much to be said. You will fathom how much when you recall that Joyce's *Ulysses* took over three-hundred-thousand words to deal with just twenty-four hours in a tiny corner of Dublin and not one of the very best tiny corners of Dublin at that. ☒ Our subject covers several years and a hundred and twenty degrees of longitude. So it's not likely this one page will do it justice. Still, advertising costs the earth and when we reach the bottom we'll just have to stop wherever we are and continue over to next week. ☒ Back to Irish Coffee and its popularity. The upshot is that thousands upon thousands of Americans have taken the Irish Whiskey without ever having fully known the goodness of it. 〖Its emphatic, burnished flavor must (fortunately) be tasted to be appreciated〗. Otherwise they'd be drinking it all the time; in other ways less darksome and exotic, to be sure, but equally satisfying. There's no need to tell *you* what these other ways of drinking fine whiskey are. It'd be like teaching your grandmother to

OH, IT'S A HORRID THING TO BE TORN BETWEEN PRIDE & PROFIT

[NUMBER II]

suck eggs. ℘ ⟦What we were saying when we (The Whiskey Distillers of Ireland) ran out of space last week is that it would be presumptuous of us to tell *you* how to drink fine whiskey. It'd be like teaching your grandmother to suck eggs, as they say. Whatever that means.⟧ ℘ Still, there's no denying that, thanks to Irish Coffee, any number of the Americans have taken Irish Whiskey without having *truly* tasted of it and that's a fact. What happens is the fragrant coffee and the sugar cube and the cool, frothy cream on top all but drown out the principal ingredient! At no *monetary* loss to us, mind. It has been a real treat to watch the dear sales curve soaring. ℘ But Profit is not all in all; Pride has its innings. We are an enormously Prideful lot when it comes to the elegant, burnished, *emphatic* flavor of our whiskies. This is why we should like you to buy them, to drink them, to cherish them for themselves alone. ℘ "Ah! but there are nine grand brands of Irish Whiskey," you say, "Which to choose?" You've stated the problem well, we think, if floridly. Look, why don't you ask the man at the whiskey store for *his* recommendation. He will be overjoyed at your humility. ℘ Now you've grasped our dilemma you'll no doubt be wishing to take your stand for Pride or Profit as the case may be. You'll appreciate that we must remain neutral ourselves, can't afford to do otherwise. But don't let our shilly-shallying prevent *you* from being forthright. ℘ To this end we are issuing badges which we trust you will wear openly and diligently. They are quite attractive and are sure to draw admiring glances from one and all. You may obtain either the Pride Badge or the Profit Badge at no cost to yourself, that is to say, absolutely free for the asking. Address your requests to: Pride, P. O. Box 186, Dublin, Ireland, or to Profit, P. O. Box 207, Dublin, Ireland, as the case may be. Air Mail is fifteen cents; surface mail, is eight cents; post cards, four cents. ℘ The lovely stamp you'll get on the return envelope is alone worth the effort, not to mention the brave badge. Perhaps you'd better write us via the air mail. It's speedier for one thing, more flamboyant, and be-

STAND UP
& BE COUNTED!
ARE YOU PRIDE OR PROFIT?

[NUMBER III]

sides you'll probably be terribly anxious to receive your Pride Badge or your Profit Badge, one. For the benefit of you latecomers we ⟦The Whiskey Distillers of Ireland⟧ are referring to the very nice badges we are sending out from Dublin to all who write us here.

We unfortunately ran off the page last week and had to continue over. No harm done, we suppose. ☞ The badges, then, are as illustrated. "Profit" to be worn by those who glory in Irish Coffee and the money it sends flowing to Ireland. And a pretty thing it is, too, watching the dear sales curve course upwards thanks to the Profit Party's interesting taste. If bizarre. Not that we condemn, no, no, no. ☞ It's just that there are the others: the Prides; proud of the taste, proud of the altogether distinctive, burnished, but emphatic flavor of Irish Whiskey. They claim the subtlety is *quite drowned out* in Irish Coffee. Strong words! Strong feelings! Before we run out of space again perhaps we'd better get our coupon in. We are given to un-

Now this isn't to say that you must already be an all-outer for Irish Coffee or a practicing Irish Whiskey drinker to qualify as a Profit or Pride respectively. All we require is a willing heart and an open mind. Choose the side that appeals to you; state your allegiance and then justify it by deeds. If you change your mind

later write in and we'll send you the badge of whichever side you defected to. No recriminations, no sidelong glances, just understanding smiles is what you'll get from us. ☞ If you're a novice, though, this great, brilliant world of Irish Whiskey is likely to set you quite agog with its variousness. There are nine grand brands. It'll do no harm to list them ⟦if you'll excuse us for a moment while we draw lots to see whose name shall go first⟧: Murphy's, John Power, Old Bushmills, Tullamore Dew, Paddy, John Jameson, Gilbey's Crock O' Gold, John Locke, and Dunphy's Original Irish. Now . . .

P. O. Box 186
Dublin, Ireland   [C O U P O N]

Pride [ ] Profit [ ] *(indicate one)*

Please send me a badge so that all may say
"There goes a (PRIDE), (PROFIT) man."

Name_____

Address_____

City_____State_____Country_____

---

derstand by those who know that a coupon ⟦rather than just saying to write in⟧ boosts the response tremendously. We hope this is true; so much advice nowadays is simply terrible.

A NEW, ALL NEW RECIPE FOR BRAZILIAN WHISKEY!

[NUMBER IV] *(if you wish the previous installments, you need only to ask)*

all Irish Whiskies share an emphatic, burnished elegance of flavor quite apart from any-thing else known to man's tongue. There are, moreover, differences *between* them. They cover a broad spectrum of taste. The man at the whiskey store will surely know and if he doesn't there's nothing for it but you must buy a bottle of each and find out for yourself. Science will be the richer for your enquiring mind. However, as we have observed in the previous chapters, these delicacies of flavor and body are largely negated when the whiskey is taken in Irish Coffee, a concoction which appears to have bedazzled the Western World. Not that we ⟦The Whiskey Distillers of Ireland⟧ are knocking it, understand. If coffee must be laced it's better we do the lacing. The question of Pride versus Profit has no easy solution. Meanwhile we must be realistic; you can't change human nature. There will always be coffee. But to make *your* choice the easier you'll note we've provided two coupons instead of the customary one. Please act promptly as we are most anxious

---

P. O. Box 186
Dublin, Ireland ⟦ PRIDE ⟧

*Please send me a badge so that all may say
"There goes a PRIDE man
(or woman, as the case may be)."*

Name_____
Address_____
City_____State_____Country_____

P. O. Box 207
Dublin, Ireland ⟦ PROFIT ⟧

*Please send me a badge.
And the recipe for Irish Coffee.
Send it to the Pride people, too. Thanks.*

Name_____
Address_____
City_____State_____Country_____

---

to know your true feelings and to send you one badge or the other so you can lord it over your friends. Air mail to Dublin is fifteen cents; surface mail eight cents; post cards four cents. Our cable address is COTRA, Dublin, if you feel you must. But bear in mind the time differential for it's probable that a Night Letter would do every bit as well as a straight cable and be thriftier into the bargain. Besides, the twenty words you'll get will enable you to be less perfunctory and more cordial. We see we've not got in the promised recipe and we're almost out of page again. Still, if we go to smaller type we may make it yet; let's make the effort. BRAZILIAN WHISKEY: 1. Fill ordinary highball glass to halfway mark with strong coffee. 2. Swirl or jostle coffee around until inside of glass is coated. 3. Pour coffee back in pot. 4. Wash glass thoroughly in hot sudsy water. 5. Pour a generous sufficiency of Irish Whiskey into glass. 6. Add ice and soda or water. We have developed a number of other recipes and weaning plans just to assist Irish Coffee drinkers through the difficult withdrawal period.

The rest of the series ran until 28th March, 1959. For Number XI Gossage persuaded the client to pay $3,300 for a full page to run next to it-and then left that page completely blank. There's an explanation for this extravagant gesture about two thirds down the page at "Just to show you how little we care for gold..."

[NUMBER XI]

HOW SHARPER
THAN A SERPENT'S
TOOTH!

Just recently we 〘The Whiskey Distillers of Ireland〙 reviewed and refuted certain charges laid against us by the partisans of Irish Coffee. They accused us of showing overt partiality to those drinkers who prefer to take the Irish Whiskey in less abnormal ways, such as with ice and water or soda. This hurt, though we tried not to show it or get choked up with emotion. We did reasonably well we think. We're not so sure we can do it again. A crueler blow has come. ℘ The other crowd, the Irish Whiskey purists, have fallen on us *and with virtually the same denunciations,* if you can believe it: cynical toadyism! Profit-mongering! They claim we are playing up to the Irish Coffee crowd only for the stimulus it gives the dear sales curve, which we admit has zoomed off into an annex atop the chart. ℘ Ah, boys, don't think for one minute that we've lost our altruism. The whiskey itself, with its elegant, burnished and, yes, *emphatic* flavor, comes first and foremost. Time and expense are no object; only the finest stone-ground grain, laboriously malted, goes into our ancient Irish Whiskey. ℘ Just to show you how little we care for gold you'll note we've engaged the page opposite and put nothing on it at all, not even "Compliments of a Friend." It's no use your protesting, we've quite made up our minds. Sometimes a stark testimonial of utter integrity is called for. ℘ Still, it would have been nice to at least run our names down the middle of the page in ever so small type. But it's a very hard matter, when you have nine grand brands among you, to decide who shall go first. Whether you do it alphabetically or draw names from a fishbowl there's still the problem. It's difficult enough to list them *here* 〘in this case alphabetically〙: Dunphy's Original Irish, Gilbey's Crock O' Gold, John Jameson, John Locke, Murphy's, Old Bushmills, Paddy, Power's Gold Label, and Tullamore Dew. That's why we generally say to discuss the matter of which of us to buy with the man at the whiskey store. He'll be grateful to you for asking his opinion and will probably talk your arm off in the consequence. ℘ There you have it and we beg you not to broach the matter again.

After the success of the first series of ads, Gossage was briefed to come up with another. They began in May 1959 and ran until January 1960. There was no let up and a third series quickly followed.

I've said that Gossage set out to entertain his audience, and he did so quite literally with these two ads. In March 1960 he'd proposed a pseudo-event, sorry, goodwill mission to New York by the heads of the distilleries featured in his campaign.

Then, like some latter day P.T. Barnum (and, as we'll see in Part 2, as a precursor of his Marshall McLuhan launch), he set up the press coverage and arranged a series of cocktail parties in honour of his overseas guests. (Right)

Gossage reckoned around 3,000 people entered the draw. Amongst the lucky winners were the Mayor of New York, the Governor, The President of the United Nations and Cardinal Spellman.

In short, an object lesson in making a brand famous - and aspirational.

These, the second series of ads, developed the initial rapport. For example, over 2,000 responded to the "Summertime" ad, just to give their opinion.

While Gossage was finishing off the last campaign for Irish Whiskey Distillers, he got a letter from Miller Harris of Eagle Shirts.

Harris had a problem, he was making shirts for the big department stores who then put their label inside and sold them as their own. Harris wanted to establish Eagle Shirts as a brand in its own right. This was Gossage's response:

IS THIS YOUR SHIRT?

If so, Miss Afflerbach will send you

your [] label

THIS is a two-color striped button-down shirt designed and tailored by Eagle Shirtmakers and sold everywhere by fine men's stores. Many of them admire our shirts so much they sell them under their own names. High praise indeed, and we should like to reciprocate by advertising their (our) shirts. But it's hard to know just where to start. Obviously we can't say things like "None Genuine Without This Label" when they are all quite genuine, you know. And it would be silly to say "Try An Eagle Shirt Today!" when it is likely you already have a drawerful; even though you didn't know it until just this minute. So all we can suggest is that you send in for your Eagle label. Write Eagle Shirtmakers, Quakertown, Pennsylvania; Attention Miss Afflerbach.

Next Miller Harris wanted to reassure people of the quality of his shirts, "how beautifully the seams had been sewn, the pockets made and how much care had been taken basting the buttonholes."

A copywriter at Weiner & Gossage, Georgiana Willis, brought in an American Airlines cocktail napkin and said she had an idea about how to use it to get swatches of Eagle cloth into the hands of potential customers.

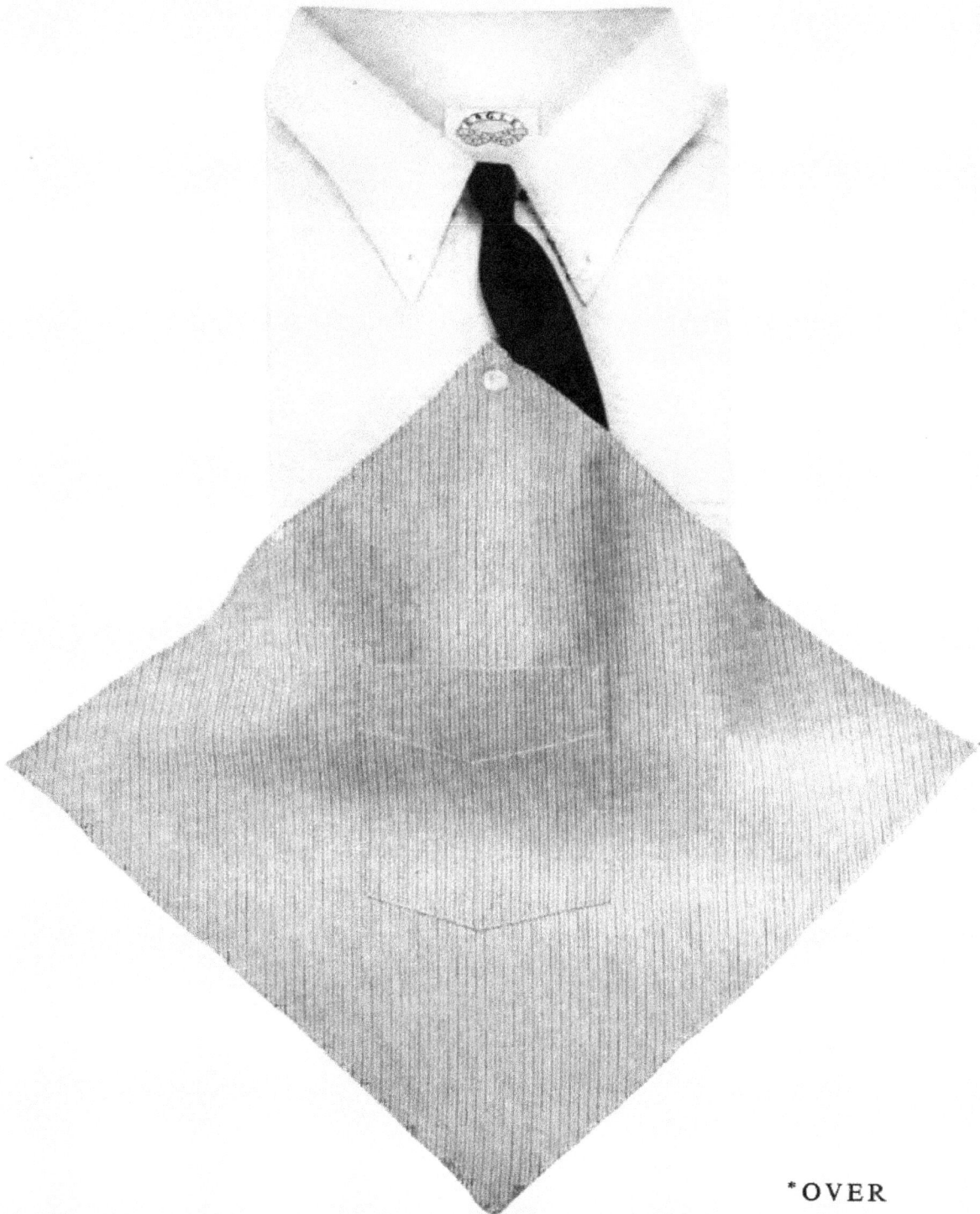

[ADVERTISEMENT]*

*OVER

What materialised was a bizarre square piece of cloth with a button hole in the top corner and a pocket in the middle. Gossage turned this "product sample" into the subject of his next ad.

[cont. from preceding page]

SEND FOR YOUR FREE EAGLE SHIRTKERCHIEF (SHIRTKIN?) (NAPCHIEF?)

AS far as we know this is a brand new invention. Perhaps you will be able to figure out how to realize its full potential. ★ It all started when we tried to devise something to send you—short of an actual shirt—to illustrate a few of the fine points of fine shirt making. A sample to take with you when you go shirt shopping. ★ So first we hemmed a piece of fine shirting; *20 stitches to the inch,* just like in our shirts. At this point you could still call it a handkerchief. ★ But it did seem a shame not to show one of our threadchecked buttonholes, so we did. It makes a pretty good shirt protector: just whip it out of your breast pocket and button it on the second from the top to avoid gravy spots. Good. And tuck your tie in behind it. ★ But then somebody in Pockets said, "Look, if you let us sew a pocket on it, it will show how we make the pattern match right across, no matter what." ★ So if anyone knows what you can use a pocket in a handkerchief/napkin for we will be glad to hear. We will give a half-dozen shirts for the best answer. Make it a dozen.

Eagle Shirtmakers, Quakertown, Pa.

Gentlemen :

Please send me whatever it is. (Signed)_____

Address_____City_____State_____

The number of returned coupons set a new record for the *New Yorker* magazine. There were over 11,000 (mostly witty) responses which led to the ad below (and which Gossage shrewdly turned into a best-selling book).

DEAR MISS AFFLERBACH
OR
Shirtkerchief Revisited

ON March 11 last we offered—to show our superb workmanship—an Eagle Shirtkerchief, a napkin/handkerchief, nicely hemmed, with a button-hole and a pocket. Unsure of what the pocket could be used for, we offered a dozen shirts for the best suggestion. Here, based on a sample of over 11,000 replies, are the findings: ★ One shirtkerchief owner in 14 keeps toothpicks culled from canapés in the pocket. Hundreds recommend it for storing eye-patches; we had no notion so many people suffered from pinkeye. Others wear it in bed to hold celery and other num-nums. One in 23 carries silverware in it at smorgasbords. Many, in restaurants, use it for tips, Tums, upper plates, olive pits and cigarettes; at gaming tables, for chips; at theatres, for ticket stubs. Space does not permit detailing of the hundreds of other splendid uses for the pocket of an Eagle Snowsheen Shirtkerchief. ★ Snowsheen; that was what it was made out of. It is a two-ply broadcloth first used for shirts 40 years ago when we ordered some sight unseen from England, not knowing that up to then it—the English called it "double poplin"—had never been used for anything but top quality umbrellas. Delighted anyway (we had to be, we had tons of it) we changed the name to Snowsheen; and what fine shirts it does make. ★ Find out for yourself by taking your shirtkerchief down to a nearby men's store (perhaps you'd best empty out the olive pits first) and saying, "I'd like a shirt that feels like this."* It won't always have the Eagle label in it—some fine stores like our shirts so much, they sew in their own label. Drop us a line and we'll tell you where to find a Snowsheen shirt near your home. ★ Oh, about the contest, the grand winner was the poignant entry of Ray Von Rosenberg of Thibodaux, Louisiana. However, so many of the entries were so good that the Macmillan Co. is shortly bringing out a book called *Dear Miss Afflerbach*. The writers of some 200 letters to be included in the tome will receive a free copy. And you other 11,000 shirtkerchief owners might want a copy, too: your names are all in the book. Look for it next spring.

*The model shown is the Keith French Cuff. *Snowsheen is also available in our flared button-down with regular cuffs. About $9 for either.*

© 1961 EAGLE SHIRTMAKERS, QUAKERTOWN, PENNSYLVANIA

Here's Gossage's take on "upselling" i.e. getting readers to make multiple purchases. As with many of his ads, he led with a sales promotion premium - with tongue firmly in cheek (have a look at his coupon copy at the bottom of the page).

SEND FOR YOUR FREE
EAGLE WARDROBE WATCH STRAP

HERE are two matching questions we feel may be of interest to shirt-wearing men. Also our answers. (1) Does the shirt now on your back match the shirt you plan to wear tomorrow closely enough to give you a feeling of continuity in an otherwise disjointed world, *but not so close people will think you're economizing on your laundry?* ANS: Probably not, unless they both come from an Eagle Wardrobe Shirt set. (2) Does the shirt on your back match your watch strap? ANS: Probably not, unless you're given to wearing leather shirts; or chromium expansion shirts. ★ Eagle realizes that many men buy their shirts three or so at a time. So we've taken three short sleeved shirts—a stripe, a check (in broadcloth), and a solid (Pima Batiste Madras)—and boxed them together at only three times the cost of a single shirt.* ★ Now, each of the three patterns comes in three

colors, blue, green, and flax, so when you reach the store (we'll tell you which one—many fine stores like our shirts so well they sew in their own labels), you'll have nine shirts from which to choose your three. ★ To improve the odds that you will actually so choose, we've had a strapwright fashion our blue, our green, and our flax checked shirting into three Eagle Wardrobe Watch Straps for you. ★ Your Eagle W. W. Strap will (a) show you our quality shirting, (b) show you our unique pattern and colors, and (c) keep your watch from falling off your arm. ★ We'll be glad to send you one in the color of your choice or, if you faithfully pledge to buy an Eagle Wardrobe Shirt set, we'll send you all three watch straps gratis. If you cannot find it in your heart to so pledge, we shall have to ask for three dollars. On your honor, then, here is the coupon: *about $6.50 each

EAGLE WARDROBE WATCH STRAP ORDER FORM AND HONOR PLEDGE

Dear Eagle Shirtmakers, Quakertown, Pennsylvania:

☐ Please send me one free Eagle Wardrobe Watch Strap in ☐ blue ☐ green ☐ flax. ☐ Please send me three free E.W.W. Straps. I pledge, on my honor, to buy a matching Eagle Wardrobe Shirt set as soon as you tell me where.

☐ Please send me three Eagle Wardrobe Watch Straps. I cannot promise to buy the three Eagle shirts, so I am enclosing $3.

Name_____ Address_____ City_____ State_____

© 1961 EAGLE SHIRTMAKERS, QUAKERTOWN, PENNSYLVANIA

Amplifying the message, Gossage turned those responses into a 200 page book:

64

Here's another Gossage send-up of conventional "marketing" practice. This one is such a outright spoof, it could easily be straight from the pages of *MAD* magazine.

SAVE 3¢ ON YOUR NEXT EAGLE INISHOWEN CHEVIOT SHIRT!

EVER interested in modern promotional techniques, exterior garment merchandising-wise, we at Eagle have devoted particular attention of late to the commercial practices of our colleagues in the tunafish, soup and soap lines. ✠ It seems that these three diverse industries have all discovered that by offering you a free discount coupon good for three cents off the purchase price of their product, they can lure you down to the neighborhood store. ✠ Well, we have been considering various ways to market (we believe that's the word they use) our Inishowen Cheviot Brooketowne. The first two adjectives describe a heavy herringbone oxford designed by our shirting gourmet who describes this fabric as meaty. Brooketowne is our tapered body button-down with the sloppy bulge we used to call flare before everyone else did too. ✠ So, tunafish on the mind, we decided to dip into that great fund of American advertising knowhow. ✠ Friends! as soon as you've written us to learn the name of your nearest Eagle dealer (not all Eagle shirts have the Eagle label in them, recall), and we answer you, and you need a shirt, run! don't walk and claim your Eagle I. C. shirt at three cents off! At once!

STORE COUPON

3¢ SAVE 3¢ ON YOUR VERY NEXT EAGLE INISHOWEN CHEVIOT SHIRT! 3¢
(Price before discount, about $7.50)

MR. DEALER: For your convenience in obtaining prompt accurate payment for this coupon, send it to Eagle Shirtmakers, Herringbone Oxford Inishowen Cheviot Brooketowne Prompt Accurate Payment Department, Quakertown, Pennsylvania (Attn. Miss Afflerbach). Offer void where prohibited, restricted, or ignored. Only one (1) coupon per customer. Cash value: 1/100 of one cent. Eagle Shirtmakers.

© 1963 EAGLE SHIRTMAKERS, QUAKERTOWN, PENNSYLVANIA

THE MALACHI HOGAN SCHEME

DOES anybody here recall the old Eagle Laundry gag? Maybe the only reason we do is because we are 94 years old. First Man: My sister works at the Eagle Laundry. Second Man: What does she do? First Man: She washes Eagles. ★ So much for the warm-up. Malachi Hogan, the Eagle (shirt) salesman out of Kansas City, has come up with an idea to show you how beautifully our shirts are finished. He contends that no man is *really* happy about the way his shirts are laundered; and that this is because laundries (or wives) just don't have the skill, equipment, experience, time, or love of shirts to do them up the way the ladies in Finishing do. ★ Therefore, Mr. Hogan – being a salesman and interested in such things – also contends* that we could at one time show up the competition and gain your goodwill by fixing your shirt up something like new; if we wanted to. O. K., we want to: the Eagle Laundry is in business. For the moment. ★ We can't make a regular thing of this, understand, so just send us your favorite shirt in good condition. If by some chance your favorite shirt isn't yet an Eagle, send it anyway. Whatever it is, we'll launder it, iron it, fold it, pin it, and then put an Eagle label in it – unless it has one already. But we won't be sad if it doesn't. Many Eagle shirts have other labels put in by the fine stores that sell them.** And even if yours isn't an Eagle, the vicarious pleasure of owning a Mock Eagle*** may eventually lead you to the true joy of wearing the real thing. ★ In any case, stuff your favorite shirt in a big manila envelope and send it off to Barry Boonshaft, our Production Mgr. He'll bring it down to the Finishing Department and stand by while the ladies give it the 8-step new-shirt treatment. Better pin the coupon with your name, address and mark to the shirt so he can get it back to you as soon as it's done. Any shirts left at the end, he'll give over to charity – except maybe the 16-35's.

*He also contends that Ray Squire, our man in New England, had the idea first and that we should mention him too. All right.
**i. e. an Eagle shirt with a non-Eagle label.
***i. e. a non-Eagle shirt with an Eagle label.

Dear Barry Boonshaft, Eagle Shirtmakers, Quakertown, Pennsylvania:
I endorse the Malachi Hogan scheme which I understand expires November 15, 1961. Here's my favorite shirt. Do it up.

Name_____ Address_____ City_____ State_____

Laundry Mark_____

Gossage and his lead art director, Marget Larsen, pushed the limits of not only what an ad said but also how it looked. In the early 1960s, there weren't many agencies reversing long copy out of a black background (David Ogilvy would have been appalled).

IS IT PERFECTLY ALL RIGHT TO WEAR BUTTON-DOWN SHIRTS AT NIGHT?

★ ★

SURE. ★ But perhaps you're looking for a more motivational-research sort of answer? O.K., try this: ★ Some men feel positively uneasy with nothing to tack down their collars except gravity and starch, two of the most dreadful contributions of science. ★ It is in response to this demand for security in a free-floating age that most Eagle Shirt collars are button-downs. We are merely doing our part in the fight to Help Stamp Out Gravity; and get starch back where it ought to be, in low cholesterol diets. ★ Now, as to why you should have wondered about the propriety of button-downs at night: It probably stems from our society's innate conviction that it is not quite moral to enjoy yourself without *something* gnawing at you; even if it is only a collar button or the suspicion that your tie knot has migrated East for the evening. ★ But there is something else, too: the button-down collar had humble beginnings, if you call polo humble. That's right, the first ones were on polo shirts. Well, the horse has largely vanished from the scene, leaving only nostalgia in his wake; and button-down shirts. ★ Speaking of button-downs, we have a new model, this one without Eagle's famous sloppy bulge. It has shorter points. ★ Speaking of horses, we call it the Derby collar. It comes with button cuff, tapered body; in broadcloth: White, Blue, and Oyster. Speaking of Oyster, it is our own color; a versatile off-white with a twist of lemon. About $6.50, and if you don't know where to find Eagle Shirts please write Miss Afflerbach, Eagle Shirtmakers, Quakertown, Pennsylvania. © 1963 EAGLE SHIRTMAKERS, QUAKERTOWN, PENNSYLVANIA

The initial work had been in black and white. Success led to a bigger budget and colour ads. To promote the colour range, Gossage asked his readers for new shades and the names that might describe them.

ANNOUNCING THE 1963-1964 AFFLERBACH FELLOWSHIPS*

◆◆

BACKGROUND OF THE COMPETITION: No matter how much time our People in Naming spend thinking up just the right color names for our shirts (Maize, Stone Green, Peat Blue, etc.), the Eagle Secret Shoppers inevitably report that you choose *your* Eagle shirts with such statements as "Gimme six of them greenish ones" or "Could I bother you for two or three dozen of those stri-ped ones." Our problem is in selecting names which will capture the imagination of the shirt-buying public. ◆◆◆ NATURE OF THE COMPETITION: The 10 Afflerbachs for 1963-64 will go to those persons suggesting the best names for our colors. Imagination-capturing names, like Well Red, Long Green, Charlie Brown, or Navel Orange. You may wish to inspect our shirts—for inspiration, if not purchase. Eagle shirts don't always have an Eagle label—some fine stores sew in their own—but if you write us, we'll suggest your nearest Eagle Shirt Color Inspection Station. ◆◆◆ STIPEND: The grand prize winner will have his (or her) choice of a Traveling Afflerbach (a grand all-expense-paid weekend at the Bush House in Quakertown—an exciting chance to become acquainted with the natives —many of whom are us, including Miss Revera Afflerbach, herself) or a Stationary Afflerbach (a dozen Eagle Button-down shirts). The 9 other Afflerbachs will consist of a grant of four Eagle Button-down shirts. Each, that is. ◆◆◆ RULES: The competition is open to all under-graduates at, as well as those who have attended, schools. Applications are due by Jan. 1st, 1963.

*This, actually, is Eagle's second competition in as many years. Those of you who partook of the first, that is, what to do with the pocket on a Shirtkerchief, will doubtless be excited to learn that the book containing many of your letters to Miss Afflerbach has now been published by the Macmillan Co. and is now available at your bookseller. We have called it *Dear Miss Afflerbach, or The Postman Hardly Ever Rings 11,328 Times*, and the price is $4.95.

◆◆◆◆◆◆◆ AFFLERBACH FELLOWSHIP APPLICATION FORM ◆◆◆◆◆◆◆

1. Name_____ 2. Address_____

3. City_____ 4. State_____

(If you live in Altoona, Fresno, or other places we've never heard of, would you help our Ladies in Address-ing by telling us what city or town you live *near:*_____.)

5. Suggested color name (s) (e.g. In Violet, Hugo Black, Whizzer White)

_____

Mail the completed application to The Afflerbach Foundation, Eagle Shirtmakers, Quakertown, Pennsylvania

© 1963 EAGLE SHIRTMAKERS, QUAKERTOWN, PENNSYLVANIA

Newspapers amplified the story. As Alice Lowe - who ran the Gossage agency - recalled: "The press services promptly picked up the color name story resulting in hundreds of additional suggestions from every state in the Union … The London *Times* ran the color name story and reportedly received 4,000 suggestions."

Here's the follow-up with the winning entries (look out for "Original Cinnamon", "Freudian Gilt", "Dorian Grey", "Medi Ochre" and "Inalienable White").

[Eagle Shirtmakers Proudly Announces]

NO. CALDWELL, N. J. MAN or a MISS LAUREN WINS COVETED AFFLERBACH FELLOWSHIP!

AFTER what is possibly the world's record rumination over who won a color-naming competition we have reached a decision. If you can remember that far back, more than a year ago we deplored the uninspired names given to colors (light green, dark blue, etc.) as well as the sheer flights of fancy that conveyed nothing at all (Kumquat Blossom Time, December Showers, Teaneck, etc.). We asked your assistance in conjuring up new, evocative names for shirt colors, but names that also had some connection with reality; such as Whizzer White, Well Red, Navel Orange, and so on. ★ To make the enterprise more tempting we dangled a Grand Prize of a Traveling Afflerbach Fellowship: a glamorous weekend at Quakertown, Pa., our HQ (with a free sightseeing trip into romantic Philadelphia), or a dozen Eagle Shirts. Additionally, there were 9 Stationary Afflerbachs of 1/2 dozen Eagle Shirts offered as second prizes. ★ Well, here it is: The winner is none other than either W. R. Goodwin of No. Caldwell, N. J. or Janet Lauren of New York, N. Y.! They were *so* close, which is what held us up, that they both win the grand prize. Second prize winners will be notified by mail. Congratulations, all! ★ Among the thousands and thousands of splendid names submitted—some of which we shall surely use—were the following:

Forever Amber	Profits Ecru	Willie Maize	Glasses Colored Rose
Chat Aqua	Goodclean Fawn	Sweet Molly Maroon	Tokyo Rose
Freres Aqua	Proud Flesh	Your Mauve	Abie's Irish Rose
Come Azure	Rudolf Flesh	Afterdinner Mint	Braint Rust
Sick Bay	Too too solid Flesh	Establish Mint	Guaranteed Rust
Editorial Beige	Another part of the Forest	U. S. Mint	Implicit Rust
Gar Beige	Unforeseeable Fuchsia	Shotan Mist	Livery Sabin
Noblesso Beige	Freudian Gilt	Mickey Moss	Old Chinese Sage
Shan Franshishco Beige	Barry Water Gold	S. F. B. Moss	Polish Sauce Sage
Hole of Calcutta Black	Bydosis Gold	Go-Easy-on-the Mustard	Lock Sand
Jungle Board Black	Common Gold	Plastered Mustard	Leapin' Lizards Sandy
Miss Affler Black	Ill-Gotten Gold	Army Navy	Hell Sapphire
Strap Molasses Black	Molly Berg Gold	Swiss Navy	Holy Mackerel Sapphire
Fountain Blue	Conquered Grape	Uncommitted Neutral	Lawsy Miss Scarlet
Gabriel Blue	Statutory Grape	God's Little Ochre	Point Sienna
Hulla Blue	Gang Green	Medi Ochre	Hiho Silver
St. James Infirmary Blue	Keep-Bucks County Green	Wicked Ochre	Bipartisan Slate
Something Blue	Lohen Green	Strip Ochre	Last Straw
Turn Blue	One-Putt Green	Tappi Ochre	Outright Steel
Elizabeth Barretting Brown	Other Fellow's Grass Green	Bringemback Olive	Eppy Taffy
Hash Brown	Sha Green	Im Peach	Barroom Tan
How Now Cow Brown	Thumb Green	Com Pewter	Charla Tan
Some-kind-of-nut Brown	Turn Green	Lydia Pink	Fan Tan
Wernervon Brown	My Darling Nelly Grey	Parlor Pink	Convertible Taupe
Blind Man's Buff	Dorian Grey	Political Plum	Room at the Taupe
Civil War Buff	At-night-all-cats-are Gray	Tuckered Out Plum	Tip Taupe
And-to-Hell-with Burgundy	Prematurely Gray	Hlanimous Puce	Unsafe Topaz
Bizet's Carmine	Stin Gray	Rest in Puce	Down Umber
De Sapio Carmine	Zane Gray	Clare Booth Luce Puce	Telephone Umbor
Carminative	Hard Hearted Henna	Ouida Purple	Unshrinking Violet
Cyd Cerise	Lie Down Honey	People Eater Purple	Bled White
World Cerise	Outdigo Indigo	Unpertur Purple	Civil White
Bit Cherry	Mood Indigo	Silly Putty	Inalienable White
Bread Chrome	Kiddledy Ivy	Better Dead than Red	'Enry 'Iggins Just You White
Hot Chestnut	Hill Mob Lavender	Blooded American Boy Red	Frankfloyd White
Original Cinnamon	Blind Date Lemon	Light District Red	Hepple White
Purr Cinnamon	Lilac à Trooper	Sea Red	Hereford Faced White
Roe Cocoa	Harry Lime	Thorob Red	White Urp
Come and Get Me Copper	Mason Dixon Lime	Shad Rose	Follow the Brick Road Yellow
Robert Shaw Coral	My Funny Valiant Lime	Billy Rose	Stonepark Yellow
Eagle's Cream	Quick Lime	Cost-of-living Rose	Sunlight on the Mustard of a
Isles Cream	Sub Lime	Gypsy Rose	Coney Island Hot
Dun Scotus	Free Loden	Hackles Rose	Dog at Sunset
Seventh Ebon	Impenetrable Maize	Hedge Rose	Yellow
		Too Black Rose	

PLEASE DO NOT FILL IN THIS COUPON!

THE only reason this coupon is here is: we are going to make this page into an easel card to sit on the counters of stores that sell Eagle Shirts; and where this space is we are going to have a pad of entry blanks which people who buy shirts (as opposed to people who merely read ads like this and who at any rate have already had a chance at color-naming) may fill out with *their* color name entries. Fair is fair. Incidentally, this sort of effort is called "merchandising", possibly because it is intended to brighten the eyes of the merchant who sells Eagle shirts. If you don't know who that might be in your town (they don't all have neon signs announcing same in their windows, you know) you might write Miss Afflerbach; you may use the coupon for *that* if you like.

Dear Miss Afflerbach
Eagle Shirtmakers,
Quakertown, Pa.:

Where is my nearest Eagle Shirt dealer? (Psst, how about

_____ for a color name?) Sincerely,

Name_____

Address_____

City_____ Zone_____ State_____

© 1964, EAGLE SHIRTMAKERS, QUAKERTOWN, PENNSYLVANIA

And this is one of the ads that came from the colour naming competition.

THE NEW HUE IN EAGLE BUTTON-DOWNS: FORESEEABLE FUCHSIA

LOOKS pink, doesn't it? ★ We chose the name for this color from among the entries in our recent competition for new color-names because of its aptness: we predict great things. Remember you heard it here first. ★ What makes our solid pink new is that it isn't solid pink: the vertical yarn (or warp) is somewhere between a Robert Shaw Coral and a Lawsy Miss Scarlet; whereas the horizontal yarn (or woof) is a sort of 'Enry 'Iggins Just You White. ★ Thus creating an illusion, but of the finest oxford cloth all the same; with button cuffs and our dear, old bulgy collar, about $7.00. If you don't know where to buy this and other Eagle Shirts in your town, please write Miss Afflerbach who does; at the address below.

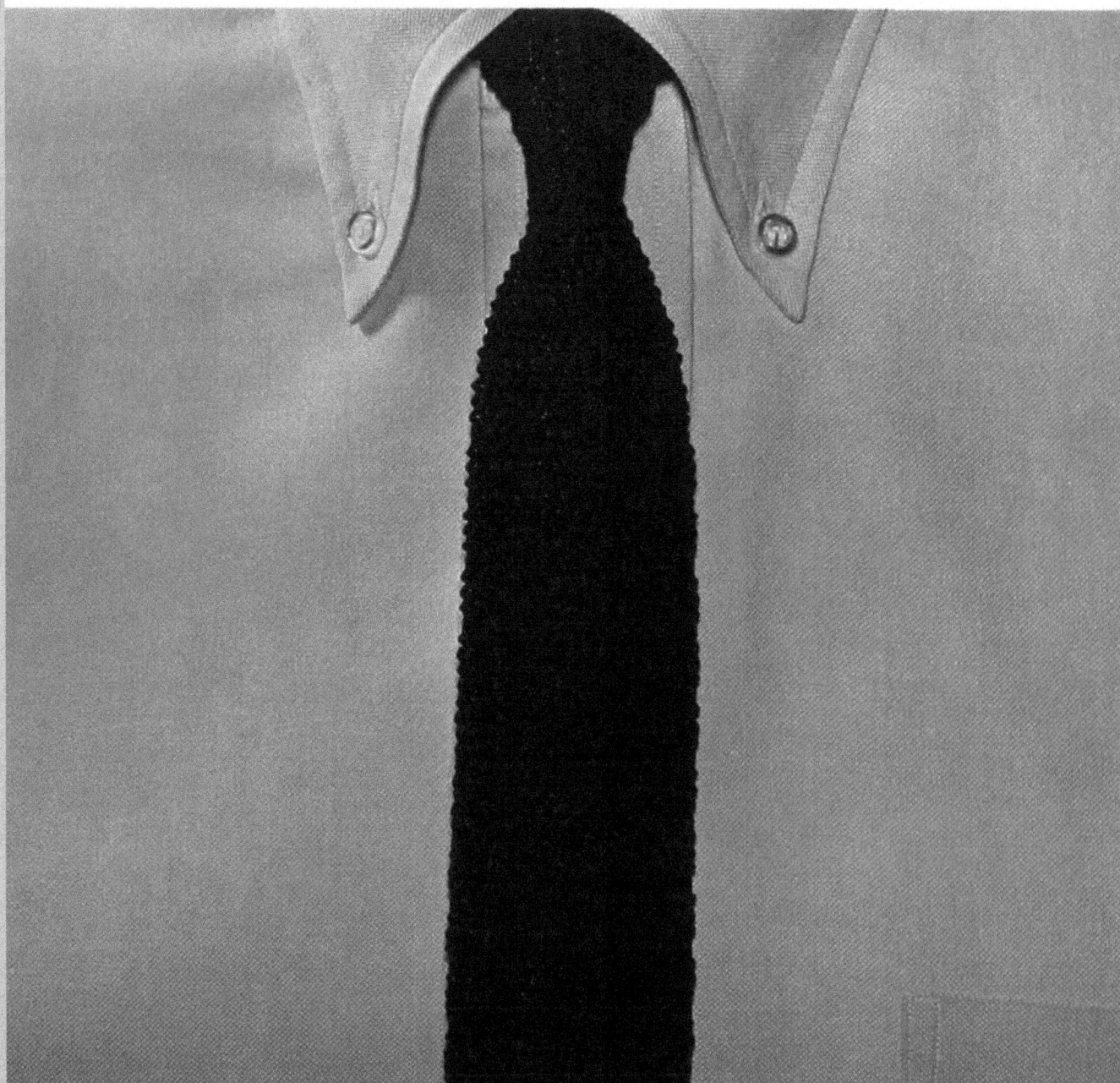

Whenever possible, Gossage sought to pull the reader in by disrupting advertising's conventions. Here the Eagle Shirts visual appears on the right hand page of the *New Yorker* - with the headline ending abruptly...

WHY WEAR LESS INTERESTING SH

...only for the headline - complete with body copy - to resume on the following left hand page.

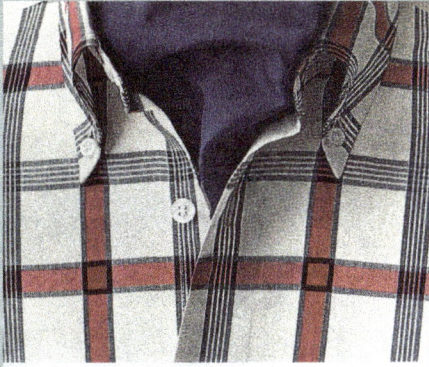

[An Eagle Naval Spectacular]

TRAFALGAR SQUARES

It appears that we are eight years too late to celebrate Vice-Admiral Horatio Lord Viscount Nelson's 200th birthday, but a nice shirt is welcome anytime. • His mother's maiden name was Catherine Suckling, which is almost the last light-hearted thing we read of him. At age 16 (see. Encycl. Brit., 11th Ed.) he prophesied, "I will be a hero, and, confiding in Providence, I will brave every danger." • On this authentic note we inform you that Trafalgar Squares come in Navy Blue, Navy Red, Navy White, and Navy Silver. • The colors themselves are from the Haywood portrait in the Trafalgar Room at Trader Vic's, San Francisco. The shirts themselves are of fine gingham and are for sale with button-down collars and short sleeves for about $10.00 wherever Eagle Shirts are sold. • If you're not certain where that is in your port, write Miss Afflerbach at the F. P. O. below.

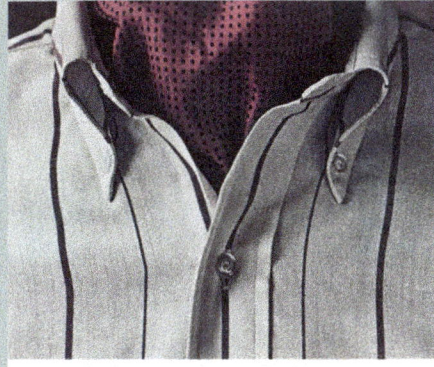

THE TROUBLE WITH SPORTS SHIRTS IS WHEN YOU WEAR AN ORDINARY TIE WITH ONE YOU LOOK LIKE A GANGSTER

However there are times that are a little too dressy for an unadorned throat (as when you're wearing a blazer), and for these the Ascot is finding increasing favor. Women apparently find them madly attractive, and men like their go-to-hell feel once they get around to wearing them. The trick seems to be in tying them, actually, there is nothing to it. All you do is slip the Ascot around your neck, inside the collar, and loop one end over the other below your adam's apple; and loop it once so it won't slip down your chest after awhile. • It just so happens that, foreseeing this demand, we have gone into the Ascot game. You will find a nice selection at your Eagle Ascot store, which is the same store where you buy Eagle Shirts. • Not to change the subject, but this magnificent short-sleeve sports shirt at about $9.00 which we have portrayed here is an exclusive Eagle pattern in two-ply cotton oxford, and comes in blue, green, or burgundy stripes alternating with skinnier black ones on an Eagle's Cream ground. • We also have a magnificent matching check; let's see if we can describe it: it's something as though we ran transverse stripes in the same colors across that pattern. No, that's a terrible description; you'd better go take a look for yourself. If you don't know where that would be, drop a line to Miss Afflerbach and she'll write right back with the news.

NOW EAGLE BUTTON-DOWNS IN ZANE GRAY: SOLID AND ALSO WITH STRIPES

This new shade of Batiste Madras, christened with one of the entries in our late, great, competition for more inspired color-names, might be more fittingly described as Bipartisan Slate; for it is certainly versatile. It is a handsome daytime color, yet unobtrusive enough to get by nicely at night. • It is available in a solid—which you'll have to imagine—and, as shown here, in stripes of red (World Cerise) or blue (Holy Mackerel Sapphire). • Buy them with short sleeves and customary baggy collars for about $7.00 wherever Eagle Shirts are sold. If you're not sure where that is in your town, please drop a note to Miss Afflerbach at the address below.

Do you recall that Great 1920's novel, the passage where the hero shows the girl his shirts? And she cries because she never saw such beautiful shirts? Sometimes we cry too.

[The G---- G----- Tromblee]*

Our 100th anniversary and we are swept into nostalgia. The shirt above, made of chambray, also comes in Zelda Red (a poignant vin ancient) and West Egg Grey, and with our lovable, baggy button-down collar if you'd rather. About $8.50. If you don't know where Eagle shirts are sold write Miss Afflerbach at the address below.

We find this all spelled out the Whitney's estate until etc.

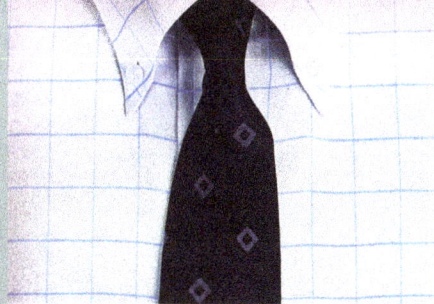

[Eagle Goes Along With The Law Of Gravity]

WINDOWPANE CZECHS

Everybody talks about the Defenestration of Prague but nobody does anything about it. • Therefore Eagle has decided to commemorate the 547th anniversary of the First Defenestration — or throwing people out the window—in which both the people and the windows were high up in City Hall. • (The Second Defenestration, in 1618, was of Ambassadors from the Hradcany Palace, and started the Thirty Years War; which is too long to go into here.) • The lesson is clear: When in Prague do as the Czechs do; and do it low down. • Now, in addition to Blue on Greenish, these checks also come Blue on Yellowish, and Yellow on Bluish. The shirting is our very own Oxford Voile; the sleeves short; the collar, Eagle's beloved, baggy button-down. • If you'd like to get in on the ground floor, you may buy Windowpane Czechs for about $7.00 wherever Eagle shirts are sold. Please write Miss Afflerbach at the address below if you aren't sure where that is in your town.

[Eagle introduces its Durable Press shirt* with Dacron; about $9]

We are 100 years old and the last time we made striped shirts that didn't have to be ironed was during the 1920s Florida land boom when the Real Estate Promoters were making so much money they bought $20 silk shirts and, although land had been discovered on some of their land, no laundries had; so they wore the shirts until they were soiled and then threw them away. Those were the days, hey Charlie?

*Durable Press means that you can wash the shirt in a washing machine and dry it in a dryer and put it on and it will look like a brand new shirt (that has been washed in a washer and dried in a dryer). This shirt of 65% Dacron® polyester and 35% cotton oxford comes in several dandy stripes, and if you want to pick one out we advise you to rush around so we whatever you buy Eagle shirts. If you don't know where you buy Eagle shirts, Miss Afflerbach at the address below will be more than glad to remind you.
Dacron® is DuPont's registered trademark*

Pictured above are just a few of the dozens of product ads that Gossage wrote for Eagle Shirts.

While he usually avoided this kind of, what he called, "treadmill" work, he made an exception because Eagle Shirts was his favourite account, and he got on very well with its boss, Miller Harris.

This good relationship paid dividends on the campaign you're about to see. Because it was the quick turnaround by Miller Harris's factories in Quakertown that enabled Gossage to pull off one of his most famous coups.

Gossage was a fan of classical music, and enjoyed listening to the small FM radio station *KSFR*.

When he found it was closing down for lack of funds, he persuaded his beer client, Rainier Ale, to send over a cheque for 13 weeks' advertising. Problem was, he forgot to do any ads and when the air date came, he had nothing to run.

Fortuitously, about two years earlier he'd seen a *Peanuts* cartoon which featured a "Beethoven Sweat-shirt".

Desperate for an idea, he pulled it from his "recall file", and wrote the radio script announcing the arrival of the Beethoven, Brahms and Bach Sweatshirts.

As Bob Freeman explained: "Nobody … but … nobody had ever screened anybody's picture on a sweatshirt or a T-shirt, or any other kind of shirt before."

Gossage put in an emergency call to Miller Harris at Eagle Shirts who quickly ran off 600 sweatshirts. These sold so fast, he decided to advertise them in the *New Yorker* and *San Francisco Chronicle* saying "What the hell, let's go for broke and print 20,000. It's nothing but money!"

The sponsor of this effort to 'strike a blow for culture', Rainier Ale, was duly accorded a tiny product shot in the bottom left with a caption exlaining the single selling point that this was a strong beer for men only (more of which later).

BE THE FIRST ONE IN YOUR PEER-GROUP TO OWN A BEETHOVEN, BRAHMS, OR BACH SWEATSHIRT™

In accordance with our policy of bringing culture to the masses, Rainier Ale sponsors an hour-long program seven nights a week on a San Francisco classical music FM station, KSFR. That this sort of entertainment is a trifle too starchy for our own taste is unimportant compared to the pleasure it gives others. Besides, we are a thousand miles away in Seattle, so we couldn't hear it if we wanted to.

(Do you want to know the real reason? O.K., the real reason is we did a survey that shows the people who like Our Product the most are either highbrows or lowbrows. It costs a lot of money to reach lowbrows because there are so many of them; and they aren't a particularly grateful bunch, either — probably because *everybody* wants to do something for them. You ask them to run down to the store and buy some, but do they?

Nope. Highbrows, on the other hand, are pitifully grateful for any little thing you do for them; it sort of gets you. They may not be numerous, but by golly they can sure sprint down to the store. In the old mercantile track meet give us highbrows every time.)

Which is why we have been offering Beethoven, Brahms, or Bach Sweatshirts over KSFR. The response was so enormous that we are extending the offer to music lovers the country over; though Rainier Ale is now only available in the West (but soon in N.Y.!).

[OUR PRODUCT]

*Rainier Ale itself is for men only; at least no woman has ever been known to drink it; they apparently don't care for it. Our Product has a good male color and a good male flavor; it is for men. But music (and sweatshirts) are for everybody. WARNING: Don't try to swill it down like beer. Rainier Ale is more substantial; it should be drunk like, and given the same respect as, a highball.

They are in "athaletic gray" and two large sizes only: Men and Women.* They fit anybody in a roomy sort of way if you shove the cuffs up. Now, on the front is a life-sized head of either Beethoven, Brahms, or Bach, exactly as pictured, each with his name below to identify him to uninitiated passers-by. The price: a mere $4.00 each. We would like to give them away, but state laws and our own prudence forbid it. $4.00, plus postage (offer limited to the U.S.A.); no C.O.D.'s or any of those tricks, please. *SEND FOR YOUR CLASSICAL SWEATSHIRT(S) TODAY!*

THREE B's
— — — SWEATSHIRT — — —
COUPON

BEETHOVEN | BRAHMS | J.S.BACH

Sweatshirts
Rainier Ale
Box 3134N
Seattle 14, Washington

Dear Sweatshirts:

Please find check or money order to cover the following sweatshirts at $4.00 apiece, plus 50¢ each to cover the cost of postage and handling.

☐ Beethoven. No. desired_____ Sex_____
☐ Brahms.   No. desired_____ Sex_____
☐ Bach.   No. desired_____ Sex_____

Name_____

Address_____

City_____State_____

Apparently Gossages' agency made more money that year from sweatshirts than they did from advertising.

Of course, Gossage was behind the sales drive. As one of his publicity ploys he sent a sweatshirt to the most famous conductor/composer in the world, Leonard Bernstein, who was then pictured in the *New York Times* wearing his whilst rehearsing with the New York Symphony Orchestra.

The craze spread from the highbrow to the hip, and soon Hollywood stars like Jane Fonda (seen above) were coming out for Beethoven. The press and public duly responded. As Alice Lowe recalled, "Stories about the sweatshirts appeared in hundreds of newspapers and magazines. Orders came in from all over the United States and many foreign countries including England, Japan and Australia."

The success encouraged Gossage to do an audacious tie-in with Pablo Picasso, putting his images on a range of apres-ski sportswear (as promoted in double page spreads in *Life* magazine) and sold courtesy of the country's most exclusive stores.

The clothes looked great - and the ads weren't bad either.

You have the frame. Now get the Picasso.
You can frame your own Picasso now... just by wearing it. Because White Stag secured exclusive rights to reproduce his works as fabric designs for apparel. And did. In the original colors. In a unique collection of sportswear for fall. Shown: the "Figures" parka with snap front in vinyl coated cotton. Sizes S-M-L, $19.
you're right, it's White Stag

Until now only walls wore Picassos.
Now you can put a Picasso on your very own frame. Because White Stag secured exclusive rights to reproduce his works as fabric designs for apparel. And did. In the original colors. In a unique collection of fall sportswear. Shown: "Triptych" fleece-back knitted cotton pullover S-M-L, $9.
you're right, it's White Stag

Can you afford a Picasso?
If you have thirty dollars, you can own this Picasso. Because White Stag secured exclusive rights to reproduce his works as fabric designs for apparel. And did. In the original colors. In a unique collection of sportswear for fall. Shown: "Musician Faun" corduroy poncho. Unsized, $30.
you're right, it's White Stag

77

As we've seen, Rainier Ale put up the money for the initial Beethoven Sweatshirt ads - and were rewarded with a footnote which highlighted the beer's major strength - which was precisely that: its strength.

In fact, according to Bob Freeman, it was so strong, the regulations said you couldn't focus on that in the advertising. He recalled: "We took on the ale partly because of the challenge of telling people it was strong without saying so."

So they positioned it as "a Man's Beer".

And to get that point across, Gossage made strong men the focus, and came up with perhaps his most successful publicity stunt of all.

It revolved around a sponsored walk from San Francisco to the Rainier brewery's home in Seattle.

The star was 80 year old John F. ("Old Iron Legs") Stahl. And the launch revolved around finding "vigorously masculine" fellow hikers to accompany him on the 1,000 mile trek.

All very macho stuff.

And commercially persuasive, too. Not only was Gossage promoting the walk, he was also soft-selling the beer and cross-selling the sweatshirts in both the body copy and the captions, bottom right.

COACH STAHL WANTS YOU TO WALK TO SEATTLE!

Yes, this is your chance to win a free trip to Seattle's Century 21 World's Fair! And the beauty of it is you will be able to enjoy the great out of doors every step of the 1000 miles from the Opera House in San Francisco to Seattle and the Space Needle. What finer way to reassure man that he will still be able to fill his lungs with fresh air amidst the marvels of the 21st Century?

However, man does not live by breath alone.

In line with Rainier Ale's policy of combining the cultural with the vigorously masculine, you will, of course, be wearing one of our Beethoven, Bach, or Brahms Sweatshirts* as the glorious miles trudge by. Expenses en route will be paid; you will be fully equipped from sweatshirt to shoes. On arrival at the Fair each of you will receive a crisp $1000 bill from an official (at the very least) of the Seattle Fair in recognition of your services to music.**

All this if you can qualify as one of the three man team to leave San Francisco the day the fair opens, April 21, 1962, and arrive whenever you get there. Applicants must be between 21 and 65 and have about three months to spare so they won't have to hurry; this is no race. Coach Stahl, shown at left, is against walking for any reason except pleasure and physical improvement. He moreover feels that this project, in line as it is with the President's fitness program, would be self-defeating if the walkers arrived too pooped to have a nice time at the Fair.

We are fortunate indeed in having John F. (Old Iron Legs) Stahl, Rainier Ale's Athaletic Director, as mentor of our squad. Coach Stahl, the dean of American walkers, has already made the arduous trip himself in a "dry run" (a figure of speech, since he gratifyingly believes Our Product to be an adornment to the training table). Mr. Stahl, 79 — he intends to spend his 80th birthday on the road to the Fair — has made walking his career since being retired from the Postoffice for physical disability in 1935. He has covered 17,832 miles the hard way during the last 27 years. His walking feats on three continents include a 3000 miler from the Canal Zone to Austin, Texas and from Fatima, Portugal, via Lourdes, to Rome. He has received many honors in recognition of his prowess, viz., he is a Papal Knight of St. Gregory and an Honorary Texas Ranger. He credits his longevity and excellent physique to walking and is anxious to inculcate an appreciation of its pleasures in young people. "The Twist is no substitute," says he, "the action is faulty."

Of the Seattle Walk Coach Stahl says, "Hitch-hikers need not apply; we do not need their sort." Those of you who are interested in joining him at the San Francisco training camp should have your applications in no later than April 9th. Write: Mr. John F. Stahl, c/o Rainier Ale, Seattle, Washington. Coach Stahl will require the data customary in affairs of this sort — age, occupation, photograph, shoe size, previous experience in long distance walking, if any; and, without seeming to pry, a report on the general condition of your health. In a pinch he would be willing to accept your say-so in this area, however a report from your personal physician would be preferable. We like to acknowledge the primacy of the medical profession in corporal matters whenever we can. It only seems fair. Oh, one other thing: men only.*** Happy Walking!

*You may still buy one — and we now have Mozart, too — by sending $4.00 plus 50c postage and handling to: Sweatshirts, Rainier Ale, Box S3134N, Seattle 14, Washington. Specify composer and size; either Male or Female.
**Since you are making the trip anyway perhaps you won't mind doing a service for us, too: return a Rainier Ale empty to the brewery; a purely symbolic gesture to remind you who put up the $1000.
***Rainier Ale itself is for men only, or so we like to think. It has a strong male flavor and a strong male color. Therefore it should not be swilled down, but drunk with the same respect as a highball. Our Product is now available on the West Coast only, but soon N.Y., and after that who knows?
© 1962 SICKS' RAINIER BREWING CO., SEATTLE, WASHINGTON

OUR PRODUC

Here's Gossage and his wife Sally seeing Coach Stahl and Co off at the Golden Gate Bridge.

Once the walk began, Gossage wrote the ad below then let the news media do the rest: "The newspaper, television and radio coverage on the coast was enormous. Front page newspaper stories with pictures - sometimes five column pictures - and absolutely no reluctance to mention the client's name."

All for what Alice Lowe calculated to be an out-of-pocket expense totalling $32,000.

[A Progress Report on the Rainier Ale Walk To The Seattle World's Fair]

COACH STAHL AND TEAM OFF AND WALKING!

Yes, by now the three man team headed by its playing Coach John F. "Old Iron Legs" Stahl, Rainier's Athletic Director, is well on the long walk from San Francisco to the Seattle World's Fair, "Century 21."

Chosen from over 700 applicants who answered our appeal, the three finalists selected by Coach represent a broad if interesting cross-section of American manhood.* They include a Scots bagpiper, a millionaire, and a soldier of fortune. They are:

CHARLES KNOWLES, 28, 6 feet 4 inches tall, Secretary of the Clan Campbell and Pipe Major of the Fraser Highlanders. Charles, not an inhibited man, will play your favorite selections at the drop of a *piobreach*. Since he habitually wears kilts anyway he is marching northward in them at a stalwart gait. At last report he was in the lead by several furlongs.

Not too far behind, however —and we must repeat that this is no race, the Coach feeling strongly that walking is for healthful, manly enjoyment— is *HERBERT HASCHE*, 62, a millionaire whose fortune is based on an invention which gives solace to each of us who rides in a car since it apparently has to do with the springing system and no American car is without one or however many it takes of whatever it is. Herb, as he has asked us to call him, is also the father of 5 children under 10 years of age. They (Gina, Nina, Tina, Herbert, Jr. and Henry II) and his pretty blonde wife (Evelyn) were at the Golden Gate Bridge to wave a cheery, teary goodbye on getaway day, May 9. (Oh, the excitement! The press was out in force and all the TV stations and newsreels; it was glorious.)

Our third man, *ROBERT LE MAIRE*, 38, is a professional adventurer-explorer who has spent his life seeing the world the hard way. Immediately he reaches Seattle he will head an expedition to certain lost cities in Central America, an area he knows well from previous scientific forays.

And, of course, there is *COACH STAHL* of whom we talked in detail last time. The Coach has done more walking than all the rest put together and will have totalled over 18,000 miles by the time he reaches the Fair; this exclusive of his pre-retirement U.S. Postal miles. He plans to coincide his arrival with his 80th birthday on August 13. Projected individual schedules by the others will have them coming in the 27th of June (Knowles), Fourth of July (Hasche; his and the nation's birthday), and the 15th of July (Le-Maire). However, the road is long and who knows what hardships and adventures may await our boys and alter their well laid plans?

They are each proceeding alone and by different routes as we see by the accompanying strip map. We hope that any of you living along, or driving along these roads to Seattle will wave or honk a friendly hello should you see any of the four. But please do not offer them a ride; it would only embarrass them since they have taken the pledge.

This concludes the news, now on to our footnote:

Gossage followed the Seattle walk with a campaign which featured his wife, Sally, as the parody of demure femininity. It was all done tongue-in-cheek but, if you think it's sexist, wait until you see what's coming up next.

RAINIER ALE

Very Few Women Are Allowed To Drink It.

* Because Our Product has traditionally been brewed for the stronger sex. Rainier Ale has never been light, feminine, or dry; it has always been dark, masculine, and very wet. A stirring record.

For this framed picture suitable for framing write: SICKS' RAINIER BREWING CO., SEATTLE, WASH. © 1963 [OUR PRODUCT]

RAINIER ALE

Very Few Women Are Allowed To Drink It.

* And southpaw banjo players are even rarer. On the other hand, however, is man's traditional right to quaff Our Product. Rainier Ale is neither light nor dry; it is dark, powerfully wet, and always has been. A blazer of a record.

For this framed picture suitable for framing write: SICKS' RAINIER BREWING CO., SEATTLE, WASH. © 1963 [OUR PRODUCT]

RAINIER ALE

Very Few Women Are Allowed To Drink It.

* Important New Evidence suggests that the reason for this is that women prefer light, feminine, dry beverages which tingle, etc. Rainier Ale is dark, masculine, and extremely wet. It feels good to your Adam's apple and goes "glunk, glunk" down your throat.

For this framed picture suitable for framing write: SICKS' RAINIER BREWING CO., SEATTLE, WASH. © 1963 [OUR PRODUCT]

RAINIER ALE

Very Few Women Are Allowed To Drink It.

*Or care to do so. This for the simple reason that Rainier Ale is neither light, feminine, nor dry. Our Product is dark, masculine, and extremely wet.

For this framed picture suitable for framing write: SICKS' RAINIER BREWING CO., SEATTLE, WASH. © 1963 [OUR PRODUCT]

Newsweek commented that Gossage "is willing to risk offending and even mystify his public as long as he can get its attention." Which certainly explains this campaign for Rainier.

The inevitable outcry came with the much publicised picketing of the Rainier factory by the League of Women voters. Which, of course, was precisely as Gossage intended.

84

Gossage was the master of the erudite, long copy press ad. His ability to paint word pictures also worked perfectly on radio. But TV is different. Usually it's the fewer the words the better. So, as you'll see from these scripts for Milky Way (which he was working on with Stan Freberg), television was not Howard's medium. Especially when the target audience was 8 years old.

FREEMAN & GOSSAGE inc.

13 August 1964

Dear Stan,

This bids fair to be the longest note you ever received. Also, if the stuff turns out to be absolutely terrible I can always say, what the hell does he expect out of personal correspondence?

O. K., let's start with the stuff Donner says she needs first, the kids' stuff for TV. Each of the following have two characters. It might not be bad to use puppets, though it might be nice if they had little bitty arms since a couple of things in the first spot seem to call for them, I think.

One character, Captain Milky Way, will appear in both spots. I see him as sort of a more clean cut Orville instead of a humanoid figure. The reason is: while space m.c.'s of kids' shows look like people because they come from Earth, Captain Milky Way comes from another planet (pick one at random), and who on Mars knows how he would look? Remember Miss Mercury from the Miss Universe Contest of 1957? A perfect 36-36-36? For all I know he's made of chocolate and might have to caution the technicians every now and then to pull back the lights because he doesn't want to have to run until the program is over. (Do they still plug putting Milky Ways in the refrigerator? It might make a lead in for another spot later). Anyway, let's start it like this (he sounds like Orville to me):

CAPTAIN MILKY WAY: Hi there boys and girls, this is Captain Milky Way from Mars. While I am not a candy bar myself, I suppose you notice my creamy complexion? Heh, heh (LAUGHS MODESTLY AND LOWERS EYELASHES) though not as delectable as the pure chocolate coating on a Milky Way bar to be sure.

- 2 -

(BRISKLY) But up and away to my
mission here which is to apprehend
my arch enemy Major Skincrawl, the
notorious candy counter-spy. He is
always spying on candy counters. Why,
I can't imagine...

MAJOR SKINCRAWL (POKES HEAD OUT FROM BEHIND WALL OF MILKY
WAYS AT REAR AND SAYS IN AN ASIDE):

Because I want to snitch a Milky Way
and copy its chocolate malty goodness,
its creamy caramel, (ECSTATICALLY) its
luscious nougat, and go in the candy
bar business for myself".

CAPTAIN MILKY WAY: What's that? (LOOKS, SEES NOTHING,
SHRUGS)

MAJOR SKINCRAWL   (POKES HEAD OUT AGAIN):
I'd buy one if I wasn't so cheap.

CAPTAIN MILKY WAY (WHIPS AROUND SUDDENLY, THE MAJOR DUCKS
BACK):

Oh, have I told you about my hobby?
It's stacking Milky Ways. This stack
here -- believe it or not -- is
43,723, no, 29, bars tall. (CONFIDENTIALLY
WITH HAND ALONGSIDE MOUTH) When you get
that high it's a pretty dangerous hobby
because if you so much...(CUT TO MAJOR
SKINCRAWL REMOVING ONE MILKY WAY FROM
STACK) ..as move just one Milky Way the

F   &   G

- 3 -

whole shebang could topple over and if
anybody happens to be under it at the
time, whew! (ROLLS EYES TO HEAVEN)

(GROANING SOUND LIKE GIANT REDWOOD STARTING
TO FALL)

MAJOR SKINCRAWL: Timber!

(THE WHOLE THING COLLAPSES WITH TREMENDOUS
CRASH. CUT TO PILE OF MILKY WAYS WITH MAJOR'S
ARM STICKING OUT HOLDING ONE BAR IN HIS HAND)

CAPTAIN MILKY WAY: Oh drat! Well...(TAKES BAR FROM
MAJOR'S HAND, SETS IT DOWN, AND STARTS
STACKING AGAIN) ...
One, two, three,...

(CLOSE IN TO GROWING STACK AND HOLD TO FINISH)

I know this has structural (and other) defects, but you
get the idea.

Now, Stanley, in this next one we'll introduce another
character, Milky the Bar. I guess he ought to look something like Smokey the Bear, sort of burly and pissed off,
but instead of a ranger hat he's wearing a pointy soldier's
hat made out of newspapers, the way kids do. I guess they
do; they used to, anyway. It goes:

CAPTAIN MILKY WAY: Hi boys and girls, this is Captain
Milky Way, from Mars. The best candy
bars on earth come from Mars, you know.
I am not a candy bar myself, of course.
Although (WAGGISHLY) some people do say
I look good enough to eat. (LAUGHS,

F   &   G

- 4 -

ORVILLE-STYLE) However, nothing, I
repeat, nothing is as good to eat as
a chocolate malty Milky Way. Just
take the wrapper off and...

MILKY THE BAR: ...And do what with it?

(CAPTAIN MILKY WAY JERKS AROUND, COWERS)

CAPTAIN MILKY WAY: Who are you?

MILKY THE BAR: Milky the Bar.

CAPTAIN MILKY WAY: You're not going to eat me are you?

MILKY THE BAR: No, I wanted to warn you about that
wrapper in your hand...

CAPTAIN MILKY WAY: I wasn't going to start a forest fire
with it, honest.

MILKY THE BAR: You've got me confused with Smokey the
Bear. I'm Milky the Bar and (TO
AUDIENCE) I want to ask every one
of you to help keep America free of litter.
Don't be litter bugs. Don't throw candy
wrappers around. Yes, when you next
take the wrapper off a Milky Way...

CAPTAIN MILKY WAY: Break it in half, eh?

MILKY THE BAR: No, throw your Milky Way wrapper in a
trash basket! (ADDRESSES CAPTAIN MILKY
WAY) Now go on with what you were saying.

F   &   G

- 5 -

CAPTAIN MILKY WAY (NERVOUSLY):

Yes, boys and girls throw your Milky
Way wrappers in the trash can (LOOKS
NERVOUSLY AROUND TO SEE WHETHER BAR
HAS GONE, CUPS HANDS AROUND MOUTH AND
WHISPERS) ...But make sure you take the
Milky Way out first.

If you like this at all there is an alternate ending to
the effect that if you want to get credit for being neat
and putting Milky Way wrappers in trash cans first you've
got to buy a Milky Way. Also, if you continue with this
character in other spots I suppose there are other things
to do with Milky Way wrappers then throwing them away:
you could make paper hats out of them. Question: Does
that go for the teeny weeny bars too? Answer: Not unless
you have a teeny weeny head.

This is only the first installment on this letter. Donner
tells me that these are the highest priority so I'll send
them off to you now.

Yours (to be continued) truly,

F   &   G

Gossage knew his limitations and attempted little TV work. As we're about to see, he was also acutely aware when his print work wasn't working.

One of his first clients was Paul Masson Vineyards and initially he did good, idiosyncratic ads aligning the brand's personality with the founder. It was a strategy that subsequently worked well for Hal Riney on Bartles & Jaymes and for Jack Daniels - as tube travelling UK readers with good memories will attest.

Paul Masson said: Tether the horses and set out my brandy!

An early riser and a hard driver. From his Vineyard in the Sky to San Francisco is 50 miles, a good day's ride. But Paul Masson, in full fig, always managed to halloo into the Palace Hotel courtyard in time for a dollop of the best *before* a lingering lunch. And *after*. "In those days I couldn't decide *when* my brandy tasted better," he'd say. "I still can't. Decisions, always decisions."

Paul Masson was the last of the bon vivants until you came along. Don't worry about decisions is what we say. Play both ends but watch that lingering.

84 PROOF ©PAUL MASSON VINEYARDS · SARATOGA, CALIFORNIA

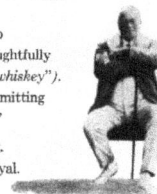

88

That early campaign was followed by dozens of ads. Some were good, like those that positioned Champagne as an everyday tipple.

█

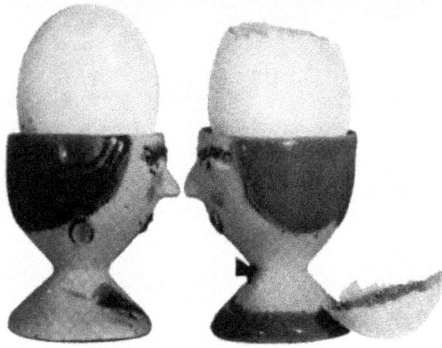

"THE CRITICAL PERIOD IN MATRIMONY IS BREAKFAST-TIME"

[Sir Alan Patrick Herbert]

You know the feeling. The married breakfast is an uneasy time, no matter how much in love the participants. You try to escape it by leaving the house before breakfast or sleeping through till lunch. Stop all that. Face up with Champagne. You break out a bottle of our effervescent stuff – midweek, say, when it feels like the bloom is off the marriage. This Breakfast Champagne comes in four different types: Brut, Extra Dry, Pink, and California Sparkling Burgundy.

And five sizes: the _____*, the Half-Bottle, the Bottle, the Magnum, the Jeroboam. When you've faced up to breakfast with it we'd like to hear from you. Fill out the coupon below, adding comments if you choose. We'll reciprocate with a brochure on our Champagnes, Wines, and Brandy. If you're in our neighborhood (Saratoga, California) stop by our splendid Champagne Cellars. We have tours daily, and we'd love to show you around.

*One ounce and littler broth, as set without a fancy name. You may call it "Split" until we tell you otherwise.

Paul Masson CALIFORNIA CHAMPAGNE
© PAUL MASSON VINEYARDS, SARATOGA, CALIFORNIA

Paul Masson Vineyards
Saratoga, California
Gentlemen:
My spouse and I had your Champagne for breakfast and: it was just the ticket □; we decided after seventeen years of marriage to seed the backyard with bluegrass □; the children missed the school bus and had to take a cab □; Other_____

Name_____ Address:_____ City:_____ State:_____

[Tonight Could be the Night! Even with seventeen relatives]

THE PAUL MASSON MAGNUM: OR HOW TO MAKE FAMILY REUNIONS TOLERABLE

For sheer amplitude there are few things more impressive than a Magnum. Even relations are impressed. If you want to get one-up at a reunion serve the 17 glass family-size of Paul Masson California Champagne.

The Magnum's uses are not confined to occasions involving blood ties, however. It is also recommended for wedding receptions, touch football rallies, executive Christmas gifts, 3 and 2/5ths basketball teams, or those who simply like a lot of champagne. The Paul Masson Magnum is available at your wine store, or write us if it isn't.

PAUL MASSON VINEYARDS, SARATOGA, CALIFORNIA (Come visit and bring the family.)

[Tonight Could be the Night! Even if there aren't enough to choose up sides]

THE TROUBLE WITH DRINKING CHAMPAGNE ORDINARILY IS, YOU HAVE TO ORGANIZE IT LIKE BRIDGE OR TOUCH

It works out like this: you say, "Who'd like some champagne?" Usually this proposal is greeted with cries of pure pleasure, but sometimes, with a small group, you can't work up a quorum. Because someone would rather have a bullshot or whatever it is that people who don't like to drink are drinking nowadays.

Do you see what the trouble is? You have predicated your suggestion on opening a bottle (fifth) of champagne.

To protect yourself from being victimized by spoil-sports, keep a couple of half-bottles, or better still, splits (quarter bottles), in the icebox. So that when everyone else wants to drink bullshots or other graceless concoctions you won't be deprived of your champagne.

You can buy half-bottles and splits of Paul Masson California Champagne at your wine store*, and probably should. It is all right to be an organization man at the office, but your spare time is your own.

*If you can't, write: PAUL MASSON VINEYARDS, SARATOGA, CALIFORNIA (or come visit the winery)

(A Reminder)

Today is the last time tonight will happen

© Copyright 1965 (We put the label on its side, too, so you could read it easier. We mention this so that when you are served Our Product labeled straight up in a restaurant you won't create a ruckus, Paul Masson Vineyards, Saratoga, California. (P. S. Doesn't "Brut" seem a thuddy-sounding name to describe something so delicious? If you can think of a more stimulating term for "Drier than Extra Dry" please let us know.)

In other campaigns, Gossage was trying to say something interesting and involving, but, as you might agree, somehow the old mischief wasn't always there.

[The World's Least Demanding Outside Interest]

COLLECTING PAUL MASSON COCKTAIL WINE LABELS IS NOT MUCH OF A HOBBY BUT IT WILL GET PEOPLE OFF YOUR BACK

NOWADAYS people look at you funny if you say you haven't got a hobby. Also, you know all those forms you fill out that have a line that asks "Hobbies:_____"? Whether you do or don't, it is a great nuisance to tell the truth about. ("Naps" or "Pingpong" sounds as bad as "None"). So we have come up with a blanket answer which will at once save face and discourage nosiness.

Just say: "I collect Cocktail Wine Labels; I am an authority". And you will be, too, if you will but write us today.

So you will know what it is that you are an authority on, cocktail wines are what we used to call "dessert wines", a misleading name, since nowadays most people drink them *before* or long after dinner; straight, on the rocks, with soda, or in all sorts of tasty mixtures. Here then...

Masson's 12 California cocktail wines: Tawny Port, Choice Muscatel, Golden Cream Sherry, Fine Sherry, Oro Fino, Rich Ruby Port, Pale Dry Sherry, Double Dry Vermouth, Sweet Vermouth, Rare Dry Sherry, Rare Cream Sherry, and Rare Tawny Port.

We'll send a description of each and some recipes along with your World's Most Extensive Collection of Paul Masson Cocktail Wine Labels. Write: Paul Masson Vineyards, Dept. Y-7, Saratoga, California.

Congratulations on your new hobby and we hope it gives you many happy question-free hours.

©1964 PAUL MASSON VINEYARDS, SARATOGA, CALIFORNIA (An hour north of San Francisco. Come on down.)

[Send for Your Free Starter Kit Today!]

WINE COLLECTING TAKES UP LESS SPACE THAN ANTIQUE CARS, IS QUIETER THAN HI-FI, AND TASTES BETTER THAN STAMPS

People always say that every man ought to have a hobby but they never mention the real reason, which is: it's the only way he can be alone at home.

Most men, therefore, will choose a hobby that is so bulky, messy, noisy, or boring that no one can bear to be near him; a high price to pay for solitude.

The wise man will forsake these self-tortures and take up wine collecting. It works just as well, no one will bother him: A) children do not drink and so are not interested; B) women love to have wine at the table, but they feel, quite rightly, that the collecting of wine is, like hunting, man's work. And so it is.

Wine collecting has one magnificent advantage over other hobbies: you can drink it. Also, it is neither expensive nor complicated to start. One may begin with two or three different reds and two or three whites; but which ones? To help you we will be happy to send you the labels of all thirteen Paul Masson table wines (plus a description of the delicious differences of each) to give you a collector's feel right away. Write: Paul Masson Vineyards, Dept. Y-1, Saratoga, California.

[Paul Masson and the New Leisure]

A hobby you can drink

A wine cellar can run anywhere from a 12-bottle rack to the point where the family is sleeping in pup tents on the lawn. For a starter it might be well to start with just a corner of the basement. We'd hate to see you rip out the furnace before you are quite sure that it is necessary.

Now, as to which wines, we can certainly recommend our own. Paul Masson's list of table wines (14), cocktail and dessert wines (13), and sparkling wines (5) runs to impressive length. (Let's see: 32).

But as a hobby table wine collecting is especially challenging; possibly because one is forever drinking up the very best specimens.

If you'd like some help on getting started you can count on us. Just write to the address below. We'll also send you the labels from all 14 of our table wines with a description of each so you'll recognize them at the wine store or restaurant. If you're already a wine collector, write anyway; you may find some items of particular interest in our catalog. Thank you.

(The inset modular stackable wine rack is our own design and is available with our wines in states which permit it.)

©1964, PAUL MASSON VINEYARDS, DEPT. J8, SARATOGA, CALIFORNIA

(Quick without looking at the picture)

What wine do you drink before (and after) the wine you drink with dinner?

We used to think we knew. Those on the left, cocktail wines; on the right, dessert wines:

Paul Masson California		Paul Masson California	
☒ Paul Masson California Cocktail Sherry		Paul Masson California Rare Cream Sherry ☒
☒ " " " Pale Dry Sherry		" " Golden Cream Sherry ☒
☒ " " " Rare Dry Sherry		" " Rare Tawny Port ☒
☒ " " " Fine Sherry		" " Tawny Port ☒
☒ " " " Sweet (Red) Vermouth		" " Rich Ruby Port ☒
☒ " " " Double Dry (White) Vermouth		" " Choice Muscatel ☒

...but we found that people don't necessarily drink them that way anymore. They drink them when and how they like them.

©1966, PAUL MASSON VINEYARDS (please visit us), SARATOGA, CALIFORNIA

91

The pressure to keep delivering on the account led to desperate measures. As para five of this letter from Dugald Stermer to Alice Lowe indicates;

DUGALD STERMER

1844 Union San Francisco California 94123 (415) 921-8281

December 27, 1984

Dear Alice:

I am but two-thirds through your
extraordinary manuscript about
Howard and found that I was impelled
to put it down and write to you.

You have done a magnificent job
of committing as much of him to
paper as possible. I don't know
how you did it, but I am in awe.

There is much there that I didn't know,
and you've filled in a great deal
that I thought I remembered. I can
only hope that Doubleday has the
good judgement to publish the book,
but one is skeptical. Jeanie Kortum
(associate editor and my wife who
allowed me to read it) will certainly
recommend it.

If they decide against publication,
let me know. Maybe Jeanie and I could
suggest alternate routes.

I few remarks. I don't know if Howard
told you this, but when he put me on
a $500 a month retainer as consultant
to the agency, it was to try to revive
his interest in Paul Masson; failing
that, I was, as honestly as possible, to
provide him with the rationale for resigning the account. Either way, I was
given six months before the decision was
to be reached.

Later he called me in to design the Paper
Airplane Design Contest advertisement,
and, as it turned out, the trophy. I
brought in Victor Moscoso, an artist and
sculptor, to make the prototype from
my sketches. The only words of mine

Dugald was another of Gossage's "discoveries" and went on to a highly successful career as an illustrator, artist and designer - creating, for example, the medals for the 1984 Olympic Games.

He couldn't, however, revive Gossage's interest in the account. Finally, the client was about to fire the agency when Gossage met him to say he was resigning the business. When asked why he replied: "I can't stand your advertising." "But", protested the client, "you *do* the advertising." "I know, that's why I'm quitting the account."

By the early to mid-'sixties, the workload was getting to Gossage. Yet remarkable he found time - and energy - to start his own business: Dean Swift Snuff.

YOU WILL FIND DEAN SWIFT® SNUFF TO BE AT ONCE ELEGANT, ASTONISHING, AND REWARDING

FEW of this age have known the ineffable pleasures of snuffing.

We of Dean Swift Ltd. think this a propitious time to reintroduce fancy snuff, hence the offering above. But first the points below:

[1] Dean Swift Snuff is *sniffing* snuff: dry, floured, aromaticked tobacco. Do not, we implore you, confuse fancy snuff with the unfortunate, orally-induced "snuffs."

[2] It is the most exhilarating form of tobacco ever devised. In the words of Coleridge, ". . . snuff! Perhaps it is the final cause of the human nose."

[3] Because it is extremely satisfying, and much more socially acceptable than smoking, fancy snuffing quite eclipsed it *for over 200 years!* People simply gave up smoking for something more rewarding. Perhaps they will again.

[4] (Smoking's comeback in the 19th Century was apparently due to two phenomena: [A] The revolt against the aristocracy. *Recall that snuff was the hallmark of the aristocrat;* [B] The invention of the "Lucifer" or sulphur match. The heady novelty of "instant fire" demanded conspicuous use. In light of this, the psychological reasons for smoking appear to be balderdash. It is a fad pure and simple.)

[5] As to healthfulness, we cannot suggest that snuff is actually *good* for you, of course. However, there is this: if we are to credit the Surgeon General's remarks, most unpleasantnesses are not present in the tobacco leaf, *but are formed during the burning process.* So much for that.

[6] While, for the present at least, the graceful, cleanly procedures of fancy snuffing could attract you quite an audience at a cocktail party, it can be accommodated without notice anywhere; even at an investiture, one imagines. And one simply sneers at "No Smoking" signs.

[7] Dean Swift Snuff is not only convenient, it is economical. A half-ounce tin should last the average ex-heavy smoker well over a week!

[8] If you are not presently a snuffer you may not be aware of the enormous range of taste Dean Swift caters to. At the moment we import nine fancy snuffs into this country: Dean's Own,* Mrs. Siddons's No. 3 & 4,* Dr. Johnson,* Cameleopard No. 5,* Bezoar Fine Grind,* Inchkenneth,* Boswell's Best,* Wren's Relish,* and Specific No. 1.* All are exceptionally agreeable. Since space forbids detailing the properties of each here (and since they possibly wouldn't mean much to you anyway until you have compared at least three snuffs), we shall include descriptive material and reorder forms when we fill your present order. The offerings then:

[9] The $5.00 Snuffing Sampler, in an exceptionally comely presentation box, brings you three assorted mixtures in half-ounce lacquered snuffbox-tins *plus* an imported paisley snuff handkerchief *plus* a numbered copy of the limited edition "A Discourse On Snuff or Its Nature Reveal'd;" with precise instructions in the modes of elegant sniffing.

[10] (It should be mentioned that a proper snuff handkerchief is highly desirable going in.)

[11] The $10.00 Compleat Offering is a magnificent unabridged presentation of *all nine* Dean Swift Snuffs in their extraordinary variety, *plus* the imported paisley snuff handkerchief *and* the "Discourse"! A truly great adventure in snuffing. Definitive.

[12] We shall also send with each order a Free Illustrated Catalogue of snuffboxes in gold, silver, pewter, horn, and precious woods; variously priced.

Thank you for your kind attention. Now back to the coupon; what better way to find out whether you are up to snuff?

*Trademarks of Dean Swift Ltd.

©1964, Dean Swift Ltd.

Dean Swift Snuff is an obscure one - and familiar only to the aficionados. It's doubtful, however, that anyone will know about the next two campaigns.

The first, Salada Tea, is typical Gossage. Resisting the usual, he ignores competitors in the tea market and aims at converting coffee drinkers. He uses a classic sales promo competition to drive responses - but a far from conventional layout.

6⅞"

TEA

ANNOUNCING:
THE SALADA TEA COMPANY'S 70TH ANNIVERSARY COFFEE BEAN GUESSING BEE!

"What does one give a tea company on its seventieth birthday?", is a question you may have asked yourself many times. A necktie perhaps? A pair of monogrammed bagging machines? We think not. Besides, we already have everything. ✑ Rather, we should like to turn the tables and give something to you in gratitude for the billions of cups of Saladá you have brewed, collectively speaking, over the past seventy years. Accordingly, we take delight in announcing: The Salada Tea Company's 70th Anniversary Coffee Bean Guessing Bee! ✑ HERE ARE THE GROUND RULES: the person hazarding the closest guess as to how many coffee beans are contained in the glass tea canister at the left, wins the sterling silver tea service pictured below, a year's supply of Salada Tea, the tea canister and beans themselves! If you're wondering "why coffee beans", you should try counting tea leaves sometime. ✑ Besides; while tea leaves make a far superior drink, coffee beans have the edge entertainment-wise. For example you may, of some long winter's evening,
(CONTINUED IN LOWER LEFT HAND BOX)

(CONTINUED FROM UPPER RIGHT HAND BOX)
do the following fun things with the beans just like on TV: (1) pour them into a mountain (2) run your fingers through them (3) scoop them up to your face (4) cascade them into the lens of your 8 mm home movie camera. ✑ Having played with the beans you may then discard them, or make them into bean bags for all the children in the neighborhood as the case may be, and get down to business. Fill up your tea canister with the Salada Tea, get out your sterling silver tea service and prepare yourself for the most terrific cup of tea you've ever had. (We hope you will permit us a bit of boasting, it being our birthday and all.) ✑ One final word: Should you prefer your Salada in bulk form, please do not run your fingers through our ambrosial blend. Our leaves are rather fine and rare and may bruise easily. Coffee beans are for playing with . . . tea leaves are for brewing.

The Salada Tea Co., Woburn, Mass.
Dear Sirs: As near as I can make out there are _____ coffee beans in the tea canister. If my guess comes closest, I understand I will win the Sterling Silver Tea service pictured above, the tea canister, the coffee beans and a year's supply of Salada Tea. If my guess comes second or third closest, you promise I will win a year's supply of Salada Tea, at least. I prefer bags ( ) bulk ( ). I understand the beans have been counted and are being held by BRINKS INC. (By the way, isn't it rather odd for a tea company to mention the word coffee in an ad?)
Yours truly,
(NAME)_____
(ADDRESS)_____

In case of tie, earliest postmark wins, Guessing Bee ends December 1, 1962.

The next ad has Gossage again trying to convert coffee drinkers - but this time he's launching a tongue-in-cheek campaign to wean them off the bean.

It's pretty certain those ads were by Gossage. They appeared in his medium of choice, the *New Yorker*. The tone of voice is his. And the competition in the first ads and the creation of a "Coffeeholics" community in the fourth are typical Gossage. Moreover, the layouts and typography are in his house style.

If you look at the coupon in the previous "Hubert Whittaker…" ad you'll see reference to "bagged by gypsies". This is both a portent of the madness to come over the next couple of pages and a clue to its origins.

The ads were written to integrate with another of Stan Freberg's extravaganzas: a seven minute musical called *Woburn!* It centres on a strike called by the American Federation of Gypsies in protest about Salada putting fortune-telling messages on their tea bags. It's as eccentric as it sounds - and great entertainment - although the product benefit doesn't get a mention until six minutes in.

The ads aren't as ornate as usual, but then again they are supposed to be bulletins from the AF of G Union. The final Call to Action offers a DO IT YOURSELF GYPSY KIT which sounds very Gossage. And the Salada factory was actually besieged by "pickets" which sounds like one of his publicity stunts.

Was it Gossage or was it Freberg? What do you think?

[An Announcement of Public Interest, By The Salada Tea Co., Woburn, Mass.]

SALADA'S POSITION IN THE GYPSY STRIKE

What with the American Federation of Gypsies holding protest meetings all over our parking lot here in Woburn so that an executive can't even step out of his car without putting his foot through a tambourine, we feel some sort of explanation is in order.

THE GYPSIES AVER: That Salada Tea, by the introduction of "Instant Fortunes" on the tags of our tea bags, has eliminated the middle man, or woman as the case may be, and virtually knocked the tea leaf reading biz into a cocked bandanna. In a complaint issued last week, the A. F. of G.'s official "spokesman," one Vladamir Krimm, grumbled, "It's a dirty deal! Why should a person bother to go to a Gypsy Tea Room any more if he can get his fortune free on the tag of a Salada tea bag?"

We'll bite Mr. Krimm…Why should he? Why should he drive all the way out to some broken down tea room and sit there in semi-darkness for forty-five minutes (The amount of time we clocked recently on a visit to one of these "union" emporiums) while some toothless old harpy pokes around in the bottom of his cup, considering that he can get an equally profound fortune on the tag of any number of Salada Tea Bags…FREE and for a lot less trouble?

SALADA'S POSITION: We are not trying to buck the Union here. Let's get our facts straight—ours is a Union shop all the way. (Practically.) Except in the case of our President and First Vice President and the Board of Directors who so far have not been fortunate enough to have such "organized" representation, we are pretty much sewn up union-wise. Our backs are to the wall pretty good, what with contracts all over the place with the A. F. of this and the United that and the American Brotherhood of what next, so let it not be said that we are anti-union. Let he who is without Union cards around here, throw the first stone. Rather, let the A. F. of G. be willing to face reality. You can't fight progress!

If Mr. and Mrs. America choose to get their fortunes direct from the tags of the world's finest tea bags, why that is their business. If they, on the other hand wish to heist themselves to some dubious Gypsy's diggings and pay through the nose for the "atmosphere," why that is their business too. It's a free country Mr. Krimm. With that in mind, Salada does not intend to pull the fortunes off their tea bags to accommodate a handful of card-carrying crystal gazers. We will not be used as a scapegoat. Isn't it a fact that the fortune biz has been on the wane for some time now, anyway? If the "art" of tea leaf reading must now take its place alongside the button shoe and the Edsel, do not attempt to pin the rap on us. Call off your picket line, Mr. Krimm. We did not throw the gypsies out of work!

[An Announcement of Public Interest by The American Federation of Gypsies]

WHO THREW THE GYPSIES OUT OF WORK?

Over 5,000 unemployed Gypsies and tea leaf readers in America today and you can lay the blame squarely at the well-shod feet of the Salada Tea Co., Woburn, Mass.

THESE ARE THE FACTS:

Salada's recent introduction of free "Instant Fortunes" on the tags of their tea bags has eliminated the middle man or woman, as the case may be, tossing the gypsy out on his/her earring and the fortune biz into a recession from which it has never recovered. In spite of this, Salada tries to weasel out on it by claiming (as would be expected) that the tea leaf reading game was going down the drain anyhow so do not attempt to pin the rap on them.

Cut out the bunk, Mr. Big Tea Tycoon! We were doing just fine until you stabbed us in the back with those fink fortunes. Oh, sure, we do not deny that we have been hurt over the years by inroads made by the weight-machine and Chinese fortune cookie people. (We have lobbyists in Washington trying to fight these interests at this very moment.) But, by and large, we have managed to eke out a living. We knew if a person wanted a real fortune told he went to a bona fide union gypsy and didn't fool around with any of that "You weigh 165 pounds and will travel" or "A letter of great importance will reach you any day now" jazz. Then Salada comes along and starts sticking fortunes on the tags of their bags, and the rest is history. Now you add insult to injury. In a recent paid ad, you implied that all Gypsies are "toothless old harpies." If any Gypsies are toothless today, it is because Salada has kicked them in the teeth. Furthermore, I could take you to a tea room within five miles of Woburn that is run by a Gypsy named Natasha Nirvana who is not exactly built like a harpy, believe you me! You should have a harpy like that running around your tea factory, brother!

THE A.F. OF G.'S POSITION:

We know Salada threw the Gypsies out of work and you know it, so do not attempt to pull the bandanna over our eyes in the name of progress. Until you take those anti-union fortunes and wise sayings off your tea bags, we intend to go right on camping in your parking lot. Maybe now you will see what a bunch of poor poverty stricken tea leaf readers look like. We do not intend to move, so don't pull any more cheap tricks like cutting your electricity at night so we can't plug in our television sets and electric rotisseries. We are asking the American public to write to Washington and protest this unfair competition Salada has entered into with the Gypsies. To make it easier on people, we have printed this handy little coupon. They should stick it on a postcard and mail it. Thank you.

Yours sincerely,

Vladamir Krimm,
President, American Federation of Gypsies

Bureau of Gypsy Affairs
P.O. BOX 1921, Washington 13, D.C.

Sirs: I think the American Federation of Gypsies is getting a dirty deal here. The Salada Tea Co. of Woburn, Mass., has thrown over 5,000 tea leaf readers out of work printing fortunes on the tags of their tea bags, thereby eliminating the Gypsy. If you ask me, the Department of Labor should go in there and tell Big Business to leave the fortune-telling to the little man or woman, as the case may be.

The Outraged _____

- text:117

- [A Final Announcement of Public Interest by The Salada Tea Co., Woburn, Mass.]

GYPSY STRIKE SETTLED!

At 11:58 P.M. Sunday last, a settlement was reached between the American Federation of Gypsies and the Salada Tea Company, bringing to an end the paralyzing fourteen-day strike which threatened to bring tea bag production to a dribble.

WHAT HAS HAPPENED UP UNTIL NOW:

The A. F. of G. in an organized move to block Salada's "Instant Fortunes" from the tags of our tea bags marched on the plant here at Woburn to protest this "unfair competition" with the Gypsy. The first of the caravan appeared at approximately 7:15 A.M. on the morning of May 1st and was spotted by our night watchman, Mr. Mulvaney, who was just going off duty. Within a matter of minutes tentstakes had been put down, and wagons rolled rudely onto our new lawn. By the time our Vice President and General Manager, Mr. Beeby, drove, or attempted to drive, up the driveway at 8:30, campfires were blazing all over the parking lot and the spectacle was on. Now we are not ones to hold a grudge here at Salada, so we will not rehash any more of these uncalled-for abuses, such as the total destruction of our new lawn, the incessant playing of "When A Gypsy Makes His Violin Cry" by The Viennese String Quartet with the volume turned up, and many other inconveniences including, but not limited to, the premature graying of Mr. Beeby's hair. "All's well that end's well" is a phrase we are fond of in Woburn, and we are proud to announce that the American Federation of Gypsies will report to work here at Home Plant No. 1, immediately.

With their knowledge of tea, they'll help us make sure only the larger, more mature leaves go into Salada Tea Bags. They will also assist in the writing of our famous Instant Fortunes which are to be found interspersed with our "Tag Lines" on the tags of our bountiful bags. Just a little reading material while you sit waiting for the world's finest cup of tea to brew. Oh, yes. The folks in Washington will be somewhat relieved to learn that "The Bureau of Gypsy Affairs" has been moved right here to Woburn as it should be, so the post office there on the hill can relax. If you're motoring around New England this Summer, and your travels take you to Boston, swing up Route 128 to Woburn, and drop in on us here at Salada Tea. Just ask our receptionist to show you to Mr. Vladamir Krimm who heads up the Gypsy bureau and will be happy to shake your hand personally, or read it as the case may be.

If you are not motoring anywhere but would give *anything* to know what this is all about, you may want to send for our...

"DO IT YOURSELF GYPSY KIT" which, we sincerely hope, will clarify the whole business for you once and for all. The kit will contain an L.P. recording of "WOBURN" the five and a half minute musical tragedy, starring Stan Freberg and a cast of dozens, which you may have heard on the radio. It tells, in words and song, of the A. F. of G. and their heartrending march on the Salada Tea Co. The kit will also contain glossy reprints (suitable for framing) of this ad and the two that preceded it, one Salada Tea Bag complete with Instant Fortune, an honorary life membership card in the American Federation of Gypsies, Local 42, and one simulated golden earring. The price for the entire ensemble is one dollar ($1.00). As the offer, from our standpoint, is a self-liquidating one, we assume you understand we are not pocketing any profits on the thing. We are merely offering you, at our cost, a few mementos of the now notorious "Woburn Gypsy Strike" in case you would care to remember it. Personally we should like to forget the whole matter.

Bureau of Gypsy Affairs
C/O The Salada Tea Company
Woburn, Massachusetts

Sirs: In an effort to get this whole thing straight in my mind, I am sending for my "DO IT YOURSELF GYPSY KIT." I understand it will include one L. P. recording of "WOBURN," three Salada/A. F. of G. strike ads, one Salada Tea bag, a life membership card in the A. F. of G. and one simulated golden earring. I enclose $1.00

NAME

ADDRESS

CITY_____ZONE___STATE___

- text:101

The next campaign that Dave unearthed is an unusual (for Gossage) foray into the world of corporate finance. The client, Justin Herman, was Gossage's friend (you'll see him pictured with Gossage and Marshall McLuhan in the next chapter.) From 1959 until his death in 1971, he was the Executive Director of the San Francisco Redevelopment Agency.

BEGINNING A SERIES OF PUBLICLY SPONSORED ADVERTISEMENTS OF COMPOUND INTEREST TO PRIVATE INVESTORS EVERYWHERE

The San Francisco Redevelopment Agency cordially requests the pleasure of your company

Or corporation, as the case may be, to participate in the development and enjoyment of the most elegantly profitable commercial enclave of the 20th Century: San Francisco's Golden Gateway. Please bring money.*

Money, however, is only money whereas the Golden Gateway is one of the rarest real estate sites in the world. Nearly 50 acres in area, it stretches from Market Street to Broadway, running along the financial district to Telegraph Hill on the west and fronting on San Francisco Bay from Ferry Building Plaza northward (see below).

Because of the unique grandeur of this location in the heart of one of America's most beautiful cities, we have been charged with the responsibility of insuring that every structure and component (parks, hotels, business and professional offices, clubs, retail establishments, recreational facilities, apartments, plazas, garden town houses, etc.) in the Golden Gateway is both dynamically and

aesthetically integrated with the area as a whole.

Which is why we are unable to sell to everybody who's willing to plonk down a few million dollars.** Not to somebody, for instance, who wanted to put up a twenty-three story building done in Neo-Pigeoncoop. It isn't that we're all that snobbish or altrustic, either. A strong vein of acumen tells us that the sum of the elegance of our Golden Gateway as a whole will increase the value of each building in it. Those already constructed provide a graceful setting for buildings yet to be designed and so future developments must compliment the present buildings; it's only fair. Also, mutually profitable.

If, by the way, you (or your company/corporation) would like to enjoy the benefits of the Golden Gateway without having to construct your own building, elegant space as mentioned above can be provided by agreement with other developers.

*About $2,310,120.00 if you'd like to buy a choice block of 74,520 square feet on Sacramento St. at Davis in the Golden Gateway. Your building (up to 23 stories) of course, would be extra.

**$4,850,680.00 for 156,480 square feet presently available on Market Street, enough land to develop 1½ million gross square feet. (Our base price is $31 per square foot and we pay your broker a 2½% fee to boot.)

R S V P FOR OUR ILLUSTRATED BROCHURE OR ANY FURTHER INFORMATION YOU'D LIKE, PLEASE DROP A NOTE TO DOUGLAS MYERS, BUSINESS DEVELOPMENT DIRECTOR, SAN FRANCISCO REDEVELOPMENT AGENCY, 525 GOLDEN GATE AVENUE, SAN FRANCISCO, CALIFORNIA. THANK YOU.

© 1965 San Francisco Redevelopment Agency

The brief was to find businesses willing to build/rent on the 50 acre stretch of real estate along the San Francisco waterfront from Market St to Broadway.

You'll never have seen Gossage as restrained. But, then again, you'll rarely read a corporate finance ad that's as relaxed and conversational.

A Modest Proposal
By
The San Francisco Redevelopment Agency

Wherein we offer a simple solution to your company's commute
problems devised to benefit your personnel and thereby increase
productivity, enhance profits and confound your competitors.

Before we digress: The plight of the commuter is not a happy one. With luck, he can leave home at seven, be at his desk from nine to five and get to see his family (if he's quick) after sundown. Between times, he's cranky, inefficient or sleeping.

On the other hand: Areas closer to the office are usually industrial, uninhabitable and overcrowded. How could a man living in such miserable surroundings be expected to do his best work?

The corporate quandary: Where to find personnel who are bright, efficient, cheerful on the job? Also awake.

A simple solution: Having eliminated all other possible answers, the solution becomes self-evident. Locate ideal conditions for your personnel and move your company to their doorstep.

Our modest proposal: It so happens that we have a choice parcel of land currently available in our Golden Gateway development you can snap up for $4,850,880.00. Then, for an additional fifty million dollars, you can build your offices in the lap of one of America's most luxurious cities.

San Francisco's Golden Gateway: One of the rarest real estate sites in the world encompassing nearly 50 acres between the financial district and the Bay, stretching from Market Street to the foot of Telegraph Hill (with splendid views of same, see below).

Up by cable car: The California Street cable climbs from this site to Nob Hill at a brisk 9½ miles per hour; if you prefer, you can walk the distance in about 20 minutes. You can also walk from Telegraph Hill, Russian Hill and, if you're energetic, Pacific Heights. If not, there are apartments and town houses in the Golden Gateway itself.

Quod erat demonstradum: Energy formerly devoted to commuting will be applied to the job. The increased productivity will enhance profits and confound your competitors!

A slightly venal note: A smaller parcel is also currently available for $2,310,120.00; our base price is $31 per square foot and we pay your broker a 2½% fee. Or suitable quarters for your company can be provided by agreement with other developers. If you'd like our illustrated brochure or any further information, please drop a note to Douglas Myers, Business Development Director, San Francisco Redevelopment Agency, 525 Golden Gate Avenue, San Francisco, California 94102. Thank you.

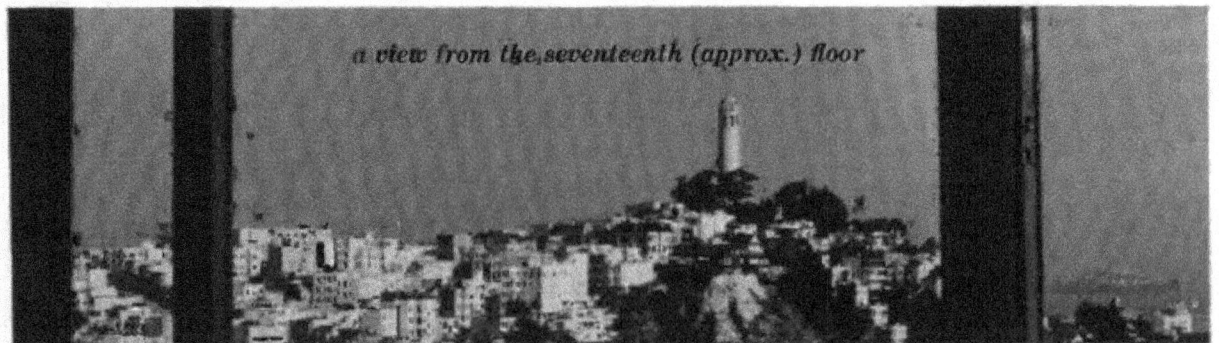

a view from the seventeenth (approx.) floor

How to Raid Your Competitors' Top Corporate Talent without Actually Resorting to Piracy

Money doesn't work anymore

As we know, the days when top talent could be lured to your company by a simple raise in salary have disappeared with the quill pen. Since then, salaries have been raised, re-raised, doubled and re-doubled until they've been taxed to a standoff. Subsequently, stock options and ingenious fringe benefits were tossed in to up the ante and the end is not yet in sight.

The Golden Gateway gambit

Since piracy is not only outdated but unethical, we (The San Francisco Redevelopment Agency) have devised a solution to this complex problem that is both honorable and effective. It is based on the observation that top talents in every line of work are so willing to work in San Francisco that salaries become secondary. So are top secretaries and trained personnel of all description. We therefore reasoned that the simplest way for an ingenious executive to acquire the top corporate talent he desired was to locate his offices here and let Mohammed come to the Mountain.

The Pen is mightier than the cutlass

Which is why we suggest you select office space in a Golden Gateway office building, reserve living quarters in one of our 2,200 apartments or 106 town houses, park your car in the 1,700 stall garage and gaze at the view shown below while your competitors' best men line up to sign your contracts with the pen shown above. And if you decide to build your own office, we'll sell you a lot for $31.00 a foot and pay your broker a 2½% fee, to boot. If we can be of further help to you, please drop a note to Douglas Myers, Business Development Director, San Francisco Redevelopment Agency, 525 Golden Gate Ave., San Francisco, California 94102. Thank you.

No doubt the intentions were good. The ads speak of staff welfare and happy employees as a benefit of locating to the Golden Gateway development. They also talk about aesthetics and deterring anyone thinking of putting up a "23 storey building in Neo-Pidgeoncoup".

But, ultimately, while the project was successful, it displaced many of the city's poorest residents. And, as seen below, it was left to Gossage's partner Jerry Mander to write the agency's ads protesting the redevelopment of the city.

YOU CAN HELP DECIDE IF OUR CITY WILL BECOME A SKYLINE OF TOMBSTONES.

Both the above pictures are of downtown San Francisco. Same spot, same weather conditions. The top one was twelve years ago. The bottom one, last year.

In only twelve years the downtown area has taken on the closed, forbidding look and feel of most other American cities. And now the high-rises are beginning to spread throughout the city, ruining views, changing the character of the landscape, and what's more, increasing property taxes city-wide.

New studies have shown that the more we build high-rise, the more expensive it becomes to live here. They are as great a disaster economically as they are esthetically. Ask a New York taxpayer.

In the next five years, 40 more skyscraper office buildings are due to be built and nearly as many high-rise hotels and apartments.

Many of them are going into new areas of town which so far have been spared. You can help slow them down.

A petition is being circulated which would stop construction on all new buildings taller than six stories until each of them is studied by the voters of this city and approved.

Tall buildings could still be built, but only after the people of the city wanted them. The pressure would be on the big developers to **prove** that these buildings bring money into the city, and that they mean long-term jobs for San Franciscans, not only commuters. Thank you.

Alvin Duskin

HOW YOU CAN HELP:
1) Sign a petition or circulate one (only registered San Francisco voters may do this);
2) help with mailings, phone calls and organizational work;
3) donate money to accelerate the campaign.

Use the coupon, or come personally anytime from 9-6, Monday through Saturday: 520 Third St., Second Floor. (397-9200)

To: The San Francisco Opposition, Alvin Duskin Factory, 520 Third Street (Second Floor), San Francisco, CA 94107
□ I would like to sign a petition and will be coming down to do so. (Only registered San Francisco voters may sign; if you are **not** registered, we **can** register you.)
□ I would like to circulate a petition, or man a signature table. □ I will be down to pick them up. □ I can't come down, but please mail them to me at the address below. (Registered San Francisco voters only.)
□ I am not eligible to vote in San Francisco, but would like to help the campaign with volunteer work at your office, or elsewhere. □ I will come down to talk to you about it between 9-6, Monday through Saturday. □ I can't come down, so will you please call me at the number below.
□ Here is a donation of $_____ to help with the costs of running this campaign: staff, mailings, printing, ads, etcetera. (Checks payable to: San Francisco Opposition.)

Name_____ Phone number_____
Address_____
City_____ State_____ Zip_____

Not that Gossage was slow to campaign for causes he believed in. For example, he wrote this ad protesting the closure of the Western Edition of the *NY Times*.

Gossage paid thousands of dollars for the ad you've just seen to run in the *NY Times* and the *San Francisco Chronicle*. Here's a letter from the appreciative publisher of a newspaper that survived because of Gossage's intervention.

PORTLAND
Reporter

PUBLISHED BY PORTLAND REPORTER PUBLISHING CO., INC.

1714 N.W. OVERTON STREET
PORTLAND, OREGON • 97208
TELEPHONE CA 6-7721

March 17, 1964

Mr. Howard Gossage
Freeman and Gossage, Inc.
451 Pacific Avenue
San Francisco, California

Dear Mr. Gossage:

I thought you might enjoying knowing your lament (San Francisco Chronicle) on the death of the New York Times west coast edition played a part in saving another newspaper -- the Portland Reporter -- from a seemingly inevitable death.

The Reporter reprinted your Chronicle ad as part of the T.N.T. (Two Newspaper Ownership Town) committee promotion material. But at the time we had no idea we would hark back to your plea that newspapers not die without prior notice.

When our "time came" your message, along with our determination that our staff <u>not</u> be slapped in the face with the death of their newspaper as so many others have been, convinced the board of directors to give prior notice of plans to suspend publication.

The reaction and response was absolutely amazing. Contributions started pouring in--and continued in a steady stream for five days. More than $50,000 was contributed and two Portland businessmen made interest free loans of $25,000 each. Contributions ranged from 14 cents to $3000.

So, Mr. Gossage, you were correct. People don't want newspapers to die and will try to save them, given the opportunity. Thousands agreed with your premise that subscribers will have to pay more for their newspapers if they are to keep them. We may even increase subscription rates unilaterally.

Am enclosing clippings concerning the "miracle" you helped wrought.

Thanks for the "sermon". It saved us.

Sincerely yours,

Robert D. Webb

For another of his personal campaigns, in 1961, he'd written an article in *Harper's* magazine attacking billboards as a medium. A couple of years later, he made it the subject of the very first ad he wrote for new client Rover Cars.

[*Some Thoughts on Advertising by a Company About to do Some*]

HOW DO YOU FEEL ABOUT BILLBOARDS?

FOR reasons which will surely keep until next time we have not been as aggressive as we might at advertising our Rover cars and Land-Rovers to you. But that is in the past, and now we are prepared to be as aggressive as you please. And we really mean "as you please"; you should not allow yourself to be imposed upon if you can avoid it.

Usually you can avoid it: if a salesman is officious or over-zealous you can, and ought to, walk out on him. (If a Rover salesman should ever prove rude or pushy—or you simply can't stand him— please let us know immediately and we will take steps and inform you of them by return post.)

If an advertisement displeases you, you can, so to speak walk out on it, too. Unless it is a billboard; it is very difficult to walk out on a billboard. Which is probably why they continue to enjoy the favour of advertisers—despite the fact that many people apparently don't care for them at all.

How many people? Well, there must be quite a lot, to judge from the enormous amount of anti-billboard legislation and other activity one reads about.

In view of this flood of public opinion it is strange that no advertiser has thought to ask the people to whom he hopes to sell his goods how they feel. It seems to us a prudent and legitimate question to ask, so we shall ask it.

You will note that the wording of the reply form is more explicit than that of the headline above. For this reason: many people who profess to dislike billboards may not, by the same token, dislike the advertising on them. They may even *like* the advertising, or some of it, very much indeed. And some people may not care a fig one way or the other. Hence the three questions.

However, we would not have you think for a minute that this effort at fairness conceals even the slightest impartiality. We don't mind saying that we personally loathe billboards, and for a highly per-sonal reason: they tend to diminish our value to you.

We make motor cars, and make them with a great deal of care so that they will please you in every possible way. The Land-Rover is unquestion-ably the finest four-wheel-drive vehicle—and the most versatile vehicle—in the world. Of the Mark II Rover (Sedan and Coupe) let us say that the only car even comparable to it in engineering or comfort costs thrice the price.

However, the single best feature about a Rover —or any car, for that matter—is the world as you drive through it from one place to another. So, it is to our interest that the world and its views be as attractive as possible; for, to the degree that they are not the car's value to you decreases. Therefore, it does not seem shrewd for a motor car manufac-turer to purposely make the world *less* attractive by publicly sponsoring eyesores.

In passing, however, it would be churlish of us not to admit that the most engaging and clever automobile advertising campaign in the country looks wonderful on billboards; but then, it looks wonderful in magazines and newspapers, too.

Well, we'd appreciate your filling in the form and sending it to us. One other thing: we haven't allowed room for pictures of our cars or much other information, but if you'd like them just check the appropriate boxes in the postscript. Thank you.

The Rover Motor Company
405 Lexington Avenue, New York 17, N. Y.

☐ I'd just as soon you didn't advertise on billboards.
☐ I have no feeling one way or the other.
☐ I'd like to see you advertise on billboards.

Name_____

Address_____

City_____State_____

P.S. I would like some information on ☐ The Land-Rover;
☐ The Mark II Rover; ☐ Your Overseas Delivery Plan

It prompted this response from David Ogilvy who clearly shared Gossage's aversion to billboards.

OGILVY, BENSON & MATHER INC.

Advertising

NEW YORK   SAN FRANCISCO   CHICAGO   TORONTO   BEVERLY HILLS

DAVID OGILVY, Chairman

2 EAST 48 STREET, NEW YORK 17
MURRAY HILL 8 - 6100

August 22, 1963

Dear Howard:

I came across a piece I wrote about posters in an
English trade paper in 1939.

It includes the following:

> "I hold no brief for or against any advertis-
> ing medium. But as an advertising agent I am
> responsible for promoting a favourable public
> attitude towards advertising in general. It
> is in the interests of advertisers, agencies
> and the outdoor industry itself to take a more
> far-sighted view of the billboard problem than
> they have had the courage to demonstrate in the
> past."

Yours sincerely,

David

I was 28 then.

Mr. Howard Gossage
Freeman & Gossage
451 Pacific Avenue
San Francisco, California

While Gossage was critical and dismissive of most of his peers, he liked and admired David Ogilvy. He took the Englishman's most famous ad and …

The Rolls-Royce Silver Cloud—$13,995

"At 60 miles an hour the loudest noise in this new Rolls-Royce comes from the electric clock"

What makes Rolls-Royce the best car in the world? "There is really no magic about it— it is merely patient attention to detail," says an eminent Rolls-Royce engineer.

1. "At 60 miles an hour the loudest noise comes from the electric clock," reports the Technical Editor of THE MOTOR. Three mufflers tune out sound frequencies—acoustically.

2. Every Rolls-Royce engine is run for seven hours at full throttle before installation, and each car is test-driven for hundreds of miles over varying road surfaces.

3. The Rolls-Royce is designed as an *owner-driven* car. It is eighteen inches shorter than the largest domestic cars.

4. The car has power steering, power brakes and automatic gear-shift. It is very easy to drive and to park. No chauffeur required.

5. The finished car spends a week in the final test-shop, being fine-tuned. Here it is subjected to 98 separate ordeals. For example, the engineers use a *stethoscope* to listen for axle-whine.

6. The Rolls-Royce is guaranteed for three years. With a new network of dealers and parts-depots from Coast to Coast, service is no problem.

7. The Rolls-Royce radiator has never changed, except that when Sir Henry Royce died in 1933 the monogram RR was changed from red to black.

8. The coachwork is given five coats of primer paint, and hand rubbed between each coat, before *nine* coats of finishing paint go on.

9. By moving a switch on the steering column, you can adjust the shock-absorbers to suit road conditions.

10. A picnic table, veneered in French walnut, slides out from under the dash. Two more swing out behind the front seats.

11. You can get such optional extras as an Espresso coffee-making machine, a dictating machine, a bed, hot and cold water for washing, an electric razor or a telephone.

12. There are three separate systems of power brakes, two hydraulic and one mechanical. Damage to one will not affect the others. The Rolls-Royce is a very *safe* car—and also a very *lively* car. It cruises serenely at eighty-five. Top speed is in excess of 100 m.p.h.

13. The Bentley is made by Rolls-Royce. Except for the radiators, they are identical motor cars, manufactured by the same engineers in the same works. People who feel diffident about driving a Rolls-Royce can buy a Bentley.

PRICE. The Rolls-Royce illustrated in this advertisement—f.o.b. principal ports of entry—costs **$13,995.**

If you would like the rewarding experience of driving a Rolls-Royce or Bentley, write or telephone to one of the dealers listed on opposite page. Rolls-Royce Inc., 10 Rockefeller Plaza, New York 20, N. Y. CIrcle 5-1144.

... produced this spoof/homage. The two men differed on the use of humour in ads. David Ogilvy was staunchly against it and Gossage was obviously for it.

Land-Rover 109 Station Wagon with Heat Shield Roof.

"At 60 miles an hour the loudest noise in this new Land-Rover comes from the roar of the engine"

What makes Land-Rover the most conspicuous car in the world? "There is really no secret," says an eminent Land-Rover enthusiast.

1. "Except for rattles, I am against silence in a car," writes John Steinbeck, a Land-Rover enthusiast, "and I don't know a driver who doesn't want to hear his engine."

2. If this is so, then you may like the Land-Rover very much indeed.

3. Our 4-wheel drive (8 speeds forward, 2 in reverse) masterpiece is not mousey. Its throaty authority is assuring in times of stress; which nowadays is usually.

4. Nor is this claim true only at 60 miles an hour. A Land-Rover is more conspicuous even when it is standing still. With the ignition off.

5. The Land-Rover stands nearly seven feet tall. All its features tend to heroic proportion.

6. Therefore, when driving, you will simply loom over traffic which previously had scared the devil out of you.

7. This is not only safe and enjoyable, but you will exult to observe how other drivers, awe-inspired by the Land-Rover's casual might, yield in deference.

8. (Small wonder that women are enormously fond of driving Land-Rovers. The easy command of such massive, maneuverable masculinity is heady stuff.)

9. You may have read of tests where "imported cars" fared badly in collisions? It's a pity we weren't in there to help out the side. The Land-Rover is built to resist the charge of a bull rhinoceros; or a bull Lincoln for that matter.

10. The Land-Rover's sturdiness of construction (the under-frame resembles a reinforced section of railway track) makes it ideal for trackless wastes, car pools of small children, wretched ordeals, et cetera.

11. There are perhaps 14 Land-Rover hardy perennials ranging from safari cars and campers to police vans and getaway cars. Our most popular passenger models are the 7-seater Model 88 and the 10-seater Model 109 Station Wagons.

LAND-ROVER WITH & WITHOUT TIRE ON HOOD

11-A. An attractive feature of the '66 Land-Rover is that it is precisely as attractive as the '65.

12. Both of these have capacious rear doors for unloading bulk or people. The unathletic may use the fold-down step.

13. The after compartment has facing seats. This arrangement, although somewhat reminiscent of riding in a paddy-wagon, is extremely sociable. Late at night, it is hilarious.

14. The Land-Rover is available with a spare tire either mounted on the rear door or on top of the hood. The tires are identical in every respect save that it costs $7.40 more to have one on the hood.

15. People who feel diffident about driving a Land-Rover with the spare tire on the hood can buy the conventional Land-Rover and save $7.40.

PRICE: The Model 109 Station Wagon illustrated in this advertisement costs **$3,906** on the Atlantic Coast, **$4,092** on the Pacific Coast; at places in between, it costs in between. The Model 88 Station Wagon (shorter by 1 door) costs about **$600** less.

If you would like to listen to the Land-Rover, or to the embarrassingly quiet Mark II Rover Sedan, or to the Rover 2000 Sports Sedan (which has "a little panty mutter when idling that rises to a whispering roar in the lower gears," according to Mr. Steinbeck), please ask any dealer here listed. (LR) signifies a Land-Rover dealer; (R), a Rover dealer; (R & LR), both.

Thank you.

©1965 Rover Motor Co. of North America, Ltd., Chrysler Bldg., New York 17.

The "Billboards" ad was the first Gossage wrote for Rover. He followed it with a two page advertorial - only in typical Gossage style, the two pages were split over two separate editions of the magazine.

113

In the previous ad, note him:

a) ridiculing the standard approach to headline writing,

b) his reference to the success of his Billboard ad,

c) how he, once again, plays with convention by ending halfway through a sentence,

d) his teaser about the next ad: "The Land Rover and Crime".

And what an unusual piece of work it was.

It's normal to do a topical ad that ties a brand with, say, a sporting success, a scientific breakthrough or a celebrity endorsement. But here Gossage aligns Land Rover with the UK's crime of the century and gleefully reports on "the dubious demonstration of its versatility" and it being an "accessory to the crime". Given he was celebrating the exploits of violent career criminals, it is probably his most subversive ad. Ultimately the Great Train Robbers didn't get away with it. How Gossage did is testimony to his chutzpah and the Rover client's boldness.

Special Report:

"THE LAND-ROVER AND CRIME"

PREFERRED BY THE POLICE OF 37 COUNTRIES
AND THE BANDITS OF AT LEAST 1

DUE TO THE GROWING POPULARITY of the Land-Rover in the commission of grand theft, an interim report seems in order. Apparently our 4-wheel drive vehicle has latent virtues which may be of interest to the prospective owner.

It is not our intent here to point out raffish ways for one to pick up a great deal of extra money in one's spare time. Rather the opposite: to abet law and order by useful suggestion.

For instance: in two recent major crimes Land-Rovers were most helpful in hauling away £2,500,000 ($7,000,-000) and £90,000 ($252,000), respectively. Now, although it is well-known that the police of the United Kingdom also employ Land-Rovers, *nowhere is it reported that they employed them on these occasions for hot pursuit of the brigands.* Perhaps that was their mistake.

NEAR LEIGHTON BUZZARD, BEDS.

The first theft, widely if grudgingly admired for its sheer bulk of loot, was, of course, the Great Train Robbery which brought the title back to England.

This Olympics of knavery took place, you recall, at Cheddington, just five miles out of Leighton Buzzard, Bedfordshire, on August 8 last, a Thursday.

Nearly a week passed before any clues turned up. Then, on Tuesday, August 13, a Times of London article datelined Brill, Buckinghamshire, reported:

"A lonely farmhouse near here, twelve miles from Oxford, was the hideout for the mail train gang and their haul of £2,500,000 in bank notes. Mailbags in three abandoned vehicles—an Army type truck and two Land-Rovers—have been found but no money."

NOT LIKE DARTS

Dismissing the Army lorry, one surmises that the Land-Rovers were given the arduous getaway assignment not only for their rugged dependability, but for their capacious rear doors, as well.

Bank notes in excess of so many tend to be cumbersome. When you are trying to on-load literally bags and bags of the stuff you simply haven't got the time to aim nicely; it's not like darts.

No, robbing a train is a very near thing at best and one has got to have the tools to do the job.

FOUND BY MUSHROOMER

Paradoxically, another Land-Rover feature, its outstanding over-all height, caused the thieves to flee the farm, it is thought. According to The Times:

Left Profile   Rear View

"On Sunday afternoon a local man went mushrooming near the farm and noticed the top of a Land-Rover sticking out of a dilapidated outhouse among the trees." This he duly reported.

The Times account continues: "Police believe that the gang fled in haste. In the garden, near a row of runner beans, was a partly dug hole about 3 ft. deep, a spade still standing in a mound of clay.

"Detective Superintendent Fewtrell,

head of Buckinghamshire's C.I.D., surveyed the hole and commented: 'Presumably they intended burying the evidence. We know they got out before they intended...they must have got the wind up'."

Naturally we are pleased that, having been an accessory to the crime, the Land-Rover was also helpful in its solution.

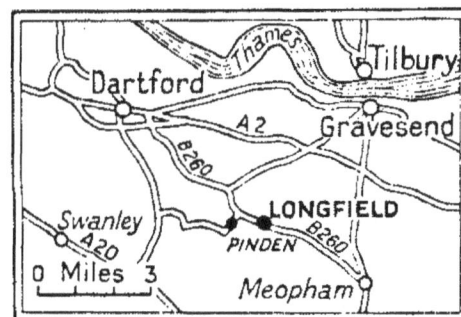

LAND-ROVER STRIKES AGAIN

Though piddling by comparison, the latest Land-Rover effort—the Longfield, Kent, job of September 27—was respectable by county competition standards. It also illustrated an entirely different aspect of the Land-Rover's amazing versatility.

Under the headlines "£90,000 Stolen In Bank Van Ambush" and "Getaway By 8 Masked Men: Guard Felled By Cosh", The London Times describes how the armoured car was high jacked. The bandits lay in wait with their vehicles along a hedgelined road at the T-junction leading off to Horton Kirby and South Darenth. And then:

"A brick was hurled through the windscreen of the bank van, forcing the driver to stop. The bank van was hemmed in by the Land-Rover and the lorry." Whereupon the bandits leaped from the ambush vehicles armed with pick-axe handles, enveloped the bank van, carried the day, and drove off towards Horton Kirby.

To our knowledge this is the first time the Land-Rover has been used in the actual *commission* of a stick-up of this magnitude. While this dubious demonstration of its versatility would seem conclusive, one wonders: what would the

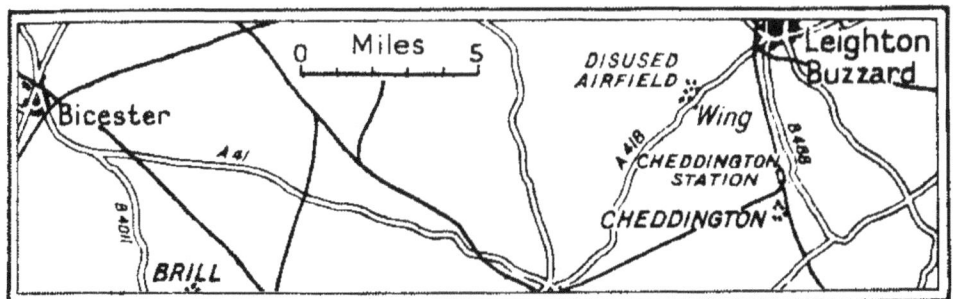

(cont. on next page)

Not for the first time, Gossage needed to run his story over to the next page - secure in the knowledge that his readers would stick with him.

He followed that ad with another oddity.

It was - and still is - almost compulsory for car ads to have a beauty shot of the product.

So Gossage parodied that with the "fashion shoot" on the right. Please read the footnotes - especially the "Pink valve caps by American Petrofina".

HONNEUR ET PATRIE

The Land-Rover Concours d'Elegance Entry for 1964

One imagines they're worried sick over at the Brand X Limousine Division.

CREDITS: Wicker work by Charlie & Nellie Bernhardi; White side walls by Pirelli; Lacquer job by Wade Looper (on overtime); Bumper chroming and Technical Direction by Ken Sykes; Gold fine-striping by Bob Funke; Coach lamps by Cost-Plus Imports; Carpeting color by Ace Dye Works; Mink lap robe by Neiman-Marcus; Flower vases by Michelob; The Two Pink Carnations by Podesta Baldocchi; Silver flask in glove compartment by Abercrombie & Fitch; Pink valve caps by American Petrofina; Basic black Model 88 Station Wagon by Land-Rover; The Thinker by Rodin.

Then he broke the convention with this ad by not leaving room for the car.

ROVER ...GRAND SPORT VERSION!

In the beginning, LAND-ROVERs were used by the world's armies (26 of them), police forces (37 of them), border patrols, big game hunters, archeologists, titled persons (mostly for country use), oil companies, farmers, lumbermen, explorers, foresters, and so on. Now, lots of other people are buying them too: commuters, doctors, skiers, gentlemen farmers and members of hunt clubs, antiquers, rock hounds, dog trainers. Even racing drivers buy them (all aluminum alloy body and eight speeds forward). The LAND-ROVER's a lot of fun—you're never frustrated—you can do anything—go anywhere—see everything—in short, it's GRAND SPORT!

You can virtually have a LAND-ROVER tailor-made—we will fit it with anything you want. Be the first on your block to own a compact fire engine, or to blow your own snow. Be the only one in town to have a Hover-Rover (cushion-of-air sort of thing). Our line of accessories would fill a book—they mow the grass, dig post holes, plow snow, saw cordwood, run your own ski tow, trail your boat, pull a house trailer (or you can dispense with the house trailer and camp in a commodious Land-Rover Dormobile). You name it, we have it!

THE ROVER MOTOR COMPANY OF NORTH AMERICA LIMITED
405 Lexington Avenue, New York 17, N.Y. YUkon 6-0220

We meant to leave more room for a picture—but our enthusiasm got the better of us. So if you'd like a profusely illustrated pamphlet, please send us a postcard.

This is the Heat-Shield Roof, one of a whole battalion of unique features.

As Gossage said: "Rover allowed me to go on defying all decency. Worse still, defying the brand name". He was referring to this ad that "callously flouted all the rules" by not mentioning either the brand or the product.

To begin with Gossage wrote most of the Rover ads. But he also enlisted help from unlikely sources. The anthropologist and author of *The Elephant Man*, Ashley Montagu, sent in hand-written ads.

Nobel Prize winning novelist, John (*Grapes of Wrath*) Steinbeck, got involved in an early form of Influencer Advertising. The idea being to give Steinbeck a car for free - so he would then reference it in his writing.

```
John Steinbeck
190 East 72nd Street
New York, N.Y.


                                              March 1, '65



Dear Howard:

I have a couple of questions I'd like to ask you because you are the only person

I know to ask.

Last fall, I sold my Ford Falcon. It was a cheap car and it never let you down

on its cheapness. This spring, almost immediately, I have to buy a new car.

Since Elaine will drive it mostly, she wants a heavier car than those so called

economy cars.

Now you drove a Rover across the country, and that's a good test of any car.

How was it -- smooth? comfortable? fast?maneuverable? quiet? dependable? I'm

asking you, not as one having the Rover account but as having driven it. How

expensive was it? To buy -- to operate?

I don't want to ask Jimmy. It would sound like a hustle and it's not. They

have already given me what amounts to a permanent loan of a Land Rover. The

theory is, I guess, that me driving it and talking and writing about it might

sell others. I doubt whether I have ever helped to move a single Land Rover.

I love the thing and pretty soon, when I can afford it, I'm going to buy it.

But we are going to have a car for the highway.

You know the pitch. There's a man in this building, Ford distributor who offers

me any kind of Ford product at cost. He, too I guess, thinks that is good public

relations. But I'm lousy at that. Besides, I would like to know about the Rover,

which should be a well built car. Do you have any specification etc. -- models?

H.P.? engines, brakes, etc. I would like your honest, non involved opinion.

What American car would you compare the Rover with? I wish you'd let me know

these things at your earliest because the time is on us for going to the country.
```

By 1966 Gossage had had enough of writing the ads - and you can detect the change here:

(Good Lord!)

Does the Rover 2000 TC really require "erotic references for proper description"? [See № 4 below.]

AS YOU MAY RECALL, here is what Car and Driver magazine had to say in their May, 1966 road test report on the Rover 2000 TC. At any rate it does no harm to repeat it. Italics theirs, numbers ours:

1] *"We have driven a Rover 2000 TC for nearly 3000 miles, on all kinds of roads and in every kind of weather, and we believe that it is absolutely the best sedan that has ever been presented in the pages of this magazine...it is an automotive milestone."*

2] "We recorded acceleration times for the 2000 TC that are better—up to about 70 mph—than those of the Porsche 912, for instance."

3] "It will maintain effortless cruising speeds in excess of anything U.S. laws will allow—yet it offers fuel economy that would do justice to a tiny austerity sedan."

4] "...bending it into a high-speed corner imparts a sensation that requires erotic references for proper description."

5] "When you're settled in your seat, with everything adjusted to your taste, you have a well-fitted, made-to-measure feeling that is quite unique."

6] "It is a supremely comfortable four-passenger sedan...Its trim and appointments and the quality of its finish throughout are equal to any of the six luxury cars we tested last year. The ride is satin-smooth...Below 80 mph the interior is virtually silent..."

7] "And it stops. Oh dear, does it stop! Our normal series of panic stops from eighty to zero were the fastest we've ever recorded and so smooth and stable that we were almost bored by the time we finished our third run."

8] "With all this, it is a bona fide 'safety' car—one designed specifically to avoid accidents whenever they *can* be avoided, and to provide the greatest possible protection to its occupants when they cannot."

9] "We...think that every so-called safety expert and every member of top management in the domestic auto companies should be required to spend a month with the Rover 2000 TC, as we did. This car...is a rare combination of virtually everything one should have in an automobile."

Test drive the 2000 TC yourself. Price: $4195. *(Technical specifications and prices subject to change without notice.)*

The Rover Motor Co. of N. America Ltd., Chrysler Bldg., New York, N.Y. 10017

That last ad is good but it doesn't read like a "Gossage."

Why? Well it's a pretty straightforward testimonial. There is absolutely nothing wrong with testimonials. It's just that Gossage wouldn't write such an ad without sending it up in some way.

It is likely that copywriting had passed to Richard Stearns, and Jerry Mander who'd just joined the agency as a new partner in the business.

According to Bob Freeman, Jerry was a "devout environmentalist and it was embarrassing having an automobile account i.e. promoting one of this planet's chief gas guzzling air polluting devices."

We may be able to detect Jerry's influence on the increasingly serious direction the work then took.

Initially though, while Gossage wasn't writing the ads, he was adding some levity by appearing in them. Here he is with his kids from his second marriage, Amy and Eben, and his third wife, actress Sally Kemp.

(NB the flourish at the end of the ad on the left as the copy bleeds off the page.)

[How to get your children to fasten their Rover 2000 safety harnesses]

Tell them how you had to walk five miles to school, in the snow, and that you weren't *fortunate* enough to have a Rover 2000 T.C. Sports Sedan ( ); and that your every waking thought, yours and mommy's, is of them, and all you are working for is to give them the advantages you never had; and that if they don't fasten them, you will blister

How to get your wife to fasten her Rover 2000 safety harness:

Tell her it drives men mad.

How to get your husband to fasten his Rover 2000 safety harness:

Tell him it's a Sam Browne belt and he looks like a World War I aviator

The Rover Motor Co. of N. America Ltd.: Chrysler Bldg., New York, N.Y. 10017; 231 Johnson Ave., Newark, N.J. 07108; 1040 Bayview Drive, Ft. Lauderdale, Fla. 33304; 373 Shaw Rd., South San Francisco, Calif. 94080; 10889 Wilshire Blvd., Los Angeles, Calif. 90024. Offices also in Vancouver and Toronto.

In 1965 Ralph Nader published his exposé *Unsafe at Any Speed* which claimed that most US cars were dangerous to drive.

Why is the owner of this Rover 2000 smiling?

Because he's alive.

This Rover 2000 Sports Sedan was photographed just after a head-on collision with a truck.

With virtually any other make of car, certain things tend to happen in these dire circumstances, among them: a) The engine tries to join you in the front seat; b) The steering column, which on most cars begins near the front wheels, competes with your chest.

Neither of these happened to the driver of this Rover 2000. (If you are wondering what *did* happen, he cracked a collar bone and two ribs because his safety harness was carelessly loose.)

Luck Had Little To Do

Luck had very little to do with it; the answer is in the car itself.

First off, the Rover 2000 is designed with the thought that, on collision, an engine ought to go down *under* a car rather than up into your lap.

Also, the forward section of the body is designed to crumple defensively; an expensive shock-absorber, but well worth it. Note that although the front lost 18 inches, the passenger compartment is intact.

Steering Column Has To Go

As to the lost 18 inches; in the ordinary car a foot-and-a-half of steering column has to go *somewhere*. The 2000's steering column begins behind the engine, and thus is not accident-prone. Moreover, the steering wheel is flexible and shock-absorbent.

The seats, front and back, are bucket seats of molded steel covered by fine padded leather. The tops of the front seats are padded, as well, to protect them from the faces of the rear passengers.

The top of the dash and the storage bins in front of your knees are also padded. Objects that are necessarily hard are carefully located and inoffensively shaped.

The Rover 2000 Sports Sedan is thought by many authorities to be the safest car in the world. Happily, it is also among the best handling, so that the likelihood of accident is far less to begin with, and it is fun to drive.

In addition to a revolutionary suspension system which makes for fantastic maneuverability, the 2000 also has disc brakes all around.

Heartless To Pretend . . .

In conclusion, may we apologize for mentioning such unpleasant possibilities? However, it is even more heartless to pretend that they don't exist—and neglect to provide for them.

The stern fact is that very few cars have *any* of the safety features we have mentioned; and only the 2000 has all of them—and a good many more besides.

Oh, yes, the price: $3998. Or you can buy it for delivery in Europe and save enough to pay for your passage. If you write, we'll tell you about that, too. Thank you.

The Rover Motor Co. of N. America Ltd., Chrysler Bldg., New York

JUNE, 1966   13

| Egg Shell | Rover 2000 Shell |
| Egg | Rover 2000 |

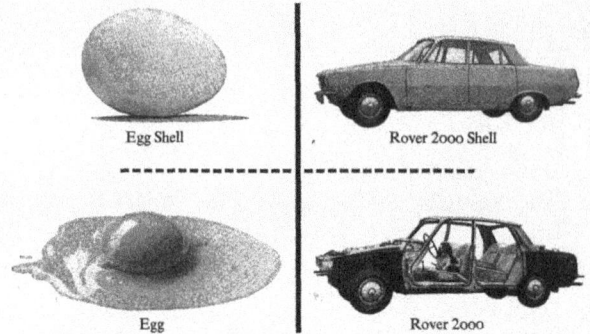

One reason why a Rover 2000 Sports Sedan is safer than a '66 Egg.

TRUE, they both have shells. However, when you remove the shell from a Rover 2000 you find something immensely strong and protective underneath.

Don't try this with a '66 Egg or any other ordinary car.

If you'd like to know more about the Rover 2000 — or try one — just ask.

The Rover Motor Co. of North America Ltd.

APRIL, 1966   33

Rover 2000 Given Gold Medal; Accepts.

THE AUTOMOBILE ASSOCIATION (British) has just named The Rover Company, Ltd., its 1965 Gold Medal winner, "for the high degree of inherent safety incorporated in the design and construction of the Rover 2000 car."

We haven't actually seen the medal yet, but we expect the Automobile Association (British) Gold Medal people will send it along shortly. And we assume it applies to the 2000 TC as well, since it's the same car with the merest addition of twin carburetors, a ten-to-one compression ratio, "mag" wheels, striped tires, a racing-type rear-view mirror outside, and a simulated wood steering wheel and gear-shift knob, and a tachometer, inside. Also some new colors, including white with a blue streak.

The criterion for the selection of the Gold Medal winner was stated as follows: "To the individual, group of individuals, or corporate body who, in the opinion of the Committee of the Automobile Association has made the most valuable contribution to the safety, comfort, economy, enjoyment or utility of motoring in Great Britain during the year."

Hear! Hear! And you can possess one of these impressive motorcars in the United States, Canada, etc.! The 2000 costs $3998; the 2000 TC, $4195.

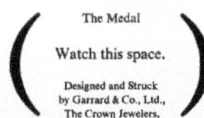

The Medal

Watch this space.

Designed and Struck by Garrard & Co., Ltd., The Crown Jewelers.

The Winner

Designed and Struck by Rover Co., Ltd., The Car Manufacturers.

And Sold? Here Here: The Rover Motor Co. of N. America Ltd., Chrysler Bldg., New York, N.Y. 10017 / 231 Johnson Avenue, Newark, N.J. 07108 / 1040 Bayview Drive, Ft. Lauderdale, Florida 33304 / 373 Shaw Road, South San Francisco, Calif. 94080 / 10889 Wilshire Blvd., Los Angeles, Calif. 90024 / Mobile Drive, Toronto 16, Ontario / 156 West Second Avenue, Vancouver 10, B.C.

Technical specifications and prices subject to change without notice.

JULY, 1966   73

Splendid design; but would you want to be riding in one when it had an accident?

1. The ordinary car has a nice shell to protect the contents, namely you.

2. The Rover 2000 Sports Sedan has a *body*, the way you do. Have you ever noticed how handy your bone structure and rib cage come in? So have we.

3. Which is why the Rover 2000, underneath all that magnificent skin, looks like this:

4. What you have just looked at is more than a safe, rigid steel cage; it is a *self-contained* car, ready to go. You can drive it like this if you don't care what anyone thinks. It is true that beauty is only skin deep; especially from the outside:

5. However, it is some skin, and pretty deep, too: 19 steel and aluminum panels, fitted to precision tolerances and bolted onto the underneath body. O.K., the Rover 2000 has *two* bodies.

6. (NOTICE: If any panel gets bashed-up you can get it repaired or replaced cheaply and quickly. To get a *whole new* front fender costs but $32.00 plus 60 minutes labor. Try this on a '65 Egg; or a '66 Egg, for that matter.)

7. We have mentioned that a Rover 2000 Sports Sedan is a sports sedan. That is true. We can't think of another car that handles as well, and that's not just our opinion.

Road Test magazine asked on its cover, "Does The World's Finest Car Cost Only $4,000?" Inside they said yes it is and does.

8. Actually, complete, it only costs $3,998; still, by the time you add on license plates and raccoon tails . . . If you want to pick it up in Europe we can beat that price all hollow.

9. It also stops: the 2000 has disc brakes all around. We figure that anything that goes that well ought to stop that well. (You'd think that Eggs would all have disc brakes too, wouldn't you? Considering.)

10. If you'd like to know more about the Rover 2000, and there's lots more, why don't you try one? See a Rover dealer or write us.

The Rover Motor Co. of N. America Ltd., 405 Lexington Avenue, New York, New York 10017.

CAR and DRIVER

124

Gossage's agency then turned to safety as their selling point. As the ads explained: "Making driving safe as well as satisfying is the whole idea behind Rover." The one below is typical Jerry Mander - taking on the government over an issue of public interest i.e. the safety of the nation's car drivers.

By the way, you'll see how the copy talks about the car having a "steel cage" thirty years before Volvo ran its famous "Cages save lives" ad.)

(Why Wait to be Safe? The Rover 2000 is Ready Now!)

o Whom It May Concern:
oes Your Government Intend to Walk
ntil 1967?

We have been thinking about the ernment's news release, reported ngth in a Times of New York dis- h (1 July 1965) under the headline: . Outlines Car Safety Standards."

It went on to say that "The eral Services Administration, the ernment's official shopper" has vn up a list of safety features that ll demand in the 38,000 1967 it will buy.

3) We don't imagine that the Government intends to walk or take trams until 1967, but apparently it *will* be making-do with cars that aren't up to safety standards.

4) Why wait to be safe? The Rover 2000 Sports Sedan is *available right now.* And frankly we'd like the business.

5) However, we realize that a U.S.

Government purchasing agency might not be authorized to buy 38,000 cars from a British maker without an O.K. from someone higher up. Which is why we are approaching you, whoever you may be.

6) Now to our sales talk:

7) To begin with, the 2000 has, in effect, *two* bodies: the inside one is of steel cage construction; its overhead

members are akin to the "roll-bar" of a racing car, and for the same conservative reason.

8) The outside, or beautiful, body is made up of nineteen panels which may be replaced *individually* in case of abrasion.

9) Which brings us to this: Supposing worse comes to worst and one of the 38,000 has an accident?

10) If fate conspires against a 2000's rear fender, say, it takes but $32.00 plus 45 minutes labor to replace it with a new one. And the Government rolls again! (In a pinch it is not necessary to stay these couriers— or whoever—from their appointed rounds at all. Just leave the ailing panel at the shop, take off, and come back later. This is the same principle that enables you to get your pants pressed without leaving your body at the cleaner's overnight.)

11) Lest you have a slight reservation that a "Sports Sedan" might be a trifle cramped in the interior or prodigal with fuel, recall that Car and Driver named the 2000 the "Car of the Year" not only for its remarkable handling but for its amplitude.

12) As to economy, the 2000's 30 miles per gallon is the automotive equivalent of only one night light in the White House.

13) Look, Sir, if you haven't road-tested a 2000 Sports Sedan yourself why don't you call your nearest Rover dealer? Or better still, just drop in and surprise him.

14) Now; in filling out the order form here, please don't feel hesitant about giving your real name and title; we assure you that they will be kept in strictest confidence.

15) Thank you for your attention. And may we say, even though it's been 150 years, how sorry we are about our servicemen burning down the White House? It looks simply beautiful now; you certainly put the insurance money to good use.

16) Finally, Sir, if it so happens that, after all, you're not the person we should speak to about the 38,000 cars, but you might like 1, please fill in the form anyway. We don't mind breaking the set. You'll hear from us, never fear. Or see your local Rover Dealer.

SHORT FORM 1776 AD
Return to Rover Motor Company of North America Ltd., Chrysler Bldg., New York, N. Y. 10017

1) Please state title, if any (as: "President," etc.) _____

2) How many Rover 2000's are you interested in? (as: (1), (2), (38,000), etc.) _____

3) Do you wish your lavishly illustrated brochure mailed in plain wrapper? _____

4) Is the Potomac navigable to a point near your place? _____

(Signed) _____

(Address) _____

(City) _____ (State or District) _____

Oh, the price: $3800 East Coast, $3898 West Coast. Places in between cost in between.

BY THE WAY: We have a most advantageous overseas delivery plan. For instance, your envoy to St. James's could pick up his 2000 for just $3080! For other places write to Mr. David Hunter at the above address.

© 1965 Rover Motor Co. of North America Ltd.

addition to satisfying to G.S.A.'s modest pleas for passenger harnesses, padded dash and visors, recessed instrument panel, unaggressive knobs, lapsible steering wheel with a column that won't attack you, etc., etc., the Rover 2000 also has disc brakes all around, non-jackknifing seats, l firewall to keep the engine out of your lap, radial tires, etc., etc.

Rover cars may have been saving lives but, in Jerry Mander's eyes, the cars were still killing the planet and eventually he expressed this emphatically in an interview with the *Wall Street Journal*. It took only a few minutes for the client to wire "Do not wish to cause further embarrassment ... STOP ... Rover account terminated."

As we've just seen, when Gossage stopped writing the Rover ads, he and his wife Sally, started appearing in them. Likewise another of the agency's accounts, the stereo sound system maker, KLH.

(SURVEY)

Question #1

How much would you pay to keep your wife one more year?

DO YOU REMEMBER the game kids used to play in school where you were asked how much money it would take to get you to sell your country's secrets? (Assuming no torture.) Or your dog?

It was a way of thinking about the value you *really* placed on a thing.

One of the first things you learned was that "features" had very little to do with it. (For example, if your country had had 20 more rivers, or your dog's tail wagged at 86 Per Minute—six less than an "average" dog's—the answer would hardly have changed.)

When KLH began making stereo equipment ten years ago, our founders (K., L., and H.) noticed that grownup manufacturers talked as though features had *everything* to do with value. We hated that. We still do.

"Feature:" Injecting 380 horsepower into cars that have no plausible market save those who commute back and forth over the Bonneville Salt Flats.

Or Again: Advertising 300 watts of power in a high priced stereo console unit to give it the *appearance* of value. (Neglecting to mention that large numbers of watts have nothing to do with hearing the music accurately, or even loudly, both of which depend on what kind of equipment you've squeezed the watts

into. 35 watts in good equipment will do far better.)

42-22-36

To define worth solely in terms of features is like determining the "market value" of a wife from her height, age, weight, width of smile, tendency to suntan evenly, and the number of pounds of food she is capable of cooking up in an evening.

It's true enough we all like to have *something* explicit to help our thinking. Even Consumer Reports will sometimes find itself detailing competitive features and statistics; akin to Playboy's 42-22-36 ratings.

But studying the centerfold and accompanying data simply doesn't give us all the information we really need. What does? Well, probably nothing short of a few years in the same house together.

BASEBALL PLAYER

Packard had it right, way back in the twenties, when its advertising rested on the confident slogan "Ask The Man Who Owns One."

(It was a new kind of "testimonial" but it's been watered down since. How is a man today to depend on testimonials to choose, say, his cigarette brand when dozens of equally beloved baseball players can't get together about which is best?)

Still, the principle of determining value through testimonials makes very good sense:

Economists, for instance, say value can be understood as "some measure of the sense of loss one experiences after being deprived of a commodity or service," or, ask the man who owns one how much he'd dislike losing it. (The boy contemplating his dog's worth figured it out the same way.)

Any other way of measuring value, like establishing a ratio between features and price, is at best only a guess, made *before* anyone could possibly know.

DEPRIVED OF YOUR WIFE

What we propose, then, is a technique of *measuring* the sense of loss as a way of thinking about "Subjective Value;" i.e., what a commodity means to someone who has it.

So. Assume for a moment that you are about to be deprived of your wife. (Substitute husband or "good friend" where applicable.) How much would you pay in dollars to keep her one more year? When you're through thinking about that one, fill in No. 1 and have a look at the rest of the questionnaire.

You see what we're up to here.

We began on this idea because we already have evidence (based upon a comparison of the number of hours owners sit listening to KLH phonographs as opposed to other brands) that our $300 stereo system is cherished somewhat more than at least one $400 system we could name; and perhaps twice as much as another $300 set.

Doubtless the same situation exists among magazines—some are surely valued more than others—or sewing machines, or autos, or toothpaste. Toothpaste? Well, we'll soon see, and if you're interested we will be pleased to let you know what we learn.

QUESTIONNAIRE

If one or more of these questions interests you, then kindly fill in the blank spaces that apply and mail to the address we have listed at lower right. For our part, we will gladly send you a tally of the results of this questionnaire, and others we are doing in subsequent ads, if you also add your name and address. Thank you.

1 (See Headline)._____.

2 Do you have a favorite magazine?_____.
Which one?_____.
If you were informed that because of financial difficulties the publication might discontinue publishing, how much would you be willing to pay for one more issue rather than be deprived of it?_____. One more year's subscription?_____.

3 Do you have telephone service at home?_____.
If yes, assume you now pay an average of $20 monthly for this service. How much additional would you pay, rather than be deprived of it?_____.

4 The automobile you now own was purchased in what year?_____. At what price?_____. What make?_____. Assuming it's in good running order, and that you couldn't get another one like it, how much would you pay to keep it during the upcoming year?_____.

5 Do you own a piano?_____. What kind?_____.
How much did you pay for it?_____. How long ago?_____. How much would you pay to keep from being deprived of it?_____.

6 Do you regularly use a particular brand of toothpaste?_____. If yes, which brand?_____.
Assuming you were informed that because of financial difficulties your brand of toothpaste might go out of business. How much would you be willing to pay, above its present cost, to have one more tube, rather than be deprived of it?_____.

7 Assume for the moment that an offer was being made for your wife's wedding dress. How much would you be willing to sell it for?_____. What does your wife say?_____.

8 Do you own stereo equipment at home?_____.
A console?_____. A one-piece table model?_____. A three-piece system?_____. Components?_____.
Which make(s)?_____.
How much did it cost you to buy?_____. How long ago?_____. If you were about to be deprived of the set you now own, and knew you could not get another of the same kind, how much would you be willing to pay to keep it?_____.

(If you worry that by putting your name below you may be subjecting yourself to a barrage of KLH literature, or that we may send a salesman around, or sell your name to some "list house," rest easy. We won't. Though if you would like to have a catalog and the name of the store near you that sells our equipment, please so indicate in the appropriate box.)

Name_____

Address_____

City_____State_____Zip_____

☐ Please send catalog ☐ Forward survey results

Mail to: Henry M. Morgan, Pres., KLH Research and Development Corp., 30 Cross St., Cambridge, Mass. 02139

The ads on page 126-7, the page opposite and top left above were part of KLH's successful "Subjective Values" campaign.

Please have a look at the campaign's launch ad. Its premise is an intellectual argument you simply wouldn't expect to see in an advertisement - then or now. But that brand of involving, idiosyncratic soft sell was, as we've seen, very much the Gossage agency house style.

The campaign was written by Richard Stearns and pulled over 5,000 responses, delighted the client and, according to Jerry Mander, was "great material for a book".

Other ads followed, with less of the Gossage touch. Until we get "The KLH Advertisement", which proved that even the best shops can turn out a turkey.

If that last KLH ad was done on Jerry Mander's watch, then I think we can cut him some slack.

Jerry, who died in May 2023, was probably the only copywriter Gossage respected. He was working as a publicist when he came to Gossage's attention in early 1966. He had created an ad for the *San Francisco Chronicle* that mocked a planned Pentagon airdrop of toys to Vietnamese children. The ad promised to collect war toys (two sarcastic suggestions: a plastic bazooka and an atomic tank that ejects napalm) for the Defence Department and drop them on the Pentagon from a helicopter.

Gossage loved the ad's audacity - and the press coverage it garnered - and invited Jerry to join the agency. With his name on the door, Jerry wrote Freeman, Mander & Gossage's two most successful campaigns. Let's begin with *Scientific American* magazine.

By 1965 Gossage had hooked up with Gerald Feigen to form his consultancy, Generalists, Inc. One of their first clients was Gerard Piel, the publisher of *Scientific American*.

He asked the Generalists how he might persuade the big spending airline companies to advertise in his pages. Gossage presented a deck which recommended: "A paper airplane derby with prizes not only for distance, but for design", all of which was to be couched in "splendidly scientific terms".

Gossage had already tried and failed to pitch that paper airplane competition to Kimberly-Clark for their Kleenex brand. This time it flew.

Jerry Mander wrote all the copy. Too much, in fact.

Here's Dugald Stermer, the campaign's art director: "The first ad was for the *New Yorker* and there was too much copy for the size of the type I wanted to use ... so I said 'OK, let's buy the back page on the reverse of the ad so that people can tear the page out and make an airplane out of it.' And we bought the whole advertising page just for that one paragraph of copy. Isn't that brilliant?

"Gossage had the power to persuade them."

1st International Paper Airplane Competition

SCIENTIFIC AMERICAN primarily concerns itself with what Man is up to these days, and our readership is known for travelling more than that of any other magazine. So it is little wonder we have spent considerable time studying the two designs for the supersonic SST airplane recently announced by Boeing and Lockheed. (See Fig. 1 and Fig. 2.)

Soon we'll all be flying around in thin air at Mach 2.7, i.e., from New York to London in 150 minutes. Quite a prospect!

FIG. 1: Lockheed SST.

FIG. 2: Boeing SST.

Still, at the close of our inquiry there remained this nagging thought: Hadn't we seen these designs somewhere before?

Of course. Paper airplanes. Fig. 3 and Fig. 4 illustrate only the more classical paper plane designs, in use since the 1920's or so, having a minimum performance capability of 15 feet and four seconds.* (See over)

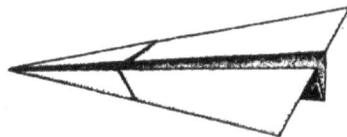

FIG. 3: Paper plane circa 1920, the classic paper plane. Smoothness of flight, grace.

FIG. 4: First developed among paper airplane designers in the 1930's. Known for spectacular darting motions. Note hooked nose.

We do not mean to question the men at Boeing and Lockheed, or their use of traditional forms. But it seems to us unjust that several million paper plane designers around the world are not also given their due, a credit which if it had been extended some years ago would have saved the pros quite some straining at the drawing boards.

Well anyway, with design having caught up with itself, we can now postulate that there is, right now, flying down some hallway or out of some moviehouse balcony in Brooklyn, the aircraft which will make the SST 30 years obsolete. No?

Consider this: Never since Leonardo da Vinci, the Patron Saint of paper airplanes, has such a wealth of flight

research and experimentation remained untouched by cross-disciplinary study and publication. Paper airplane design has become one of those secret pleasures performed behind closed doors. Everybody does it, but nobody knows what anyone else has learned.

Many's the time we've spied a virtuoso paper plane turn the corner of the office hallway, or suddenly rise up over

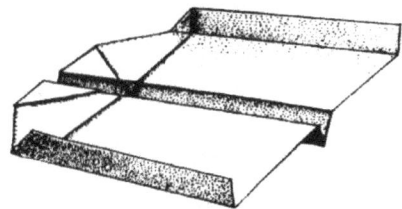

FIG. 5: Drawn from memory, this plane was last seen in 12th floor stairwell at 415 Madison Avenue. Do you know its designer? Where is he?

the desk, or on one occasion we'll never forget, veer first down the stairs to the left, and suddenly to the right, staying aloft 12 seconds in all. (See Fig. 5.)

But who is its designer? Is he a Board Chairman or a stock boy? And what has he done lately?

All right then. In the interests of filling this information gap, and in light of the possibility that the future of aeronautics may now be flying in a paper plane, we are hereby calling for entries to the 1st In-

ternational Paper Airplane
Competition.

RULES

1. Scientific American has created The Leonardo (see Fig. 6) to be winner's trophy in each of these four categories: a) duration aloft, b) distance flown, c) aerobatics, and d) Origami.

2. A silver Leonardo will go to winners not involved professionally in air travel, and a titanium Leonardo (the metal being used in the SST) to professional entrants, that is,

FIG. 6: The Leonardo.

people employed in the air travel business, people who build non-paper airplanes, and people who subscribe to Scientific American, because they fly so much.

3. We have left the page nearly blank so you would rip it out and fold at will. If this paper is not suitable to your particular design, feel at liberty to use your own paper of any size or description. (Rag content and water marks will not, however, have any bearing on the final decision.) Or, send for your free Official Entry Form Pad — reprints of this ad, padded, which you can stand on your desk, or hang near it, and with which you and your associates can make literally dozens of Official Entries.

4. You may enter as often as you like, being sure to include your *name, address, employer,* if any, and the *classes* in which you would like your entry to qualify.

5. Send your entry to us, somehow, at this address: Scientific American, Airplane Design Dept., 415 Madison Ave., New York 10017, postmarked by January 16, 1967. On January 21 all entries will be test-flown down our hallways by a panel of distinguished judges whose identity we'll announce at a later date (so as not to influence anyone's design).

6. Except that we will publish scale drawings of the winning designs, all other rights to same remain reserved to the designer. We, however, will do our bit towards assuring immediate production. Thank you.

*(In paper plane circles, of course, a *better* time is a *longer* time. If a plane can stay aloft, floating on the air as it were, for 15 seconds, *that* is a virtue, as indeed it was for the Bros. Wright. One would assume that today's commercial designers, who seek planes to get from here to there and *down* as quickly as possible, would not have been much interested in the study of paper planes, or the Bros. Wright. In light of the illustrations, our assumption appears to be wrong.)

The launch ad was followed by:

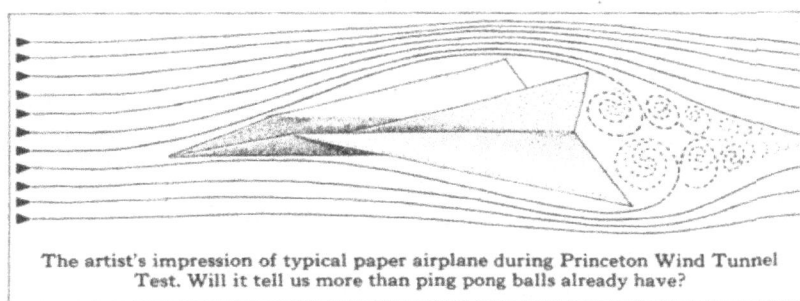

acteristics between these *low* speed objects, and *hypersonic* Mach 20 aircraft attempting to safely negotiate the difficult re-entry and landing procedure. "By now," Professor Hazen reports, "we know more about the aerodynamics of ping pong balls than anyone else in the world."

Now who would have thought, in this age when the primary virtue is the getting from here to there as *quickly* as possible, that the testing of *low* speed objects could have such profound importance?

Well, that's the point of all this. There's little enough chance for any of us to really get on the inside of things these days so let's just proceed as though the world of aviation and space travel is a book with blank pages and we are in charge of the text. (Or shall we merely rip them out, fold, and fly?)

Thank you.

PANEL OF JUDGES: SCIENTIFIC AMERICAN 1ST INTERNATIONAL PAPER-AIRPLANE COMPETITION.

(In alphabetical order)

MR. SURENDRA BAHADUR
President, Go Fly A Kite Store, New York City; one of few men in the world to have flown a kite to upwards of 4,000 feet.

CAPT. LEE CERMAK
Pilot-In-Charge, Goodyear Blimp ("The Mayflower").*

MRS. SUSAN CLEMENTS
U. S. Women's Skydiving Style Champion, 1964, 1965, 1966 (in which parachutist does four 360° turns and two backflops in shortest time possible); Women's Overall Champion, 1965; veteran, at age 22, of 470 jumps.**

PROF. DAVID C. HAZEN
Assoc. Dean of Faculty, Princeton University; senior member, Dept. of Aerospace and Mechanical Sciences; pioneer researcher in low-speed flight at Princeton Subsonic Aerodynamics Lab. (also see adjoining page)

PROF. EDMUND V. LAITONE
Chairman, Aeronautical Sciences Div., Univ. of California, Berkeley; former member Nat'l Advisory Committee for Aeronautics (NACA), specialist in high speed aerodynamics; former Section Head, Flight Research Engineering, Cornell Aeronautical Lab.

MAJOR S. S. PIKE
President, Skywriting Corporation of America; inventor of precision 5-plane Sky-Typing; supervisor of skywriting project which brought the name Pepsi-Cola to 8,000 cities and towns, 160,000 times.

CDR. R. E. SCHREDER
U. S. National Soaring Champion, 1958, 1960, 1966; holder of three world speed records for gliders; designer and builder of 14 aircraft, both sailplane and powered types; member of Helms Soaring Hall of Fame.

MR. BUNJI TAGAWA
Sage Fellow in Philosophy, Cornell University; prominent technical illustrator; Instructor in Origami, P.S. 29, New York.

*The word blimp, according to Goodyear, is not derived from the descriptive phrase "Balloon, Type B, limp" as has been suggested from time to time, but in fact dates to 1915 when a certain Lt. Cunningham of the British air forces became amused at the sound he heard on the occasion of flipping his thumb at the gasbag.

**Mrs. Clements reports that the U. S. has 20,000 sky divers, and the Soviet Union 3 million. Does this suggest a skydiving gap?

RULES: In honor of Leonardo da Vinci, the Patron Saint of Paper Airplanes, Scientific American commissioned San Francisco artist Victor Moscoso to create The Leonardo, as winner's trophy in each of these categories: a) duration aloft, b) distance flown, c) aerobatics, and d) Origami. A silver Leonardo will go to winners not involved professionally in air travel, and a titanium Leonardo (the metal being used in the SST, provided to us in the public interest by the Titanium Metals Corporation of America) to professional entrants, that is, people employed in the air travel business, people who build non-paper airplanes, and people who subscribe to Scientific American, be-

The Leonardo.

cause they fly so much. Be sure to include your name, address, employer, if any, and the classes in which you would like your entry to qualify. Except that we will publish scale drawings of the winning designs, all rights to same remain reserved to the designer. We, however, will do our bit towards assuring immediate production. Send your entry to us, somehow, at this address: Scientific American, Airplane Design Dept., 415 Madison Ave., New York 10017, postmarked by Valentine's Day, 1967.

With the winners announced here:

1st International Paper Airplane Competition; A Last Backward Glance

Fig. 1. Six members of the Panel of Jurors at the 1st International Paper Airplane Competition shown during Final Flyoffs observing one of 43 finalists launched for their study and the press. The particular entry they are watching was entered in the distance category, and flew some 87 feet before crashing into a CBS camera, at one foot three inches above ground. It was reflown.

By now, most of you are acquainted with the names, performances and other details of the Final Flyoffs held Washington's Birthday Eve at the New York Hall of Science. (As one news account put it, the event "drew international press coverage not seen since the visit of Pope Paul.")

Fig. 2. The Leonardo. Proud possession of 7 winners whose paper planes were judged best of 11,851 entries.

For ready reference, however, we record the winners elsewhere on this page, together with performance data where applicable.

Our *primary* purpose now, is to review with you what we have learned from this experiment.

This much *is* certain. At long last the hitherto uncelebrated and uncatalogued achievements of aircraft design's "underground" have had their day in the sky.

And, there's this: A mere eight weeks after our competition was formally announced the long lost notebooks of Leonardo da Vinci, the Patron

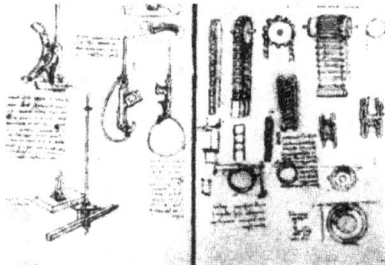

Fig. 3. Two pages of drawings by Leonardo da Vinci, Patron Saint of Paper Airplanes, discovered eight weeks after competition was announced. This development alone is said to have made the entire project worthwhile.

Saint of Paper Airplanes, whose name graces our winner's trophy (see Fig. 2 and Fig. 3), were suddenly discovered.

If no further benefit accrued to science during this project, would not this discovery be ample?

But, going on....

One of our distinguished panel of jurors, Prof.

David Hazen of Princeton's Aeronautics Dept., when asked if indeed we *had* found the key to the SST of the year 2000 flying about in a paper airplane, stated categorically, "No, we have learned nothing new at all."

Berkeley Protest

Not wishing to excite controversy within academia, we must yet observe that another juror, Prof. Edmund Laitone of Berkeley protested, believing Prof. Hazen may have spoken hastily.

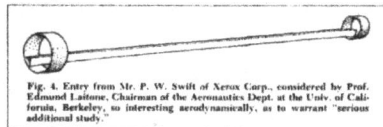

Fig. 4. Entry from Mr. P. W. Swift of Xerox Corp., considered by Prof. Edmund Laitone, Chairman of the Aeronautics Dept. at the Univ. of California, Berkeley, so interesting aerodynamically, as to warrant "serious additional study."

Several of the entries need further study, Prof. Laitone indicated, particularly one dart-like object distinguished by flight-perpendicular ring air foils (hoops) both forward and aft. (See Fig. 4.) Prof. Laitone felt "it raises important questions concerning an aspect of aerodynamics that has had virtually no study."

"I would like to know," he added, "exactly what the optimum diameter-length ratio for cylindrical lifting surfaces would be at various Mach and Reynolds numbers? We may find it demonstrates lift characteristics and stability potentials applicable to *both* supersonic and subsonic speeds."

An exciting prospect to be sure.

And now on to the statistical data.

U. S. Government

In all, 5,144 people entered 11,851 airplanes. They came from 28 countries including Liberia and Switzerland, though the largest number of foreign entries were from Japan (some 750), mostly in origami categories. The U. S. government, while not admitting that it considered the winning of this competition vital to national interests, was represented by entries from 18 of its agencies.

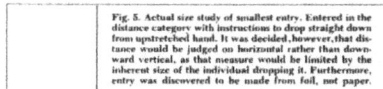

Fig. 5. Actual size study of smallest entry. Entered in the distance category with instructions to drop straight down from upstretched hand. It was decided, however, that distance would be judged on horizontal rather than downward vertical, as that measure would be limited by the inherent size of the individual dropping it. Furthermore, entry was discovered to be made from foil, not paper.

The smallest entry received measured .08 x .00003 inches (see Fig. 5) submitted by the Space Particles and Field Dept. of Aerospace Corp. The largest entry was 11 feet. Entered in the distance flown category, it flew two times its length.

Dr. Sakoda

The most interesting statistic, we believe, is that against an estimated 5,000 entries from children, the seven winners were all grownups and between them have devoted 314 years to paper airplane design and experimentation. All seven are engaged in science and engineering, even the ori-

gami winner, Dr. James Sakoda, a professor of anthropology who specializes in computer programming.

Frederick Hooven, of Ford, whose flying wing (see Fig. 6) won in duration aloft, learned his aerodynamics as a student of Orville Wright's, using Mr. Wright's own wind tunnel for early testing.

And Capt. R. S. Barnaby, an aerobatics winner, was founder of the N. Y. Model Aero Club back in 1909.

England, 1934

Captain Barnaby presented us with the startling news that the very model that won him first place in our competition won him second place in a paper plane competition in England, 1934.

Does this suggest that aerodynamics has retrogressed over the years? It is hard to say since who knows *what* won first place in '34?

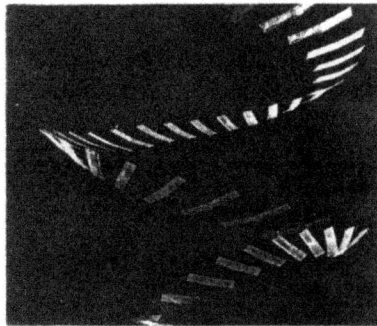

Fig. 6. Flying wing which won duration aloft category. It is shown here in stroboscopic illumination taken at 17 images per second.

You see, without continuously available data, we have merely our imaginations to guide us, which brings us to this special good news:

Commander Richard Schreder, another of our jury who is also national Soaring Champion, has suggested that the American Soaring Society will be pleased to keep our effort aloft, as it were, by sponsoring the 2nd International Paper Airplane Competition, a suggestion we heartily endorse.

For, even as a magazine whose readership is devoted to technological advance and for whom air travel is a way of daily life, we still remain convinced that there is a world of discovery, pleasure and satisfaction in all manner of subsonic activity, from the walking through forests to the flying of paper airplanes. Or as Capt. Lee Cermak, still another of our judges and pilot of the Goodyear blimp Mayflower put it:

"I don't care how much you fly, you won't ever see a jet stop, just to take a better look at the sharks."

Winners of the Leonardo

Duration aloft Nonprofessional*	Jerry A. Brinkman Assistant Sales Manager Globe Industries, Dayton, Ohio	9.9 seconds aloft	Aerobatics Nonprofessional	Edward L. Ralston, University of Illinois, (and Clark, Dietz & Associates, Consulting Engineers) Urbana, Illinois
Duration aloft Professional**	Frederick Hooven, Special Consultant to the General Manager, Ford Motor Co., Detroit	10.2 seconds aloft	Aerobatics Professional	Capt. R. S. Barnaby, USN (Ret.), Exhibits Consultant to the Director, Science Museum, Franklin Institute, Philadelphia, Penn.
Distance flown Nonprofessional	Louis W. Schultz, Engineering Group Manager, Stewart Warner Corp., Oak Brook, Illinois	58 feet, 2 inches	Origami Nonprofessional	Prof. James Sakoda, Professor of Sociology and Anthropology, Brown University, Providence, Rhode Island
Distance flown Professional	Robert B. Meuser, Lawrence Radiation Lab. Univ. of California, Berkeley	91 feet, 6 inches (At this point, while still aloft entry hit rear wall of Hall of Science.)	Origami Professional	The judges did not consider that any entry in this category was worthy of The Leonardo.

NOTE: All entries were pre-tested by students of the NASA Goddard Inst. of Space Studies who reported that entries performed considerably better in preliminary testing than in the finals. The reason for this was not nervousness before the judges, but rather that the TV lights created severe thermals invariably hazardous to paper plane flight.

*"Nonprofessionals" were defined in our rules as those not involved professionally in air travel.

**"Professionals" were defined as "people employed in the air travel business, people who build non-paper airplanes, and people who subscribe to Scientific American, because they fly so much."

There were over 11,000 entries from 28 countries. As *Western Advertising* reported, the campaign "generated the kind of press reaction usually reserved for Super Bowl games or heart transplants. Over 150 newspapers showed up for the Final Fly-offs in New York, more coverage than was accorded the Pope."

To keep the campaign in the public eye, Lewis Lowe, the industrial designer and husband of Alice Lowe, created a set of deluxe paper airplanes that were sold at the exclusive Manhattan toy shop, FAO Schwarz.

Next was *The Great International Paper Airplane Book* by the art director and photographer George Dippel, Jerry Mander and Howard Gossage.

It was an instant best-seller, with 10,000 copies on order before the day of publication.

237

Great paper airplane event

It's here — the Official Book of the 1st International Paper Airplane Competition conducted by *Scientific American*. Photographs, diagrams, 20 cut, fold, and fly-them-yourself pages of winners and other

notable aircraft (the cream of 11,851 entries from 28 countries) including the Flying Wing that won *Duration-Aloft/Professional* and the superbly flightworthy helicopter disqualified for reasons of protocol. Plus the behind-the-scenes story & official records of the Competition, with facsimile documents and some pretty profound commentaries on historical, esthetic, technological aspects of the Paper Airplane, its mystique and implications for the future.

The Book that Board Chairmen, Schoolboys, Engineers, Housewives, Computer Programmers, Poets, Office Boys, Government Aeronautic Experts and other secret paper airplane people dream of finding in their Christmas Stockings.

THE GREAT INTERNATIONAL PAPER AIRPLANE BOOK

By Jerry Mander, George Dippel and Howard Gossage.

Paperback $2.95; Glamorous clothbound presentation edition $10.

Simon and Schuster, Publishers

Alas, the client quickly lost faith in the Gossage house-style and approach to circuitous selling. Yes, the copy had mentioned that the magazine's readers flew a lot. But, for the next campaign, the client wanted more focus on the product.

Within nine months the agency had been fired. Note, on the client's letter below, Jerry's handwritten comment to Al(ice) on the whole sorry affair.

SCIENTIFIC AMERICAN

Established 1845

415 MADISON AVENUE, NEW YORK, N.Y. 10017   MURRAY HILL 8-3900

October 6, 1967

Al.
Have a look
at this. Depressingsville

Mr. Jerry Mander
Freeman & Gossage
451 Pacific
San Francisco, California

Dear Jerry:

I am back from a few days of vacation and now it is my turn to pick up the correspondence Gerry Piel has been having with Howard and you.

You will recall that last March (see attached letter addressed to Messrs. Gossage, Mander and Feigen) I wrote and told you that we want to aim our Generalists' effort at "select consumer" advertisers rather than just airline advertisers. Since the letter of six months ago spells it out I won't continue the discussion here but ask that you consider this very seriously as you think of possible new campaigns.

Further, I think the campaign should be to the point - or at least more to the point than we have done in the past. Let's not go too far around the back of the barn.

And still another addition: We want our advertising to be remembered as coming from SCIENTIFIC AMERICAN rather than from an unusual agency which has produced similar campaigns for Irish Whiskey, KLH, et al. We would like a change of pace and physical appearance. And there is no requirement it be humorous.

I think you achieved this in some of your Sierra Club ads. Unfortunately the Destination Syndrome and KLH efforts are so similar they would be confusing to the reader if both were published in a short time period in The New Yorker and The New York Times.

more....

137

Jerry Mander's other great contribution to Freeman, Mander & Gossage had a happier ending. It began when David Brower approached the agency for help. Brower was executive director of The Sierra Club, a non-profit organisation dedicated to the conservation and enjoyment of America's natural habitat.

For five years they'd been fighting the government's plans to dam the Grand Canyon. By May 1966, with bulldozers preparing the foundations, the fight seemed lost. Brower's last act of resistance was to be an ad in the *New York Times*. He'd already written the copy, he just wanted Gossage's brilliant designer, Marget Larsen, to art direct it. Gossage suggested they test Brower's ad against one written by Jerry Mander.

Here's Brower's ad:

And here's Jerry Mander's. The challenging headline and the copy are his...

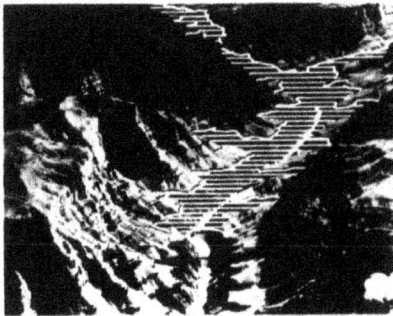

... but the coupons going down the right hand side of the ad were Gossage's idea.

Each one carried a message to, and the address of, respectively the President of the United States, the Secretary of the Interior, the Head of the Interior Committee of the House of Representatives, and the reader's representatives in Congress and the Senate.

As Jerry Mander explained: "Gossage did the important, brilliant thing with those multiple coupons. That had never been done before. They were very, very important because in those days people used coupons, they were their internet."

Indeed, Gossage had used "their internet" to create a feedback loop that linked those who were opposed to the dams directly with those who were responsible for approving or rejecting them.

One of the latter, Secretary of the Interior, Stewart Udall later conceded: "That really was a stroke of brilliance. Of course he knew how to put the heat on you. If you were in my position you had to act."

Gossage also knew how to "put the heat on" in other ways.

I said at the start that it was his aim was to make his clients famous. Or in this case, to make the issue into headline news. You'll see one classic ploy in the second paragraph with the reference to the creation of a 130 mile lake.

By all accounts that wasn't true. But it was exactly the kind of, what we now call, "fake news" that Gossage and Brower knew would make the front pages and galvanise popular protest.

More publicity came when, in response to the ad, the Internal Revenue Services revoked The Sierra Club's charitable status. This act of, what the public perceived as governmental bullying, rallied even greater support to the cause.

Which was then capitalised upon by the follow-up ads in the campaign:

SHOULD WE ALSO FLOOD THE SISTINE CHAPEL SO TOURISTS CAN GET NEARER THE CEILING?

EARTH began four billion years ago and Man two million. The Age of Technology, on the other hand, is hardly a hundred years old, and on our time chart we have been generous to give it even the little line we have.

It seems to us hasty, therefore, during this blip of time, for Man to think of directing his fascinating new tools toward altering irrevocably the forces which made him. Nonetheless, in these few brief years among four billion, wilderness has all but disappeared. And now these:

1) There is a bill in Congress to "improve" Grand Canyon. Two dams will back up artificial lakes into 148 miles of canyon gorge. This will benefit tourists in power boats, it is argued, who will enjoy viewing the canyon wall more closely. (See headline). Submerged underneath the tourists will be part of the most revealing single page of earth's history. The lakes will be as deep as 600 feet (deeper for example, than all but a handful of New York buildings are high) but in a century, silting will have replaced the water with that much mud, wall to wall.

There is no part of the wild Colorado River, the Grand Canyon's sculptor, that will not be maimed.

Tourist recreation, as a reason for the dams, is in fact an afterthought. The Bureau of Reclamation, which backs them, prefers to call the dams "cash registers." They are expected to make money by sale of commercial power. *They will not provide anyone with water.*

2) In Northern California, four lumber companies are about to complete logging the private virgin redwood forests, an operation which to give you an idea of its size, has taken fifty years.

Soon, where nature's tallest living things have stood silently since the age of the dinosaurs, the extent of the cutting will make creation of a redwood national park absurd.

The companies have said tourists want only enough roadside trees for the snapping of photos. They offer to spare trees for this purpose, and not much more. The result will remind you of the places on your face you missed while you were shaving.

3) And up the Hudson, there are plans for a power complex —a plant, transmission lines, and a reservoir on top of Storm King Mountain—destroying one of the last wild and high and beautiful spots near New York City.

4) A proposal to flood a region in Alaska as large as Lake Erie would eliminate at once the breeding grounds of more wildlife than conservationists have preserved in history.

5) In San Francisco, real estate developers are day by day filling a bay that made the city famous, putting tract houses over the fill; and now there's a new idea — still more fill, enough for an air cargo terminal as big as Manhattan.

There exists today a mentality which can conceive such destruction, giving commerce as ample reason. For 74 years, the 40,000 member Sierra Club has opposed that mentality. But now, when even Grand Canyon can be threatened, we are at a critical moment in time.

This generation will decide if something untrammelled and free remains, as testimony we had love for those who follow.

We have been taking ads, therefore, asking people to write their Congressmen and Senators; Secretary of the Interior Stewart Udall; The President; and to send us funds to continue the battle. Thousands *have* written, but meanwhile, the Grand Canyon legislation has advanced out of committee and is at a crucial stage in Congress. More letters are needed and more money, to help fight a mentality that may decide Man no longer needs nature.*

David Brower, Executive Director
Sierra Club
Mills Tower, San Francisco

☐ Please send me more details on how I may help.
☐ Here is a donation of $_____ to continue your effort to keep the public informed.
☐ Send me "Time and the River Flowing," famous four color book which tells the complete story of Grand Canyon, and why T. Roosevelt said, "leave it as it is." ($25.00)
☐ Send me "The Last Redwoods" which tells the complete story of the opportunity as well as the destruction in the redwoods. ($17.50)
☐ I would like to be a member of the Sierra Club. Enclosed is $14.00 for entrance and first year's dues.

Name_____

Address_____

City_____ State_____ Zip_____

---

*The previous ads, urging that readers exercise a constitutional right of petition, to save Grand Canyon, produced an unprecedented reaction by the Internal Revenue Service threatening our tax deductible status. IRS says the ads may be a "substantial" effort to "influence legislation." Undefined, these terms leave organizations like ours at the mercy of administrative whim. (The question has not been raised with any organizations that favor Grand Canyon dams.) So we cannot now promise that contributions you send us are deductible—pending results of what may be a long legal battle.

The Sierra Club, founded in 1892 by John Muir, is nonprofit, supported by people who, like Thoreau, believe "In wildness is the preservation of the world." The club's program is nationwide, includes wilderness trips, books and films — as well as such efforts as this to protect the remnant of wilderness in the Americas. There are now twenty chapters, branch offices in New York (Biltmore Hotel), Washington (Dupont Circle Building), Los Angeles (Auditorium Building), Albuquerque, Seattle, and main office in San Francisco.

AGE OF TECHNOLOGY
FIRST MAN 2 MILLION YRS. AGO
FIRST ELEPHANTS 60 MILLION YRS. AGO
FIRST REDWOODS 130 MILLION YRS. AGO
FIRST MAMMALS 160 MILLION YRS. AGO
FIRST DINOSAURS 180 MILLION YRS. AGO
FIRST TREES 280 MILLION YRS. AGO
FIRST REPTILES 275 MILLION YRS. AGO
FIRST FISHES 400 MILLION YRS. AGO
GRAND CANYON 550 MILLION YRS. AGO
FIRST CORALS 575 MILLION YRS. AGO
FIRST SPONGES 650 MILLION YRS. AGO
BIRTH OF THE EARTH 4 BILLION YRS. AGO

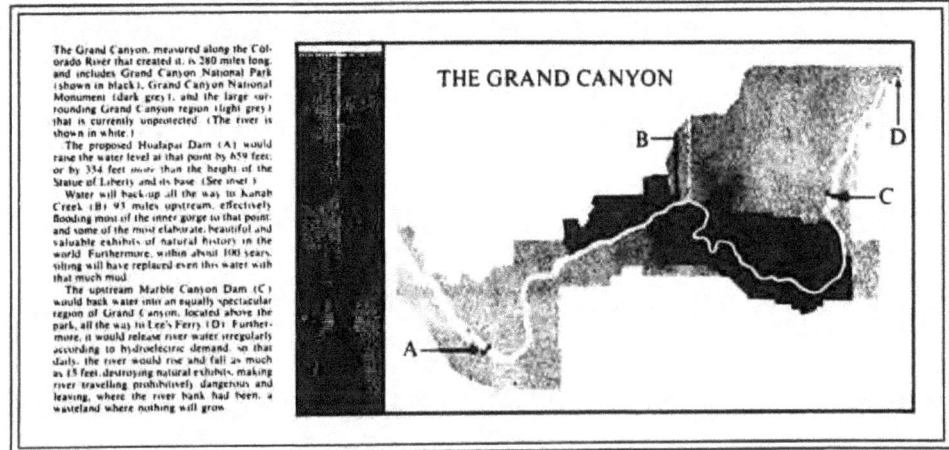

142

With the ads keeping the issue centre stage, the bill designed to OK the building of the dams never made it to the floor of the House or Representatives.

The campaign did much more than stop the damming of the Grand Canyon. Jerry Mander felt that the ads "put the environmental movement very much in play."

David Brower's son, Kenneth agreed: "The ads focused the campaign, they brought a lot of activist people in … This really was the first time that Americans confronted government in this way and I think the ads were crucial."

According to Jerry, the ads also transformed the Gossage agency. "We had gained public attention for having invented a new style of advocacy advertising … The ads had not only affected policy, they catalysed and organised the public, because they allowed a new level of involvement."

Jerry then applied this "new style of advocacy advertising" to a series of Sierra Club causes. And, in so doing, added further momentum to the Green Movement's development.

The President
The White House
Washington 25, D.C.

Mr. President: There is one great forest of redwoods left on earth; but the one you are trying to save isn't it.

...Meanwhile they are cutting down both of them.

The lumber industry has already cut nearly two million acres of redwoods down to two possible sites for our much-talked-of Redwood National Park.

One of them — Redwood Creek — is magnificent still. The other — Mill Creek? Well, it is less unacceptable to the lumber companies.

Soon Congress will decide which of these to save from the saws — which in the meantime buzz on, despite a so-called moratorium on cutting.

It's an old story, Mr. President. In the 1920's there were four great forests left: 1) that along the Eel River and on the Bull Creek and the Dyerville Flats, 2) along the Klamath River, 3) along Redwood Creek, and 4) on the Smith River at Mill Creek.

Considering these as possible sites for *that* year's Redwood National Park, Madison Grant, a founder of the Save-the-Redwoods League, said: *"Each has its peculiar beauty and it is difficult to choose among them."* And so they didn't.

The lumber companies did, however:

I have just seen the rip-rapped banks of the Eel, and its slash- and gravel-choked side streams. I saw the high, steep slopes pitifully scarred and eroded by logging. I drove through the great groves left along the Eel — on a high-speed freeway which has effectively and forever ruined the integrity and peaceful beauty of this place.

I walked in the Rockefeller Forest, among the sky-scraping giants, and then saw the glacier of gravel up Bull Creek — the product of catastrophic logging and floods — moving inexorably and lethally toward them.

There is no longer a chance for a great Redwood National Park on the Eel River.

I have just seen the final throes in the destruction of a superlative landscape on the Klamath.

The waters of this river — only a short time ago among the most gorgeous in the northwest — are muddy and roiled and swollen with silt. The high hillsides through which they travel, once clothed in dark, magnificent forests, are now shorn and scraped bare. They are shucking off huge fans of topsoil in a classical display of erosion.

Side streams, long beloved of fishermen, are now gutted and filled with slash — their bright fish gone.

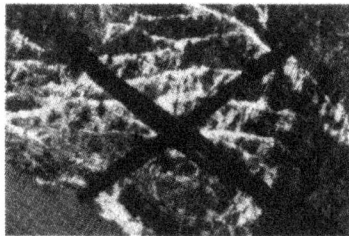

No one talks about a National Park on the Klamath any more.

A few exquisite fragments of the Smith River groves at Mill Creek still remain. They are already protected in California's Jedediah Smith and Del Norte Coast State Parks.

I walked through these in a few hours.

Outside these state parks less than 1,100 acres of superior old-growth redwoods remain in Mill Creek. More than half its forests have been logged.

The proposed park is girdled along the Smith River by summer homes, motels, gas stations and grocery stores. The heart of it has been completely cut out, and now boasts a splendid multi-million dollar industrial complex.

Hardly the stuff a great National Park is made of.

Yet Mill Creek would cost us an estimated 60 million dollars.

Much of that would go to buy developed private property. The rest would add only 7,500 acres of virgin redwoods to the existing state parks. (Consider Olympic National Park: nearly 900,000 acres. That, indeed, is preserving the marvelous Douglas Fir forests of Washington for the enjoyment of people for all time. Can we seriously be talking about adding *only 7,500 virgin acres* to our present state parks to preserve the incomparable redwoods? And this for $60,000,000?)

Yet this is the site that the Secretary of the Interior has espoused on behalf of the Administration, because he "wanted to pick a park, not a fight." Not a fight with the lumber industry, anyway.

One last chance remains: Redwood Creek.

In 1920 Madison Grant called it "peculiarly adapted for a national park." In 1964, after fifteen months of study, National Park Service planners called it the finest large block of redwoods left, in terms of park values.

This was confirmed, at one time or another, by conservation groups throughout America. And it was re-confirmed *this year* by the Hammon, Jensen and Wallen report to the Secretary of the Interior.

I was four days exploring Redwood Creek and its drainages this trip. Even then I saw only a fraction of the area I and other Sierra Club members have been looking into for four years. For there are great reaches of it not yet penetrated by logging roads — a unique circumstance in what is left of the redwood country.

The last long stretches of virgin acres in all the redwood region are at Redwood Creek: 20 miles and 34,000 acres of them. And there are more than 10,000 acres of superior old-growth stands. *Ten times what is left at Mill Creek.*

The last virgin forests on both sides of a river are at Redwood Creek: over four miles of them, including the magnificent Emerald Mile.

In short, the last chance to preserve the entire ecological variety of the redwood species — from the ocean shore at Gold Bluffs Beach through inland stands of near rain-forest luxuriance to 3,000 foot high mountain ridges, is at Redwood Creek.

And it is here that the National Geographic Society discovered the tallest tree on earth — and where the second, third, fourth, sixth, eighth, ninth, and tenth tallest trees were subsequently discovered.

Clearly then the $60,000,000 mentioned as the price of a park at Mill Creek would buy far more at Redwood Creek. If indeed $60,000,000 — the equivalent of but 2 days' work on federal highway construction projects — is all the money available.

$140,000,000 — *but 3 more days of highway building* — would give us the great national park we ought to have.

Meanwhile they are cutting it down. The area the National Park Service recommended for preservation *in 1964;* that named at Senate hearings as the best possible Redwood National Park by 94% of those who favor any park at all; the subject of Senate and House Redwood National Park bills sponsored by 17 Senators° (S. 514) and 41 Congressmen°° (H.R. 2849, for example) *is being cut down.*

Mr. President, the Sierra Club and most of its 53,000 members, the 58 Congressmen listed below — and we believe *all* conservationists, were some of them not afraid that lumber interests had ruled it out already — are convinced that Redwood Creek is the only national park this wealthiest nation in history can *afford* to establish.

Speaking for them, and for future generations with every interest in the creation of the park — but no voice in it — I urge you to reconsider the site of the Administration's proposed Redwood National Park, while there is still time.

Yours sincerely,
Edgar Wayburn, President
Sierra Club, Mills Tower, San Francisco

P.S. to other readers. *Your* letters, giving the President and the following Congressmen your opinion in the Redwood National Park crisis, could just do it.

Senator Henry M. Jackson, Chairman
Committee on Interior and Insular Affairs
Senate Office Building, Washington 25, D.C.

Members:
Clinton P. Anderson, New Mexico
Alan Bible, Nevada
Frank Church, Idaho
Ernest Gruening, Alaska
Frank E. Moss, Utah
Quentin N. Burdick, North Dakota
Carl Hayden, Arizona
George S. McGovern, South Dakota
Gaylord Nelson, Wisconsin
Lee Metcalf, Montana
Thomas H. Kuchel, California

Gordon Allott, Colorado
Len B. Jordan, Idaho
Paul J. Fannin, Arizona
Clifford P. Hansen, Wyoming
Mark O. Hatfield, Oregon

Representative Wayne Aspinall, Chairman
House Committee on Interior and Insular Affairs
House Office Building, Washington 25, D.C.

Members:
John P. Saylor, Pennsylvania
James A. Haley, Florida
Ed Edmondson, Oklahoma

Walter S. Baring, Nevada
Roy A. Taylor, North Carolina
Harold T. Johnson, California
Hugh L. Carey, New York
Morris K. Udall, Arizona
Phillip Burton, California
John V. Tunney, California
Thomas S. Foley, Washington
Richard C. White, Texas
Robert W. Kastenmeier, Wisconsin
James G. O'Hara, Michigan
William F. Ryan, New York
Patsy T. Mink, Hawaii
James Kee, West Virginia
Lloyd Meeds, Washington
Abraham Kazen, Texas

Santiago Polanco-Abreu, Puerto Rico
F. Y. Berry, South Dakota
Craig Hosmer, California
Joe Skubitz, Kansas
Laurence J. Burton, Utah
Rogers C. B. Morton, Maryland
Wendell Wyatt, Oregon
George V. Hansen, Idaho
Ed Reinecke, California
Theodore R. Kupferman, New York
John H. Kyl, Iowa
Sam Steiger, Arizona
Howard W. Pollock, Alaska
James A. McClure, Idaho

°Senators Lee Metcalf, Montana; Mike Mansfield, Montana; Quentin Burdick, North Dakota; Joseph S. Clark, Pennsylvania; Thomas J. Dodd, Connecticut; Ernest Gruening, Alaska; Daniel Inouye, Hawaii; Robert Kennedy, New York; Eugene McCarthy, Minnesota; Gale McGee, Wyoming; Walter Mondale, Minnesota; Gaylord Nelson, Wisconsin; Claiborne Pell, Rhode Island; Abraham Ribicoff, Connecticut; Joseph D. Tydings, Maryland; Ralph Yarborough, Texas; and Stephen Young, Ohio.

°°Messrs. Jeffrey Cohelan, California; John P. Saylor, Pennsylvania; William R. Anderson, Tennessee; Jonathan B. Bingham, New York; George E. Brown, Jr., California; John Conyers, Jr., Michigan; John G. Dow, New York; Don Edwards, California; Donald M. Fraser, Minnesota; Richard Fulton, Tennessee; Cornelius E. Gallagher, New Jersey; Henry Helstoski, New Jersey; Chet Holifield, California; Joseph E. Karth, Minnesota; Richard D. McCarthy, New York; Joseph G. Minish, New Jersey; William S. Moorhead, Pennsylvania; John E. Moss, California; Lucien N. Nedzi, Michigan; Barratt O'Hara, Illinois; James G. O'Hara, Michigan; Arnold Olsen, Montana; Richard L. Ottinger, New York; Claude Pepper, Florida; Joseph Y. Resnick, New York; Henry S. Ruess, Wisconsin; Peter W. Rodino, Jr., New Jersey; James H. Scheuer, New York; Frank Thompson, Jr., New Jersey; John V. Tunney, California; Lionel Van Deerlin, California; Jerome R. Waldie, California; Charles H. Wilson, California; Phillip Burton, California; Ogden Reid, New York; Thomas P. O'Neill, Jr., Massachusetts; Edward Boland, Massachusetts; Philip Philbin, Massachusetts; William D. Ford, Michigan; Dominick V. Daniels, New Jersey; and John D. Dingell, Michigan.

The Sierra Club, founded in 1892 by John Muir, is nonprofit, supported by people who, like Thoreau, believe "In wildness is the preservation of the world." The club's program is nationwide, includes wilderness trips, books and films — as well as such efforts as this to protect the remnant of wilderness of the Americas. There are now twenty chapters, branch offices in New York (Biltmore Hotel), Washington (Dupont Circle Building), Los Angeles (Auditorium Building), Albuquerque, Seattle, and main office in San Francisco.

Edgar Wayburn, President
Sierra Club, Mills Tower, San Francisco

☐ I have sent the letters.

☐ Please tell me what else I can do.

☐ Here is a donation of $_____ to continue your effort to keep the public informed. (I understand that you can't promise this will be tax-deductible.)

☐ Send me "The Last Redwoods," which tells the complete story of the opportunity as well as the destruction in the Redwoods. ($17.50)

☐ I would like to be a member of the Sierra Club. Enclosed is $14.00 for entrance and first year's dues.

Name_____

Address_____

City_____ State_____ Zip_____

144

This ad railed against everything from deforestation and pesticides to building dams in Egypt, Alaska and Laos.

The members of the Sierra Club Board felt that David Brower had gone way beyond his remit. His days at the Sierra Club were numbered.

When, in May 1969, he was ousted, he set up his own activist organisation which, according to Sally Gossage, her husband named "Friends of the Earth."

Gossage immediately gave Brower office space and offered to do his ads. The responsibility for which fell to Jerry who increasingly shifted the agency's output towards these and other political and cause-related issues.

145

"….The need is not really for more brains, the need is now for

A GENTLER, A MORE TOLERANT PEOPLE THAN THOSE WHO WON FOR US AGAINST THE ICE, THE TIGER AND THE BEAR.

The hand that hefted the ax, out of some old blind allegiance to the past, fondles the machine gun as lovingly. It is a habit man will have to break to survive, but the roots go very deep." *(Loren Eiseley)*

Please write your congressmen and senators. In particular, write letters, or postcards or send wires to the list of senators who, at this time, have not gotten off the fence on this issue. [See coupon below for their names.] It is as significant an ecological act as blocking the SST, or turning in a car, or *not* buying a fur-coat, or getting the lead out of gas. It is an act in favor of life.

Thank you.

FRIENDS OF THE EARTH
30 E. 42nd St., N.Y.C.—451 Pacific Ave., San Francisco
David Brower, President; Gary Soucie, Executive Director

THIS ADVERTISEMENT is being placed by FRIENDS OF THE EARTH, a conservation group, but it concerns the war in Southeast Asia, and also wars in general.

Until recently conservationists have been thought of as content to fight the tragedy of a dam, the outrage of pollution, the spread of ugliness and environmental degradation, and also the economic and political solutions to that sort of mindless destruction.

Wars have been someone else's problem.

It has been as though war is not as destructive as dams. Or that an air pollution hazard in Los Angeles is a more significant danger to life than bombs landing upon non-combatants in a war, or the laterizing (turning to rock) of thousands of square miles of formerly living soil by widespread use of napalm. It is as though DDT in *our* vital tissues is worse than wartime chemical defoliants in the tissues of pregnant women.

It is not true. They are all of equal order, deriving as they do from a mentality which places all life and its vital sources in a position secondary to politics or power or profit.

Ecology teaches us that everything, *everything* is irrevocably connected. Whatever affects life in one place—*any* form of life, including people—affects other life elsewhere.

DDT on American farms, finds its way to Antarctic penguins.

Pollution in a trout stream eventually pollutes the ocean.

Smog over London blows over to Sweden.

An A-bomb explosion spreads radiation everywhere.

The movement of a dislodged, hungry, war torn population affects conditions and life wherever they go.

It is all connected. The doing of an act against life in one place is the doing of it everywhere. Thinking of things in any other way is like assuming it is possible to tear one stitch in a blanket without unravelling the blanket.

Friends of the Earth, therefore, its Board of Directors and staff, wishes to go on record in unanimous support of the recent telegram to Mr. Nixon, signed by the leaders of the nation's conservation organizations, reproduced below.

We would further like to urge readers of this ad to become involved in supporting the several resolutions now in the Congress which will hasten our withdrawal from Southeast Asia, as follows:

1) The Cooper-Church amendment which requires the withdrawal of all American military from Cambodia by June 30;

2) The Repeal of the Gulf of Tonkin resolution, used as the "legal" basis of the Vietnam involvement;

3) The McGovern-Hatfield Resolution, which requires total American disengagement by 1971.

147

(SST: "Airplane of Tomorrow")

BREAKS WINDOWS, CRACKS WALLS, STAMPEDES CATTLE, AND WILL HASTEN THE END OF THE AMERICAN WILDERNESS

FRIENDS OF THE EARTH is a conservation organization and we have been reading, with mixed feelings, all the recent reports about threats to our environment and the "massive efforts to win the War on Pollution."

It's a good thing, clearly, to recognize that we've only a few years to meet such problems. However we have the sinking feeling that what we've witnessed so far is only *apparent* activity; *cosmetic* solutions which are creating an impression in the public mind that things are somehow being taken care of.

But things are *not* being taken care of.

For example, this:

1) In the same message that he spoke so eloquently about environmental pollution, President Nixon announced that he was budgeting $275 million for this year's work toward a commercial supersonic transport (SST).

2) Mr. Nixon said that he made that decision in order to (a) create jobs, (b) help the balance of payments, and (c) add to our national prestige. He did not say anything about the virtues of the plane itself. It is easy to understand why.

3) The SST has been a subject of controversy mainly because it produces a "sonic boom." If you've ever heard one (from the much quieter military supersonic fighters that occasionally fly by) you'll remember it as a shattering experience. Something in the magnitude of a factory explosion down the block. It is that sudden and scary.

4) Sleeping through a sonic boom is out of the

RELATIVE NOISE LEVELS

	Perceived decibel level
Room in a quiet city dwelling at midnight	32
Average city residence	40
Small 2-engine private plane (sideline noise @ 1,500 feet)	80-85
Heavy truck, 25 ft. away	90
Train whistle, 500 feet away	90
Subway train, 20 feet away	95
DC-3 (sideline noise @ 1,500 feet)	95-100
Loud outboard motor	102
Loud motorcycle	110
Boeing 707, DC-8 (sideline noise @ 1,500 feet)	110-115
Rock 'n' Roll band playing at loudest moments	120
Large pneumatic 3" riveter	125
SST (sideline noise @ 1,500 feet)	122-129

Increases in decibels, by the way, are not arithmetic, they are logarithmic. Therefore every increase of ten decibels is a ten-time increase in noise!

According to the FAA, 100 decibels is a level that a high percentage of the population will find intolerable, and so which they'll react strongly. Yet the FAA's new noise standards permit 108 ! The first question, then, is why they are permitting noise standards above what the population will find tolerable ! And secondly why are they supporting the SST which will be many times worse than is now permissible ! If the argument is that most of this urban noise — during take-off and landing — will be right around the airport we should point out that the SST's take-off noise won't be confined to the airport vicinity. It will produce over 100 decibels for 13 miles in either direction from its flight path.

question. Booms can break windows, crack walls, and stampede cattle and have done so throughout the country. If they're used for everyday commercial travel, stay off of operating tables at boom-time.

5) The boom affects an area 50 miles wide for the entire length of a flight. If the SST flew the usual air routes in this country, the boom zones would cover practically everything. (See map.) In some places — Cape Cod for example — the

average day might be punctuated by twenty bangs loud enough to make you duck for cover. Even wilderness areas — the one place where man's technological feats give way to nature's quiet — will offer no escape.

6) Boeing Aircraft — which is receiving a 90% subsidy to build the thing — likes to call it the "airplane of tomorrow." As for the boom, they call that "a 20th Century sound."

People in Oklahoma City, however, don't call it that. In 1964 they put up with five months of military supersonic testing and reacted this way: 15,000 complaints to authorities, 4,000 damage suits and the declaration by a quarter of the population that they could never live with it.

7) Mr. Nixon, apparently sensitive to this point, said we shouldn't worry, that the SST would fly at boom speeds only over the oceans, or other sparsely populated areas.

But the FAA has *not* said that, though if it did, it wouldn't mean much. Its membership changes, remember, and so by the way does the President. Ten years hence, if SSTs prove unprofitable without high speed land routes which do you think the airlines will do: scrap them? Or lobby to change the ruling? You know the answer.

8) But *what about* the oceans?

No one knows the effect of sonic booms upon sea life. If the enormous vibrations should disperse the fish concentrations off Newfoundland (over which most trans-Atlantic SSTs would fly), it could disturb the fish industries there. That's 40% of the U.S. fish catch and 12% of the world's.

We *do* know what happens to animals living under the boom. They panic. A boom killed 2,000 mink in Minnesota during 1966; a boom drove a herd of cattle off a cliff in Switzerland in 1968; and simulated booms have significantly changed the birth patterns of test rats at the University of Oklahoma.

9) As for the sparsely populated areas, *those* are what we now call wilderness; places still free of the crunch of technology.

Or they're farmlands, or reservations, or else national park lands where a visit would no longer be the same. Not with a boom every little while, and the trees rattling, and animals going crazy from the shock.

So much for sonic booms. They are a terrible prospect, but they're only part of the story.

10) Before making his decision, Mr. Nixon established a committee of many of the top figures in his own administration to advise him concerning whether he should cancel the whole SST project.

They said yes, he should.

The feeling of their report is typified by the remark of Mr. Hendrik S. Houthakker of the President's Council of Economic Advisors who, on the question of prestige, put it this way: "...we do not believe that our prestige abroad will be enhanced by a concentration on white elephants." (See also Footnote.)

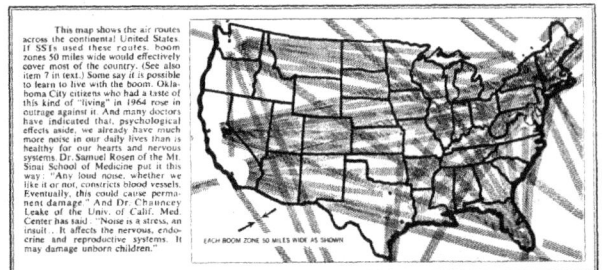

This map shows the air routes across the continental United States. If SSTs used these routes, boom zones 50 miles wide would effectively cover most of the country. (See also item 7 in text.) Some say if it is possible to learn to live with the boom. Oklahoma City citizens who had a taste of this kind of "living" in 1964 rose in outrage against it. And many doctors have indicated that, psychological effects aside, we already have much more noise in our daily lives than is healthy for our hearts and nervous systems. Dr. Samuel Rosen of the Mt. Sinai School of Medicine put it this way: "Any loud noise, whether we like it or not, constricts blood vessels. Eventually, this could cause permanent damage." And Dr. Chauncey Leake of the Univ. of Calif. Med. Center has said: "Noise is a stress, an insult. It affects the nervous, endocrine and reproductive systems. It may damage unborn children."

EACH BOOM ZONE 50 MILES WIDE AS SHOWN

11) There is evidence that the SST will pollute the upper atmosphere in such a way as may result in terrible alterations of global weather.

12) It will be far more dangerous than present aircraft because of severe problems of metal fatigue, landing speed, visibility and maneuverability.

13) It will have a relatively short range (4,000 miles). And despite the fact that it will be smaller than the 747, it will be *more* expensive to build. and will use *three times* the fuel.

As a result, it will be much more expensive to fly in. It will be an elitist's flight.

That's your "airplane of tomorrow!"

Notwithstanding all the talk, it appears that *basic* attitudes remain unaltered.

The SST is being built because people continue to believe that there's an advantage to being able to get from N.Y. to Paris two hours sooner than at present; that if technology can do a thing, then it ought to be done.

But this attitude — the tendency to place technology ahead of considerations of our living environment — has gotten us into this mess. More luxury technology may have seemed a good idea at one time in history, when we were an underdeveloped country. But now we are an overdeveloped country.

The little bits of wilderness that still exist are being threatened daily by our *more, faster, bigger* attitudes. Industry needing more space, or trees, or ore; ever more people buying more of what industry makes and then seeking a place to escape from it.

Talking about "pollution" is not sufficient. If industry, "newly awake to its responsibilities," as the media like to say, *does* come up with a non-polluting auto engine, will it then be okay to cover-up the rest of America with highways and cars? (Mr. Nixon's budget also contains $5½ billion for highway construction. The result will be more damage than all of his anti-pollution programs could possibly correct.)

And even if there were no boom, the more noise we have in cities and over America's parkland, the more it will confirm the nightmarish

feeling: *We are locked in a small room, and the walls and ceiling are closing in on us*

Friends of the Earth is interested in promoting the proposition that we had better come up with alternatives to endless technological expansion, considering that we live on a planet of fixed size.

We have established a number of task forces to investigate the implications of an economy in which growth of exploitive industries is curtailed; a society which doesn't measure "progress" as an outgrowth of GNP. We wish to build for a system which you might call microdynamic, while macrostatic.

Meanwhile, we are also opposing specific government and industry projects that seem to us to typify the sort of thinking that will lead our species into an unnecessarily short and miserable life. The SST is one. New highway construction is another. Nuclear power. Water diversion. The Alaska Pipeline. Pesticides. Airport expansions. The killing of wildlife for furs. Etc., Etc.

Coupon #6 above will permit you to learn more about what we are up to. The others contain messages to specific individuals who can be effective in stopping the SST. But please do not stop there. The congressional vote on the SST will be coming up *within the next few weeks.* Write, telephone and wire your own congressman, the Department of the Interior, the Department of Transportation, the FAA, and urge others to do likewise.

Thank you.

David Brower, *President*
Gary Soucie, *Executive Director*
Friends of the Earth
451 Pacific Ave., San Francisco, CA 94133, or
30 East 42nd St., New York, NY 10017

FOOTNOTE

On the other two issues Mr. Nixon felt were paramount in his decision in favor of the SST, his advisory committee felt as follows:

JOBS: "The net employment increase from SST production would likely be negligible and would occur in the professional and technical categories where shortages already exist. The project would have practically no employment benefits for the disadvantaged hardcore unemployed." BALANCE OF PAYMENTS: "If the U.S. overall balance of payments is considered, there is substantial reason for delay in proceeding to the next stage of the SST project." The reasoning went this way: Mostly Americans, and mainly rich ones, would fly on SSTs. They would spend large sums abroad, thereby worsening the balance of payments.) FOR A COMPLETE COPY OF THE PRESIDENT'S ADVISORY COMMITTEE REPORT ON THE SST, SEE COUPON #6.

(NEXT: INITIATIVE TO OUTLAW PRIVATE CAMPAIGN DONATIONS)

HOLD THE CONFETTI EVEN IF "T" WINS—THE BUILDERS STILL RUN THIS CITY

The reason we have tall buildings in San Francisco—where they make no sense at all—is simply this:

The people who build the buildings are the campaign backers of the officials who let them get built.

Voting Yes on Proposition T will slow the Manhattanization of this city, but a still more basic issue remains: Breaking the power of the very rich private donor—private investor, really—and the favors (high-rise is just one example) that always result.

We cannot call this a democracy while only the rich and the darlings of the rich get elected and then run things from their point of view.

Here is how it works and a plan for what we can do:

I. IF THE VERY RICH WERE LIKE EVERYONE ELSE

There are *three* weeks before the voting but you can already tell the really serious candidates from the rest. The ones with money are the serious candidates. The others are not.

This arrangement is not unusual. Box A shows you how the last campaigns worked out—the people with wealth or backing got elected—and it's an accepted political homily that this will always be the case.

So in this year's Mayor's race, for example, we have Alioto, Dobbs, Feinstein, maybe Newhall as the "serious" candidates. Tony Serra, Fred Selinger, Nate Weinstein, John Brent et al are *not* considered serious, but it has nothing to do with their opinions. No one hears their opinions because a) they have very little money to advertise, and b) the working press—knowing the *real* rules of the game—does not take them seriously either. There *are* some reports

BOX A. **YOU GOT THE MONEY, YOU GET THE VOTES**

	Votes	Total Campaign Expenditures
1967 Mayoralty Campaign		
ALIOTO	110,405	$395,975
DOBBS	94,504	289,742
MORRISON	40,436	45,293
1969 Supervisor Campaign		
FEINSTEIN	93,519	81,368
TAMARAS	92,251	74,142
BOAS	91,135	85,277
BARBAGELATA	82,331	33,329
VON BEROLDINGEN	80,996	59,320
BLAKE	80,566	54,629
MORRISON	73,094	65,926
CHINN	70,513	36,256
LAU	55,927	14,000
ROURKE	41,872	12,170

Source: San Francisco Registrar of Voters

These charts show the campaign spending for all of the leading candidates in the most recent mayoralty and supervisor races.

In almost every instance, there was a direct proportion between how much a candidate spent and how many votes he (or she) received.

If Dobbs had spent more money he would be mayor now. Alioto "charisma" translated apparently just means dollars.

On the supervisor side, Blake didn't quite make it. He spent the sixth amount of money and alas, he came in sixth. He was beaten by Von Beroldingen who spent the fifth amount of money and, surprise, she came in fifth!!

As for Dianne Feinstein's "miracle" victory, it wasn't so much a miracle as it was proof of the way the system works. She raised the second most money and came in first. Not a very big miracle.

The only *real* exceptions to the rule in both of the races were Barbagelata, who spent disproportionately little, and Morrison, who ran behind his spending for supervisor. Possible explanations: Morrison, a long-time well known liberal, had consistently voted his conscience and was on the losing end of many 10 to 1 votes. (He was the only vote against Transamerica.) This produced an active, hostile, downtown opposition. Barbagelata, on the other hand, enjoyed a large "bullet vote," a technique to protest against and vote out incumbents, i.e., his supporters voted *only* for him, giving him the advantage he needed.

But the rule of thumb is clear. If you want public office, cuddle up to big money. Nine times in ten you'll make it and you'll have a lot of new rich friends inviting you out to lunch. There's your democratic election.

on them but more for what newsmen call "color"—they are curiosities, really—rather than people trying for office. Yet several of these non-serious candidates *might* make better public officials than the people we're likely to get—most of whose idea of representative government is that big business is represented and the rest of the people are not.

It always works out this way because campaigns are financed by *private contribution*, a notion which sounds all democratic and free and American but in practice is the opposite. Only the very rich can afford to contribute and enjoy the resulting privileges. (Could *you* get to see the Mayor? Donate Two Grand and see what happens. Same for any other office.)

Private financing would be democratic only if the very rich were typical of everyone; if there were an equal number of very rich orientals, very rich blacks, very rich Taraval residents, very rich small businessmen, very rich young people and old people, very rich artists, and oh yes, very rich poor people. This is not the case.

According to data from the Registrar of Voters' records, *all* of the campaign contributions in the last two elections here came from *one-third of one per cent* of the people. And, of course, almost all of the *large* donations came from a handful of the *very* rich people who are hardly typical of everyone.

The very rich in San Francisco are (1) real estate interests (that's where high-rise comes from), (2) big merchants, (3) corporate lawyers and bankers and (4) assorted members of the Chamber, the Pacific Union and the Concordia Club (the same people, incidentally, who have put up nearly a half million to defeat Proposition T).

They are almost all white. They almost all work downtown. They almost all know each other. And they almost all devote themselves exclusively to making more money than they presently have. *And*, God save us, to politics.

II. KNOWING FIVE SUPERVISORS PERSONALLY—FAR BETTER THAN KNOWING NONE

In case you retain the belief that these few very big donors are doing it just to keep the democratic process flowing, or because of the moral questions involved, consider this:

A very common practice in this crowd is to give donations to people *running against each other* for a specific public office. Hedging their bets, so to speak.

And forty-five very large donors—more than half of them real estate bigwigs—backed *five* of the *winning* supervisors.

Now why do you think they do this?

It's *access*; five supervisors will make time to see them. How many can *you* drop in on?

Money donated in the way they do it downtown, you see, is not so much donated as it is invested. An officeholder is inclined to be friendly to a big donor and he always knows him personally. So when a Supervisor, say, feels he could vote either way on some issue—high-rise zoning, for example—well, he might as well favor his "friend" as that anonymous mass out there.

What we get because of this system is that representative government breaks down—some people get represented more than others do; we get government by business pressure. Here are a few examples:

1) Yerba Buena Center, a construction bonanza which costs the city $50,000,000, is enthusiastically okayed. But a *special* election on high-rise is too expensive at 1/200th of the cost.

2) Streets are closed for new buildings—the vote is always unanimous—but a street fair on Grant is refused. ("Dangerous to close the street.")

3) A $600,000 bridge across Kearny is approved, though it ruins a Chinatown playground. But four

BOX B. **THE "RATIONAL" URBAN DESIGN PLAN**

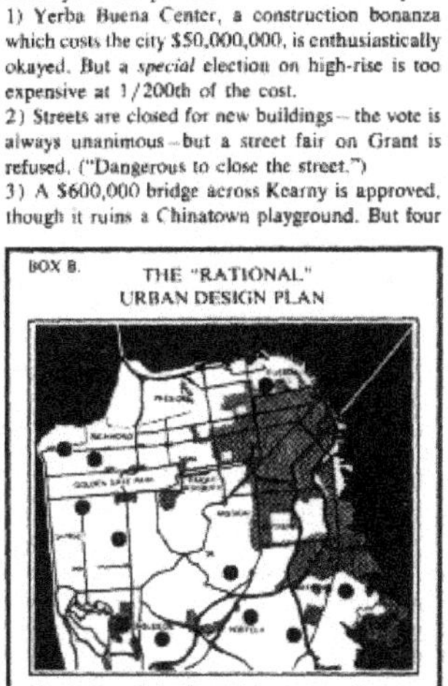

The new Urban Design Plan, hailed as a "rational" solution to San Francisco's high-rise problem, is shown, in part, above. All of the areas in gray would allow buildings taller than what Proposition T, if passed, would allow, unless the people vote. Notice that it introduces high-rise into areas which have thus far been spared—the Sunset, Ingleside, Richmond, along Golden Gate Park and so on. The round black circles, furthermore, are what the planners call "point towers." This means that very tall buildings would be okay in spot locations, even where the 40 foot limit exists.

But there's an important added thing to say. The Plan is only a Plan. If it ever gets voted in—which is highly doubtful—the version that passes will be far worse than this already bad one! And even then, there are variances and exceptions and thinking of the "developer's investment," as they did on the new Holiday Inn. (Box C.) The only real solution is to outlaw *all* tall buildings until some plan without loopholes exists, and is voted on by *all* the people. First step then is Vote Yes on Proposition T. Second step: Remove the power of the rich to control how public agencies vote.

day-care centers—which would free working mothers—are ignored. "Too expensive," at twenty thousand.

4) Candlestick Park is "remodeled" 11 million! Non-polluting buses? Too costly. As usual.

These procedures go on down at City Hall every day. The list of examples is endless. But there *are* two *amazing* new items—

5) About three weeks ago, the City Planning Commission issued this dictum—a public vote on high-rise was "too extreme." The Urban Design Plan is better, they said. It is a "rational solution." The Chamber of Commerce agreed, as everyone knew it would. (The Plan allows high-rises just everywhere a builder would dream of—in the Sunset, the Richmond, Portola, wherever you happen to live. See Box B.) But going on with this "rational" plan.

A few days after the cheering—the *first* time the plan was tested—the Planning Commission caved

BOX C. **PRESENTING: THE NEW HOLIDAY INN**

At the left we had intended a photograph of the new Holiday Inn, 25 stories, on Van Ness Avenue. This does not fit the "rational" Urban Design Plan, but the Planning Commission voted it in anyway, giving us all some idea of what will happen even if the plan is adopted. The Commission—which refused to provide us a picture of the building—voted for it because "the developer had so much money invested ... it would have been unfair to him otherwise." Never mind if it's unfair to you and me and our children over the next 100 years.

The rulings always go that way. Protect the developers; forget the rest of the city.

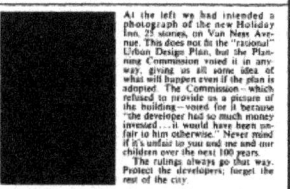

in to commercial pressures and overruled its own plan itself. A portent of things to come.

They didn't approve just anything, of course, but the largest Holiday Inn in the world. We asked for a picture of the thing—it *is* a public agency—but were told we could not have one. (See Box C.)

So much for "rational solutions."

But the worst is yet to come.

6) Be sure to look at Box E. It will give you details on what the Supervisors have been up to lately. Just this: Quietly, without any public notice, they have placed two *new* items on the ballot. A propo-

BOX D. **A LITTLE OF KANSAS CITY PLANNED FOR RUSSIAN HILL.**

Elsewhere in this ad we talk of public agencies representing the people—some people just a little bit more than others. Now to the Board of Permit Appeals.

Some developers from Kansas City dreamed-up a thing for Russian Hill. (For some idea of how it would look in context, see above at left.) The builders said, "Russian Hill is destined for high-rise ... no more backyard gardens." The permit board, surprisingly, said "no." Doesn't fit the Urban Design. But just a moment. Not to discourage the builders, the Board suggested they make a few changes; make it fit the Urban Design, which they obligingly did. (At right.) So having beaten one great horrible slab, we get two great horrible slabs instead, with a little alley between them. They call that alley a "view corridor" down at City Hall. Although this new "improved" design is actually *wider* than the first, yes, it fits the Urban Design.

sition which could mitigate "T" however the vote should go, and another one which *doubles* the signatures you and I will need to get anything onto the ballot.

The point is painfully clear: If a thing benefits poor people, old people, "underground" people, homeowners, working mothers—people who don't put money on candidates—it's too expensive.

If it benefits downtown commercial interests, it's "good business," important to San Francisco.

This is not going to change as long as the Board represents only big business, and as long as big business controls the Board. So here is what I am planning, hopefully with your support.

III. THREE PART PLAN

1) I am running for Supervisor and my name is on the ballot. I want to present an alternate to the prevailing corporate view that we have to give up clean air and clear water, a city to walk in and raise our children, a city with a special diversity and pace of

BOX E. **REPRESENTATIVE DEMOCRACY IN ACTION, DOWN AT YOUR BOARD OF SUPERVISORS**

The Board is the official legislative body of San Francisco, charged with representing the people equally.

In practice, some people are represented more equally than others, and if the rest of this ad hasn't convinced you of that, here are two brand new delightful tidbits that I'm sure you never heard about:

1) When it was clear that the Board would not control high-rise, we went out into the streets, collected 45,000 signatures, and expected a special election in June, which is what the law required. The Board said we couldn't have it—too expensive. Okay, lawyers cost a lot, so we went for November. But the Board had learned a lesson. The people who live here can enact laws *directly* when the Board refuses to act; the initiative process. So, to correct this disturbing loophole, the Board did this: Proposition K. It *doubles* the number of signatures needed to qualify for a general election, and it gives the Board a virtual veto over future special elections. This subversion of the initiative process was introduced by Ron Pelosi and it passed 11 to 0. And that's one of the reasons why I am personally not voting for any incumbents.

2) So now that future initiatives may be stopped, what could they do about Proposition T, the high-rise vote? What if it wins? Could they let that sort of thing stand? Pelosi to the rescue again. Unanimous again. This time it's *for* Proposition M, which could give the Board or the Planning Commission permission to override the 72-ft. height limit *if* it is passed. Or to make exceptions and variations in the Urban Design Plan, which has too many variances as it is.

If you ask down at City Hall, they'll tell you that Proposition M won't negate the Vote-on-High-Rise Initiative. It's supposed to be just a minor touch-up of the City Charter. Like the Holiday Inn on Kearny Street was to be the Chinese Cultural Center. *Now* we know it's a Holiday Inn.

So. Vote Yes on T. Vote No on K and M. Pass it on.

life—all so that business and industry can push their growth curves onwards and upwards.

2) We are working to get as many votes for Yes on Proposition T as possible. The Chamber is spending $400,000 to tell you T will be too expensive—like day care, clean buses, and street fairs.

3) We are beginning an initiative to outlaw the private financing of campaigns and substitute something like one of the public financing systems that have already been introduced in Congress for national elections. The process has begun: On October 5th, we placed this legal notice in the San Francisco Recorder.

Notice of Intention to Circulate a Petition (Section .4002, General Elections Code).

DECLARATION OF POLICY ON CAMPAIGN Financing to be submitted directly to the voters.

.... Because financing political campaigns by the use and/or solicitation of private funds denies many qualified people of the opportunity to win election to public office and thereby converts public service into a matter of privilege and because the need for campaign contributions makes public officials particularly obliging to special interests that finance their campaigns, it is declared by the people of San Francisco to be their policy that no private funds shall be used in a campaign for public office. All private campaign contributions in the form of funds, goods and services—with the exception of voluntary personal services—shall be henceforth prohibited. Instead a new system of public financing of campaigns shall be instituted by which all candidates for public office shall be entitled to campaign financing out of public funds.

A fund to finance campaigns shall be established and the income into that fund shall approximate 1/20 of 1% and shall not exceed 1/10 of 1% of the annual city budget. ....

We do not specify which system of public financing to use, but the one I like is the "voucher system." This gives every voter a one-dollar voucher which he could donate to any candidate. That is *all* he could give the candidate. And money collected that way is all the candidate spends. (If he's personally rich, he's no better off.)

The result would be that money-raising would be strictly a grass-roots effort. A hotel man gives a dollar; a developer gives a dollar. So do you and I. No more Nob Hill Cabinets. The cost is 1/20th of one percent of the total city budget and yet it will break the power of the richest men in this town. Everyone will have the same influence. The *people* will have the power.

We will begin collecting signatures on October 30. That will be an apt day because about then you'll be getting the brunt of the Chamber spending *against* Proposition T. (They will tell you, as usual, with radio and tv and computer letters that small buildings will cost you money and lose you your job—the usual stuff; just the Chamber watching out for your interests. If you want *our* study, showing how high-rises raise your taxes or rent and drive people out of the city, check the coupon.)

Our own campaign to drive the Chamber out of City Hall will begin with a mass meeting at 10 a.m., the 30th, 510 Third Street.

Thank you, Alvin Duskin.

To: Alvin Duskin, 510 Third St., San Francisco 94107

Dear Alvin,

Good idea. I'll be at the meeting on the 30th ☐

Please send me a copy of the just-published report, "The Ultimate High-rise" on the economics of high-rise buildings, and how they raise my taxes ☐. (Enclose $2.00 for this, please.)

Here is my donation of $________ to help pay for this ad and subsequent efforts. (Checks to: Committee for a Vote on High-Rise.)

Name ________ Phone ________

Address ________

City ________ State ________ Zip ________

(The California Water Project is illegal. Nobody told the voters that.)

Suing California

WHEN *Californians voted on Proposition 7 the other day, most were not aware that they were actually voting on the California Water Project. There was no way of knowing this from the way the thing was worded—a Yes vote just seemed like a harmless bit of legalese. But in fact we voted to support, through a bond issue, a project which is costing a minimum of $4½ billion; is benefiting no one save 50 or 100 of Southern California's largest real estate operators; would dam the last of our wild rivers; and, according to a recent Federal report, would destroy life in San Francisco Bay as surely as paving it over with asphalt.*

On top of all that, it is illegal. A lawsuit was filed yesterday. More suits will follow shortly, as more money is raised. You are invited to help.

Here are the details:

1) A few months ago I placed an advertisement pointing out that, in the judgment of every leading conservation group in the state, the California Water Plan is potentially the most destructive single project in our history.

2) The plan includes damming our last free-flowing rivers, and diverting water from them and from the Sacramento River southward to Los Angeles. Just incidentally, it would flood lands of the Round Valley and the Wintu Indians in the Dos Rios area. It would deprive fishermen, other sportsmen, and people who just like to look, of some of the most scenic country we still have left. And it would reduce the natural "flushing action" of fresh water through San Francisco Bay, killing the birds and fish as effectively as shooting each one with a gun. (See Fig. A.)

3) Once it arrives down south, at a cost of some $4½ billion, the water will not be used for drinking. It will be used to benefit private real estate operators needing greater water flows to turn what is now open space into more of Los Angeles. The effect will be to increase crowding, smog, water pollution and the sort of creeping, random ugliness that have made California not nearly as marvelous or as healthy a place to live as it used to be.

4) Thirty-six thousand people responded to the earlier anti-Water Plan advertisement, sending opinion coupons to Mr. Unruh, Mr. Reagan, and others.

Mr. Unruh took the occasion to denounce the plan on its merits. But when a reporter asked Mr. Reagan's press secretary what the Governor thought of this outpouring of feeling about the California environment, all he could manage was this already famous remark : "We have better things to do than count silly coupons."

While perhaps not on a par with the Governor's classic "bloodbath" remark, the "silly coupon" comment has its own special place in the Hall of Fame of anti-democratic remarks.

5) One of the "better things" they had to do in Sacramento was to prepare ballot Proposition 7, which, without ever mentioning the Water Project, would allow the state to finance it with high-interest bonds. Californians, unaware that the entire project was being conducted in an illegal manner, making the bond issue a dubious one at best, voted Yes. But that's not the end of the story.

6) About the time of the voting, the United States Geological Survey submitted a report to Secretary of the Interior Walter Hickel on environmental effects of California's water diversion plan. The report reads like an autopsy after the death of our state. The U.S.G.S. said that if things went as planned, the bay would "turn into another Lake Erie...a dead sea." It said that because of the lower rate of fresh water flow into the bay, chemicals would collect in the south bay and elsewhere, causing algae blooms which would suffocate all aquatic life.

7) If that isn't sufficient reason to stop the project, then there is also the recent independent report by the Rand Corporation, the famous Santa Monica "think tank." It reported, amazingly, that in fact there is *no* shortage of water in southern California, nor will there be in the foreseeable future. "A political water coalition," said the report, "has created what appears to be an already excessive and costly supply; the coalition continues to seek out vast new increments [the California Water Plan] although supplies now arranged for cover gross needs for 30 to 50 years."

And after that time, as everyone must surely realize by now, California will be so jammed with people and tract houses that accommodating any further growth, with its companion crowding and crime, would be nothing short of suicide.

8) So, misleading ballot measures notwithstanding, I have formed a non-profit committee which is currently planning a number of lawsuits against the state, intending to point out the variety of illegalities in the project, and stop it once and for all. We have been raising money for this purpose, and to date have raised $18,000. We will need, in all, some $50,000 for these suits, and we ask that you use the coupon below to help us if you agree with the cause. The money will be used for the legal struggle, ads to finance litigation, and for no other purpose.

The first suit was filed in Federal District Court in San Francisco yesterday.

9) This particular suit is based upon Federal reclamation law which states that, when Federal funds are used for water projects—as some are in this project—no individual beneficiary may achieve a financial gain upon more than 160 acres of land. The law was intended to support small landowners, you see. Yet the accompanying Fig. B will show you how the *big* promoters are doing, in what appears to our attorneys to be an obvious violation of the law.

Fig. B

THE REAL REASON FOR THE CALIFORNIA WATER PROJECT

Because the California Water Project would provide sufficient water to make it profitable for big developers to turn farm land and other open space into subdivisions and industrial developments, huge corporations have been busily buying up California land and waiting for Mr. Reagan to bring home the bacon. Already, simply because of the prospect of the project's being completed, land values have made spectacular increases. This chart indicates how a few companies have already made out:

Land Owner	Amount of Land	Approximate Economic Gain Thus Far
Tenneco	162,560 acres	$93,797,120
Standard Oil	101,120 acres	58,346,240
Tejon Ranch	54,400 acres	31,388,800
Southern Pacific	37,120 acres	21,033,240
Miller & Lux	25,000 acres	14,405,000

All this despite the fact that Federal reclamation laws prohibit the use of such water to achieve profits upon more than 160 acres. The purpose of the law is to disallow just the sort of rampant big company speculation that is going on here and now.

Furthermore, to the extent that large corporations have bought up the land, and the land is substantially appreciated in value, it is unavailable for purchase by family farmers at reasonable prices. This is also contrary to the intent of the reclamation laws.

And, while they wait for the opportune time to subdivide, the big landowners compete unfairly with small raisin and almond growers, glutting their markets. Or they raise un-needed crops, such as cotton, which are subsidized still further by us taxpayers.

10) Among others, the California Water Project is in violation of the following Federal and State laws:

5th and 14th Amendments U. S. Constitution
Federal Reclamation Laws 43 USC Sections 423, 430, 523–525
The San Luis Act 74 Stat. 156
Rivers and Harbors Act of 1899 33 USC Section 403
National Environmental Policy Act of 1969 83 Stat. 852
Fish and Wildlife Coordination Act 16 USC Sections 661-663
Migratory Bird Acts 16 USC Section 701
Anadromous Fish Act of 1965 16 USC Section 757
Federal Water Pollution Control Act, as amended by Federal Water Quality Improvement Act 33 USC Section 466 et seq.
Federal Administrative Procedure Act 5 USC Sections 500–559
National Estuarine Areas Act 16 USC Section 1221 et seq.
Act of September 22, 1959 16 USC Section 760
California Counties of Origin Act, California Water Code Section 10505
California Watershed Protection Act, California Water Code Sections 11460-11463

11) We will be backing at least two and possibly seven other suits against the state, based on some of these violations. So, if you agree with our position, and can afford to help us fight the legal battle, please do.

Thank you.

Alvin Duskin for the Legal Committee
To Stop The California Water Plan
510 Third Street, San Francisco, CA 94107

Fig. A

HOW THE CALIFORNIA WATER PROJECT WILL DESTROY THE DELTA AND THE BAY

The California Water Project will reduce the flow of fresh water into San Francisco Bay from 15½ million acre feet per year to as little as 2½ million. The United States Geological Survey says the effect will be to decrease the natural "flushing action" of the fresh water, which removes from the Bay the variety of chemicals and pollutants that otherwise kill life in the water, as well as other life which feeds upon it, such as birds and animals. When the flow of the river is reduced, the inflow of the ocean will increase, thereby drastically altering the natural ecology not only of the Bay but of the Delta, pushing far upstream the salinity, and a lot of dangerous chemical garbage, that was formerly swept out through the Golden Gate. The Geological Survey reports that the result of all this, if the project is not stopped, will be to make San Francisco Bay as "dead as Lake Erie."

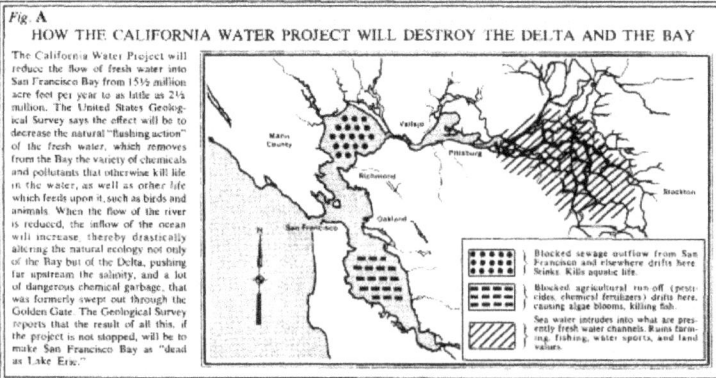

Blocked sewage outflow from San Francisco and elsewhere drifts here. Stinks. Kills aquatic life.

Blocked agricultural run-off (pesticides, chemical fertilizers) drifts here, causing algae blooms, killing fish.

Sea water intrudes into what are presently fresh water channels. Ruins farming, fishing, water sports, and land values.

More Smog, More People, More Traffic, More of Everything We Don't Want

DO YOU WANT the state to finish a project which costs $2.82 billion, which will benefit a handful of real estate promoters, a few businessmen, and make your daily life more difficult than it is right now?

I am a dress manufacturer and I live in San Francisco and I am not in the habit of buying advertisements which talk about anything but dresses. But I've lately begun to understand that unless *I* finally do something, *and you do*, the mindless development of California might proceed until there'll be no air to breathe at all, and no place to escape to.

What's the use of a nice house in the countryside when the countryside is increasingly becoming a place it's not worth going to? Have you been to Palm Springs lately? It's getting just like the city, and I won't be surprised if before long we all have the delightful experience of buying a whiff of oxygen from a vending machine, as they already do in Tokyo. You put a coin in, out comes a mask, you get to breathe again.

There was a time when big commercial development projects in our state made some good sense; but that was when the population was low and there was ample room and resource. But California is no longer an underdeveloped state; it's an overdeveloped state and life here just isn't what it used to be.

But if you think the crowding, ugliness and poison air have got as bad as they can possibly get, then you don't know about a development called the California Water Plan. Listen to this:

1. The idea is to bring water down to Southern California from up north. The water isn't for you, it's for *growth*, the one thing nobody in Los Angeles needs. It's to encourage new industry and more population on the presently undeveloped outskirts of Los Angeles. In other words, to make more Los Angeles.

2. To accomplish this, the state is creating the most complex (and expensive) series of canals, dams, pipelines and tunnels ever built in the

I. THE POLLUTION "BODY COUNT"

THE BROWN PELICAN · THE BAY CRAB · THE BAY SHRIMP · THE PONDEROSA PINE FORESTS

Here you have some lovely pictures of living things which are on the way to extinction. Well, Ponderosa Pines are not going to be extinct, very soon, but 1,300,000 of them in the San Bernardino National Forest may soon be dead from smog. The future is a little more definite for the peregrine falcon and the brown pelican. *They* may be extinct when the *current* generation dies. The pelicans have eaten enough fish contaminated with pesticides that as a result, when they lay eggs, the shell is not thick enough to support its own weight. It cracks open and all the offspring die. No next generation. We don't know what happens to the human reproductive process from digesting these same fish, but it isn't good, that much we know.

world (see map). When put into operation the result will be terrible destruction of some of California's most spectacular regions but that's the least of it.

3. While the new water *will* produce profits for

(a) real estate developers eager to turn the countryside into suburbs (b) industry, which wants the water for development, and (c) mechanized agriculture, the accelerated development will dramatically increase smog, traffic, and poisonous chemicals. It will encourage only the more unpleasant aspects of life in Los Angeles.

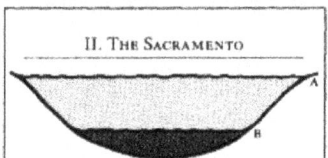

II. THE SACRAMENTO

Fresh water flow of the Sacramento River today [A] and when and if the California Water Plan is completed [B]. All the fresh water between gets shipped to S. California to help real estate and industrial interests near Los Angeles

While helping some business in the short run, it *will* do so at the expense, the health and the comfort of 99% of the population.

4. Here is what will happen up in San Francisco. After the water is diverted from its natural flow, the fresh water in the Sacramento River Delta will be reduced from 18 million acre feet per year to 2 million. (See Box II.)

5. With less fresh water flowing through the rivers and delta, the pesticides, nitrates and industrial chemicals that wash into it will have much greater destructive power than even now. They are likely to kill off millions of fish (as happened recently in Germany), species which eat the fish, plantlife along the shores, birds which need the plantlife and, finally, the oxygen producing marine plankton along California's continental shelf. (Smog aside, 70% of the oxygen we breathe is produced by plankton.)

6. It's a kind of chain reaction. Everything needs the next thing, you see; that is the miracle of nature. We are in the process of destroying the chain, forgetting for the moment that if *it* is disrupted, so are we. A few too many chemicals in the fish and birds we eat, and we can all forget the buying and selling of dresses.

7. These same chemicals flow into San Francisco Bay and eventually we will have as dead a Bay as Lake Erie. But let me get to one other little point. Poison Lake.

8. As it heads south some of the water will be used for irrigation. Eventually this water will be leached from the land into a giant open ditch (The San Joaquin Drain) which will be provided because this water will be so filled with nitrates and pesticides that it would begin to poison the soil.

9. Originally, the plan was to take this poisoned water and, by a marvel of engineering creativity, dump it back into San Francisco Bay. This technological "advance" has since been discredited, but as nobody can figure just what *can* be done with such a deadly water supply, the solution that's been devised is this one: collect it all in a poison lake (Kesterson Reservoir) and then leave it there until someone figures out how to clean it all up. That's the solution!

10. Now all this imaginative thinking is not

free. You and I voted in 1960 (during Governor Brown's regime) to pass the $1.75 billion Water Bonds Act to execute this thing. What did *we* know? Who could figure it out? But this water is not for drinking, it turns out, and the real cost is more nearly three billion dollars and guess who is going to foot the bill for the difference? You know the answer. (See Box III.)

11. There's a lot more to this, of course, than I can possibly tell you on this page, and I'm not the expert anyway.

If any of you want the full technical story, please check the appropriate box above, and I'll tell you where to find reports which all discuss alternative less expensive and less destructive ways of getting water where and when it is really needed, including reports by scientists who *are* experts and who will scare you more than I have.

It should be obvious to everyone living in California that the time for placing first importance on commercial development of anything in this state has long since passed.

We must all purge from our minds the belief that all industrial growth is *necessarily* good. We cannot afford any longer to give commerce and industry first sayso over the landscape and the wildlife and the environment, not if we once get it in our heads that we are also wildlife; we are only one strand of the web of life on this

planet and in order to survive we have got to save everything else.

The California Water Plan will accelerate development at a time when we're choking from what we already have. Just because, in our

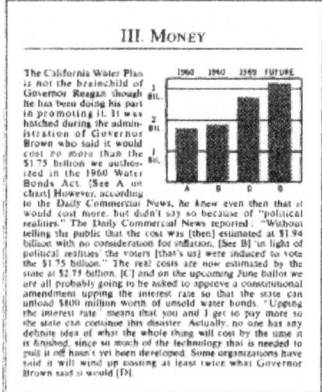

III. MONEY

The California Water Plan is not the brainchild of Governor Reagan though he has been doing his part in promoting it. It was hatched during the administration of Governor Brown who said it would cost no more than the $1.75 billion we authorized in the 1960 Water Bonds Act. [See A on chart] However, according to the *Daily Commercial News*, he knew even then that it would cost more, but didn't say so because of "political realities." The *Daily Commercial News* reported: "Without telling the public that the cost was [then] estimated at $1.94 billion with no consideration for inflation, [See B] in light of political realities the voters [that's us] were induced to vote the $1.75 billion." The real costs are now estimated by the state at $2.79 billion. [C] and on the upcoming June ballot we are all probably going to be asked to approve a constitutional amendment upping the interest rate so that the state can unload $400 million worth of unsold water bonds. "Upping the interest rate" means that you and I get to pay more so definite idea of what the whole thing will cost by the time it is finished, since so much of the technology that is needed to pull it off hasn't yet been developed. Some organizations have said it will wind up costing at least twice what Governor Brown said it would. [D].

naivete, we supported it ten years ago, does not change that it's a disaster in today's world and should be scrapped.

A critical element of the project—The Peripheral Canal—is now on Gov. Reagan's desk. Hailed by the State as a "compromise," this canal would divert water from above the Delta instead of from the Delta itself which makes it about as much of a compromise as one bullet in the heart instead of two. The *entire plan* is out of date and all work on it must be stopped, if we want a livable California.

Please join me in trying to halt this project, by mailing the coupons above and encouraging others to do likewise.

Thank you.   Alvin Duskin
                    510 Third Street
                    San Francisco, Calif. 94107

This is a unsimplified map of how the California Water Plan will work. The North Coast Development would stop-up the natural flow of all the major wild rivers in the area (as has already been done around the Oroville Dam). The flow of water down into the Sacramento River will be controlled, and below Sacramento, instead of flowing into San Francisco Bay as it naturally has, 82% of the water will be pumped into the California aqueduct toward Los Angeles. Along the way some of it will irrigate farm lands in the San Joaquin Valley, and then collect in the San Joaquin Drain and then in what I have called "Poison Lake." No one has determined what will be done with this poisoned water (no clear idea is to dump it in San Francisco Bay). As for the *good* water, it will go towards servicing an expanded population and industry in an area where there is already too much.

As you see from the final three ads, Jerry had graduated to doing overtly political ads for progressive causes. Gossage, who was himself Left-leaning, was all for, as he put it, "stirring up the mush". So he was happy to let Jerry do his activist thing.

But more than that, he was probably just delighted someone else was doing the ads.

He'd had an extraordinarily fertile decade - from the Qantas Kangaroo to the *Scientific American*'s Paper Airplane. And it had taken its toll.

In his early days he'd told his first wife, Francis, that writing copy "was like giving birth to a baby grand piano." And it never got easier. He knew that "advertising was a privilege, not a right" and this heightened sense of responsibility to his audience made it impossible for him to turn out anything but his best efforts.

Under such pressure, he was, as Alice Lowe recalled, "popping pep pills like candy" and they didn't appear to be helping. "Fresh ideas were more difficult to come by for old accounts. At such times, he paced the floor restlessly, becoming steadily more edgy, as he sought first rate ideas in vain. With each passing day, he became more sullen and withdrawn ... The slightest provocation triggered him into violent rage. Except for these outbursts of temper, he scarcely spoke to anyone, concentrating every bit of energy on that desperate inward search for inspiration.

"At such times he was given to reciting the Chinese legend of the man with the golden brain. All his friends and relatives came to him and begged for gold to live. So he gave them each a little fleck for their support. Eventually he was found dead with an empty skull and a lot of gold flecks under his finger nails."

Gossage was afraid that when *he* was found dead, all he'd be remembered for was the Beethoven Sweatshirt.

And it was this, the trivial and transient nature of advertising, that made him question whether all the exhausting work was worth it.

Yes, he was adamant that it "requires a superlative talent, if the results are to be superlative." But he doubted if it was worth expending all that talent and effort on something as relatively insignificant as an ad. It was, as he observed, like having a concert pianist being asked to play "Chopsticks".

As early as August 1963 he'd confided to John Steinbeck his hope that "I will discover some other way of living that will obviate doing advertising."

By September 1965 he was writing to his friend Barrows Mussey seeing "no prospect at all except the treadmill, I am getting tired."

Fortunately for Gossage, by early 1966, he'd met Jerry Mander: "the only person who ever understood what I was up to and is able to do it in his own way."

We saw on page 130, he'd also found another kindred spirit, Dr Gerry Feigen. Together they set up the consultancy, The Generalists, Inc., whose end product required neither tortuously come by headlines nor body copy.

For Gossage, it wasn't just a way out of advertising, it was also a means of indulging his love of sitting around and shooting the intellectual breeze.

Jerry Mander explained, "Howard was a fantastically entertaining, very, very funny man. He really liked to be around creative people, of any kind, or intellectuals. He was hungry for that ... What he lived for was the exchange of ideas and the exchange of experience, and I think that was his greatest craving."

To Gossage's great surprise, it was also a way of making money.

As he said, "There was the heady revelation that people were willing to pay us for advice, just for talking to them. Up 'til then, we had been doing that for nothing. Indeed, if put to the test, I would probably pay people to listen to me, I enjoy talking so much."

So he left the ads to Jerry and Co, and set off in search of more interesting problems to solve, more fun to be had and a much bigger stage and audience.

SELLING CELEBRITY

We've just left Gossage exhausted by what he called that "race without a finish", advertising. After ten years' hard slog, he was desperate to surrender his lane to someone else.

But what next?

Well, it was around the mid-'sixties that psychologist Abraham Maslow observed, "To the man with a hammer, everything looks like a nail." As far as Gossage was concerned, this "Law of the Instrument" hit the ad industry on the head. It seemed wrong to him that every time a client had a problem, their agency proposed an ad campaign.

Adman Gossage found a perfect foil in Gerald Feigen who was, in no particular order, a painter, television commentator, ventriloquist, lecturer and the country's leading proctologist.

According to journalist Warren Hinckle, "Traffic slowed down when they crossed the street, heads turned when they walked into a room. Feigen looked like the prototype of the mad professor while Gossage chain-smoked Gauloises like a Pittsburgh chimney."

By early 1965 this odd couple had set up in business as Generalists, Inc.

As long as the problem was interesting enough, Gossage and Feigen were willing to take any client. For example, at one point they were advising both Berkeley University's revolutionary Free Speech Movement and the Chancellor of the University - although as Gossage told his friends Dagmar and Barrows Mussey, "the kids nor the University know of the other".

Their aim was to solve clients' problems with ideas before or beyond advertising. But not just that. They took on bigger societal issues. And, if they couldn't find the answers themselves, they'd seek out visionaries who could offer their own theories on the peculiarities and pathologies of modern life.

AS GOSSAGE DECLARED: *"WE ARE GURU DISCOVERERS"*

The first "guru" was Jesuit priest, Father John Culkin, who was pioneering what we now know as Media Studies at Fordham University. As you'll see from the letter below, it was Father Culkin who turned Gossage on to another leader in that field: Marshall McLuhan.

February 25, 1965

Marshall McLuhan, Ph.D.
University of Toronto
Toronto, Canada

Dear Dr. McLuhan:

Father Culkins and I talked about "Understanding Media" at length recently. He showed me his abstraction. I thought it deserved expansion into at least fifty volumes; it is the most remarkable work of our time.

Would you be free to come to San Francisco for a weekend soon? There are two or three of us who would like to talk to you very much indeed. We would be happy to pay the freight, of course, for you and your wife too.

With kindest regards,

Howard Luck Gossage

P.S.

If this sounds too vague, but you are interested, my telephone number is YUkon 1-0800. I am an advertising man, but don't let that scare you; it doesn't have anything to do with it. Except that we have turned over "what mankind is all about" to an idiot child.

When they spoke, Gossage asked McLuhan if he wanted to be famous. Apparently, he answered "yes", but he was too busy grading end-of-term papers. Gossage's idea of fame would have aligned well with Jeremy Bullmore's definition on page 15: being known by people way beyond your target market.

Conversely, if you'd asked McLuhan to identify the target for his books and theories he'd probably have said fellow academics. Or even students. After all, the book that ultimately made him famous, *Understanding Media*, had its origins in the syllabus he'd written for an eleventh grade high school class.

At that stage, McLuhan was known to his peers but not, according to Gossage, greatly respected. As he put it: "At a high level educational conference on mass media at Washington, reference to his theories were accorded that profound non-response usually reserved for stomach rumblings in chapel".

For Gossage and Feigen those educational conferences were a thing of the past. McLuhan's long time collaborator, Edmund Carpenter recalls in *That Not-So-Silent Sea* the plan was "to convert McLuhan into an internationally recognized media guru, then peddle him as a business consultant, fees to be established."

"A SUSTAINED CAMPAIGN OF CREATING 'NEWS'"

We'll pause here on the above reference to "peddle". Because it harks back to Paul Feldwick and the premise of his book, *Why Does the Pedlar Sing?*" As we saw on page 16, the pedlar, the hawker, the huckster sing because they're trying to attract and entertain an audience so they can then make a sale.

Feldwick says such showmanship found its finest exponent in the 19th century impressario P.T. Barnum. And to explain Barnum's ballyhoo at its most ambitious he cites a campaign very similar to that planned 115 years later by that other master of media manipulation, Howard Gossage.

In Barnum's case, it was the launch of "The Swedish Nightingale", Jenny Lind. According to Feldwick, "Barnum waged a sustained campaign of creating 'news' about Jenny Lind which the newspapers could not resist amplifying."

By May 1965, Generalists Inc., were embarked on their own "sustained campaign of creating news." With $6,000 of their own money, they took their 53 year old protege to the East Coast where, in restaurants affordable only to those on corporate welfare, he was introduced to the nation's leading media owners, newspaper reporters, TV journalists and admen.

One of the media men was journalist Tom (*Bonfire of the Vanities*) Wolfe who was covering McLuhan's tour for the *New York Herald Tribune*. "Looking back, I can see that Gossage, but not McLuhan, knew what was going to happen to McLuhan over the next six months. Namely, that this 53 year-old Canadian English teacher, grey as a park pigeon, would suddenly become an international celebrity and the most famous man his country ever produced."

The soon to be most famous Canadian certainly seemed a little overwhelmed in this June 1965 letter to Gossage:

University of Toronto
Toronto 5, Canada

CENTRE FOR CULTURE AND TECHNOLOGY

Marshall McLuhan, Director

June 10, 1965

Dear Howard:

Greetings and blessings. A great deal to tell you. Mostly, however, I am simply without the time to even say 'thanks' to people like yourself who are the mainstay of my efforts.

Will tell you about a number of new things when I get back from a trip to Quebec city.

Most cordially,

Marshall

HMM:ms

McLuhan was at the centre of Gossage's publicity generating "ad platform technique". But this time the adman hadn't bothered with the "ad". Instead, in August 1965, he amplified the message by orchestrating a series of seminars at his agency.

In the top photograph, that's Gossage, far left, and McLuhan, far right. It all looks very intense. and everyone seemed more relaxed once they'd decanted to *Klamath*, Walter Landor's luxurious ferryboat, where the photograph overleaf was taken.

From left to right (top): President of Freeman, Mander and Gossage, Alice Lowe; *San Francisco Chronicle* columnist, Herb Caen; San Francisco city developer, Justin Herman; Generalist, Gerry Feigen; Marshall McLuhan and wife, Corinne McLuhan.

Front: Industrial designer and branding guru, Walter Landor; Howard Gossage; and pioneer of the New Journalism school and, later, novelist, Tom Wolfe.

Gossage, Herb Caen and Tom Wolfe then took the cloistered academic to a topless restaurant on Broadway. Here's Caen's column of the following day:

HERB CAEN

FLASH: In town is Prof. Marshall McLuhan, fabled, fabulous, revered, and even sainted by the New Intelligentsia, Director of the Center for Culture and Technology at University of Toronto, author of "The Mechanical Bride," "The Gutenberg Galaxy" and "Understanding Media," darling of the critics ("Compared to McLuhan, Spengler is cautious and Toynbee is positively pedantic"—New York Herald-Tribune), the man who stands "at the frontier of post-Einsteinian mythologies."

Hot on the trail of this titan, I thought to myself, "Where is the last place in town you'd expect to see Marshall McLuhan?" and that's where I found him—at Off-Broadway in North Beach, lunching amid the topless waitresses with Writer Tom Wolfe, Adman Howard Gossage and Dr. Gerald Feigen.

★ ★ ★

A TOPLESS fashion show ensued, commentated by a young lady who was fully dressed and in good voice. "Now here, gentlemen," she said, "is the ideal opera gown for your wife." A gorgeously-endowed blonde appeared in a full-length gown open to the waist. The audience, composed mainly of Tuesday Downtown Operator-like types, gaped silently. "You're all dead out there," chided the commentator. "Where's the applause?"

"Now the word applause," interjected Dr. McLuhan, "comes of course from the Latin 'applaudere,' which means to explode. In early times, audiences ap-

which means to explode. In early times, audiences applauded to show their disfavor — they clapped their hands literally to explode the performer off the stage. Hence you might say that that the silence here is a form of approbation, at least in the classical sense."

★ ★ ★

The show over, Tom Wolfe asked Waitress Marilyn: "Why do you wear pasties?" "Have to," she dimpled. "It's the law, when food is being served. For health reasons, you see?" Nobody saw. We invited Marilyn and Rochelle to join us for a drink. "Before we can sit with customers," said Marilyn, "we have to put brassieres on." She and Rochelle left and reappeared wearing black bras.

"I think brassieres look sexier than pasties, don't you?" Marilyn inquired. Everybody nodded. "Besides, you can walk faster with a brassiere." Everybody looked blank. "What I mean is," she went on, "you don't JIGGLE so." The discussion switched to the recent police raids on Off-Broadway, and Rochelle said "I guess it was just a test case, we haven't been bothered since. "I see," said Dr. McLuhan. "To mix a metaphor, it was the thin edge of the trial balloons." I'm sorry to report this, but it's fact that he tittered at his own remark.

We walked out into the sunshine, filled with innocence and good feelings, to find a young man on the sidewalk, handing out blue pamphlets for the "Scandinavian Massage Studio, Miss Ingrid, Director." The copy read "Six young and trained Scandinavian girls are ready to serve you. For the tired executive we offer private massage rooms, private telephones, stock quotations, the Wall Street Journal, music."

It didn't sound relaxing at all. Not half as relaxing as lunch among the nymphs with Dr. Marshall McLuhan and his merry men.

★ ★ ★

Tom Wolfe returned to New York to file his copy for "What If He's Right?"- the *NEW YORK* magazine article that supercharged McLuhan's media career.

McLuhanacy gathered pace and, in 1966, he was the focus of 120 major features in magazines across the US, Canada and the UK. *Newsweek* splashed him on its cover, and *Life* magazine announced the coming of "the oracle of the electric age".

All seemed convinced that, at last, North America had produced a thinker, with a unified theory of everything, who could rival the best of Europe's intellectual heavyweights - past and present.

Certainly no thinker had ever benefited from the kind of marketing and electronic media coverage that was jet propelling McLuhan to fame.

He had become, to quote his biographer Douglas Coupland, "A superstar .... At a certain point in the mid-1960s he stopped being merely a brainy academic from Toronto. He became a massive brand, as famous and synthetic and misunderstood and misquoted as fellow 1960s media construct and artist Andy Warhol ... He was everywhere. He was hip and cool and groovy and far out. He was a fraud, a monster, a genius, and a hoax. Young people loved him. Talk shows were incomplete without him."

But even then, he was reliant upon Gossage. Here he is asking advice on how much to charge his corporate clients and who should publish his next book (note also his prescient concern about becoming a "fad").

u n i v e r s i t y   o f   t o r o n t o
CENTRE FOR CULTURE AND TECHNOLOGY
toronto 5, ontario, canada. h.m. mcluhan, director

February 1, 1966

Dear Howard:

      I am much in need of your advice apropos the Container Corporation of America. I had a letter from Mr. John Massey, Director of Design, Advertising and Public Relations, asking me to consider being the lead-off man in a kind of Aspen Conference series in New York City. I phoned them and was told that their plan was to have "ten top leaders of industry and business" at dinners. No audience except these. They expected to begin fairly soon and to have monthly meetings. Three or four of them. They added apropos payment that they "wanted me to be satisfied."

      If I were to do three or four two-hour dialogues with them, what would be a reasonable way of charging them? I raised the matter to a corporation lawyer friend yesterday. He agreed that money meant nothing to these people. He cautioned that I should not underprice myself since in such company both my name and my price have snob-value. So that, if I were to say to them that my price was $5,000 a meeting in addition to $1,000 per hour, plus expenses, they could then say "We had McLuhan for $5,000." This, in turn, becomes a prestige item for them.

      The Life Magazine piece is due to appear in about two weeks. When they saw the copy and pictures they were quite pleased and decided to speed it up. There is also a bit in Fortune currently, and a Saturday Evening Post representative is now in town to spend a week working on a piece. He is quite a bright boy. Just back from a Fulbright year in London. His name is Richard Kostelanetz. He warns me that all this publicity will tend to build me up into a fad, which inevitably leads to the bursting of the balloon. How about that? And how do all these things bear on the Container Corporation proposal?

      Your idea of sub-title for Cliché to Archetype as "The Environments of Man" strikes me as perfect.

      By the way, Howard, another publicity item concerns a Mr. Ellis, Washington editor of the Time Bureau. He is coming here next Monday to visit the seminar. He says he wants to do a Time essay on our theme of the Future. I think we can accommodate him quite handily since we have eighteen or so students doing individual projects on The Future of the Book, the Family, Architecture, the City, the Planet, Art, Muesology, Crime, Language, Education, Politics, the Unconscious, Work, Entertainment, Old Age, etc. We have made some quite fascinating discoveries in all these areas, so Mr. Ellis should have a good essay out of it. I have not assigned these essays to any publisher yet. Do you have any suggestions?

Fondly
marshall

EXPLAINING McLUHAN TO McLUHAN

Alice Lowe felt that: "McLuhan was pretty hard to understand because he goes round and round and round. Howard would say 'you mean…' and turn it into something an ordinary person could understand. On the wall at the Firehouse there was a lot of graffiti and I think it was Marshall McLuhan that had written 'The Medium is the Message'. Some disrespectful person had crossed out the 'M' and put a 'T'."

To further clarify things, Gossage wrote a feature article in *Ramparts* magazine titled "Understanding Marshall McLuhan". In a preface to the article, the *Ramparts* editor Warren Hinckle noted that McLuhan "once remarked that Gossage understood McLuhan better than McLuhan understood McLuhan."

Hinckle was close to Gossage and witness to McLuhan's reliance upon the adman. He described their relationship: "Gossage was always kind of translating for the potty prophet. 'What Marshall means by all this is that…' But a lot was added in the translation and McLuhan would look at Gossage like the Mad Hatter peering over the tea cup and say, in a voice that was part confused innocence, part modest genius, 'Gee, Howard, that's exactly what I meant when I wasn't saying it'."

Whatever it was that McLuhan wasn't saying, the public was lapping it up.

At the beginnning of this chapter, we noted that being famous means being talked about by people way beyond your target audience. Gossage had achieved that for McLuhan. By the late 'sixties he had become a celebrity.

Daniel J. Boorstin, who brought us the pseudo-event in his book *The Image*, also gave us a definition for that creature of modern media: the celebrity was simply someone who was "well known for being well known." Famous, yes, but not for anything that the mass audience might use, enjoy or understand. But simply because by good luck, a gift for self-promotion, a marketable asset or a sizeable advertising budget they've captured public's attention.

While McLuhan's *The Medium is the Massage* sold nearly a million copies, it's a good example of a book that lots of people buy but not that many read.

Having said that, there was one group of people who understood his insights, and acted on them: the hippies and members of the counterculture who, at that time, were gravitating toward San Francisco.

The counterculture's intellectual heavyweights set about making McLuhan's prophecies real. And not by projecting them onto TV screens, as McLuhan predicted, but by plugging them into a network of what would soon be known as personal computers.

As the electro-hippies experimented with ever more effective ways of creating such a network, their old mentor, McLuhan suffered the inevitable fate of the celebrity and faded from public view.

So much so that today he is primarily known for such aphorisms as "The global village" and "The medium is the message". However, those who know their digital history will tell you it was McLuhan who inspired the hobbyists and hackers who became the internet's most influential innovators.

Indeed, they paid tribute to his genius when, in 1993, Kevin Kelly launched *Wired* magazine and pronounced McLuhan the "Patron Saint of the Digital Age".

If McLuhan was ahead of his time then, as we've seen throughout this book, so

was the man who made him famous.

As Symbolism.org's "The Medium of the Messenger" had it: "McLuhan may have been a major precursor of cyberculture. But the promotion of him was also a major precursor of contemporary celebrity manufacturing. Perhaps one of the original textbook cases. Gossage's mixture of marketing and news, design and promotion, PR and planted 'newsworthy' journalism – almost Joycean in effect with its barrage of various media – in many ways previewed postmodern marketing and public relations."

It seems that everything came together in the launch of McLuhan via that "mixture of marketing and news, design and promotion, PR and planted 'newsworthy' journalism".

And, perhaps to Gossage's relief, it didn't entail having to write an ad.

THE NEXT GURU

The success of the McLuhan launch proved that Feigen and Gossage were much more than a couple of eccentrics working on the marketing world's margins. They'd created their own niche speciality, and it wasn't long before they'd found their next guru.

Here the "genius" was political scientist, Leopold Kohr. He contended that the problems besetting humankind proceeded from bigness and could be solved through the devolution to smaller, self-governing communities and city states - a theory later popularised by E.F. Schumacher's *Small is Beautiful*.

This certainly appealed to Gossage who had himself, half-jokingly perhaps, advocated San Francisco seceding from the Union.

Either way, as with McLuhan, the first contact was made by letter. And, once again, Kohr was to be promoted via a series of seminars at the Firehouse.

Gossage felt "there will be much interest from the press and TV and Etc". But this time, there was no Tom Wolfe to focus media attention, and Kohr went off to teach Economics and Public Administration at the University of Puerto Rico.

Then, a few months later in Spring 1967, Kohr contacted Gossage to tell him the people of the Caribbean island of Anguilla had declared independence from the

HOWARD LUCK GOSSAGE

451 PACIFIC, SAN FRANCISCO

15 December 1966

Dear Professor Kohr:

I'm glad I had a chance to talk with you this morning,
however unsatisfactory it may have seemed for you. There
is some information conveyed through such a personal
contact that eliminates a good deal of tentative probing
for me.

I am writing you at greater length, since there is much
to say, but for the moment I just want to confirm our
proposal and suggest a firm date. What would you say to coming here on Saturday, 20 February, and leaving the next
Friday or Saturday?

This would give us a couple of days to get acquainted
and talk about whatever we have planned for the week
ahead. "We" in this instance being Dr. Gerald Feigen, our
~~my~~ colleagues in Shadetree Corporation (see attached to
give you some notion of its Kohresque structure; though
it has been amended somewhat-- more about this in following
letter), and such other worthies as may group themselves
around your coming.

At the moment it is hard to say what it will all turn into.
I have a notion that we may find we have tapped into an
enormous fund of interest; we are, after all, dealing with
the most fascinating and troublesome problem of our time:
how man groups himself so he doesn't lose himself in the
process. (On the whole, unsavory as the choice is, I have
always preferred Cleopatra and her asp to the Laocoon Group.
Then, of course, ~~xxxxxxxxxxxxxxxxxxxxxxxxxxx~~ all comparisons
are upward from there.)

Thematically, I doubt we have to look much beyond "Sociality,
Religiosity, and Politicality" for starters.

And I imagine there will be much interest from the press and
TV and Etc. Can't think why not, at any rate.

I can assure you it will be informal, and pleasurable.

Let me know if the date suits you and I will send a ticket.
The modest $100 a day (plus expenses, naturally) is from
arrival to departure and nothing is required of you beyond
the pleasure of your company. No preparation is necessary
though there may be a couple of surprise quizzes.

Thanks,

Howard Gossage

over)

island federation of which they'd been a member.

The British government frowned on the break-up of one of its Commonwealth dependencies and put pressure on the rebels to get back in line. They needed help. As Gossage explained: "Kohr called me from San Juan to tell me excitedly that he had found a 'marvellous island' upon which to experiment his carefully developed theories of smallness."

Nation-building is an expensive business and to achieve it Gossage and Feigen partnered with Scott Newall, the buccaneering, wooden-legged executive editor of the *San Francisco Chronicle* and other like-minded adventurers to set up a line of credit for $80,000 dollars.

Much of it was invested in thousands of silver Liberty Dollars which were shipped to Anguilla to be used as the new currency. The heads of the breakaway government were then flown to New York to speak at the United Nations.

From New York they were taken to a celebration of independence at the St Francis Hotel in San Francisco for which Alice Lowe was delegated to come up with the catering and Marget Larsen was tasked with running up the new nation's flag.

"THE BEST AD I EVER WROTE"

It wasn't, however, going to be that simple. With a British frigate preparing to land 40 policeman and the rebels' resolve wavering, Gossage fell back on his core competence and produced what he later said was "the best ad I ever wrote".

Readers of the *New York Times* and *International Herald Tribune* were promised an honorary Anguillan passport for every $100 they donated. The money rolled in and, with the media spotlight on the island, the threat of a bit of latter-day British gunboat diplomacy faded.

But so, too, did the ideals that had originally inspired the Anguillan rebels. Not only did they start to seek outside investment, they also disowned the *New York Times* fundraising advertisement, which left Gossage and his partners open to accusations of fraud.

(The Anguilla White Paper)

Is it "silly" that Anguilla does not want to become a nation of bus boys?

THE NEW YORK TIMES, in its editorial of August 7, described the Republic of Anguilla's desperate efforts to remain independent as "touching and silly."

With a pat on the head, the Times advised us to return to the awkward Federation of St. Kitts-Nevis-Anguilla, itself newly formed, from which we had withdrawn shortly after its arbitrary inception on February 27.

We say "arbitrary" because, as you can see from the map, Anguilla does not, even geographically, have much in common with the other two islands. St. Kitts and Nevis are right next door to one another and share a common one-crop, sugar cane, economy dominated by huge, foreign land holdings. Anguilla's land is owned by the islanders themselves; each family has its own little plot and lives off it. Why, then, did Britain lump us in with the other two islands? Because we were their last odd-parcel of real estate in the Caribbean; it's probably that simple. (The Times disregarded these basics, if it ever knew them.)

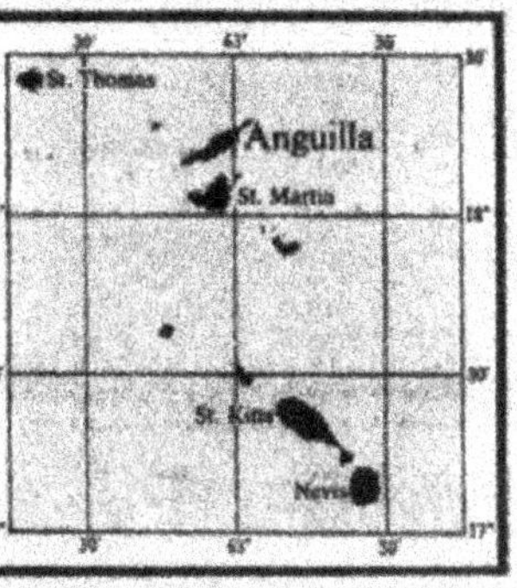

The Times then dismissed our aspirations to independence by pointing out that, "Anguilla has an area of only 35 square miles and a population of 6000. Its people subsist on agriculture and fishing and *lack such modern amenities as telephones.*" (Italics ours.)

This is a terrible indictment in New York eyes, we suppose, but do you know what one Anguillian does when he wants to telephone another Anguillian? He walks up the road and talks to him. Primitive as this arrangement is, it is hardly grounds for justifying the Times' conclusion that Anguilla cannot hope to go it alone.

The fact is that we *have* gone it alone economically, socially, and politically for centuries. The British have neither bothered us, nor bothered about us. We have never been exploited, possibly because there has been nothing much to exploit.

UGLY DUCKLING

To understand this, you must know that Anguilla is referred to in guidebooks as "the ugly duckling of the Caribbean." Objectively that may be so, though to us Anguilla is beautiful because it is our homeland.

There is not enough water on the island for major crop cultivation, nor is it a "tropical paradise"; it is not the prettiest island in the West Indies. The highest point on Anguilla is but 200-and-some-odd feet. There used to be a lot of trees we are told, but these were burned for charcoal long ago. So we must bring in wood to build Anguilla's famous knife-like schooners and sloops.

OLDER THAN U.S.

Anguilla has been left to herself, with generations of the same people, since the 17th century. We are, therefore, a very old nation by any standards. It can even be argued that, as a distinct nation with a stable people, we are older than the United States.

Anguilla is only "new" in the sense that the New York Times had never heard of us before, nor have we had to assert ourselves recently. The last time we were threatened was 250 years ago when the French attempted an invasion with 600 men. They were thrown back by 60 of us, men whose names nearly all Anguillians still bear in direct descent.

There is also this, and it is all-important: Anguilla has proved its self-reliance. It can feed itself, and does. How else do you suppose it could have withstood a blockade—the impounding of our funds, and even our mail—plus the threat of siege by the St. Kitts Government for more than three months now?

"ERRATIC PROCEDURE"

Back to the Times editorial, there is more than a suggestion that Anguillians, though enthusiastic for freedom, are also undisciplined, unrealistic, and given to "erratic procedure." In a word: natives.

We would point out that, whatever the British failed to do on Anguilla, they did give us 300 years of grounding in democratic institutions; and they did establish schools: Anguilla's literacy rate is over 70%, by far the highest in these islands.

Which brings us to the Times's unfounded assertion that "there is no truly representative government to speak for the island." That is quite untrue. Anguilla is ruled by a duly elected Council. The premise for this statement was the supposition that Mr. Peter Adams, who has served as a member of the Council, "had a mandate to negotiate for Anguilla" with the British. This is not true either.

Mr. Adams was in the United States seeking help and recognition for us when he, already at the point of exhaustion, enplaned in the middle of the night for Barbados to meet with Great Britain's Minister for Commonwealth Affairs, Lord Shepherd. He flew there from San Francisco arriving after 15 hours of hard travel, with no luggage—only the clothes on his back.

UNREMITTING PRESSURE

It is impossible to know the pressures that were subsequently exerted on this man whom we know to be ordinarily unswerving and extraordinarily dedicated. But after a week, virtually incommunicado toward the end, he submitted to the following demand (in writing) by Lord Shepherd:

> "If you now reject the settlement which we regard as being very reasonable, I must say, in all seriousness, that the British Government cannot continue to countenance the present situation in Anguilla, which constitutes a threat to the stability of the whole Caribbean.
>
> "I shall therefore have to consult with the other Caribbean Governments as to the steps which shall have to be taken to deal with this serious situation."

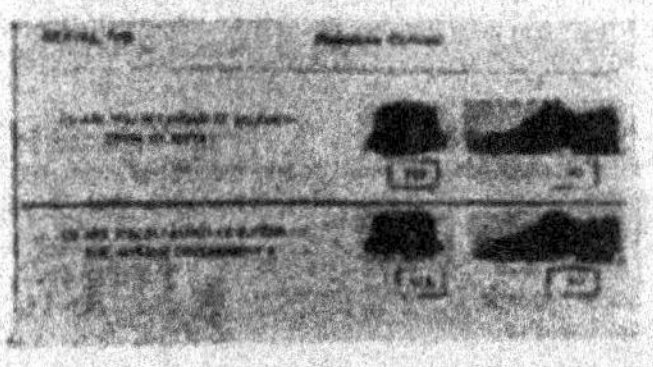

This "serious situation" was simply that Anguilla, after withdrawing from the embryo Federation in May, had, on July 11, held a plebiscite by secret ballot (above) to confirm its independence beyond question. To insure complete accuracy and believability to the world, this election was supervised, and the ballot count confirmed, by outsiders; correspondents, chiefly.

The returns were embarrassingly lopsided: 1813 For independence, 5 Against. It is therefore utterly impossible that Mr. Adams carried with him what the Times calls "a mandate to negotiate"; i.e., to give up.

BRITISH THREAT NOT EMPTY

Why did he succumb? Well, the British threat of force has seldom been an empty one. Also recall that the St. Kitts government's Prime Minister Bradshaw had, in addition to blocking our mail and our money, threatened—and continues to threaten—our small island with armed force; with no success thus far, though it has meant manning our beaches all night every night for months.

Meanwhile, a British frigate with a force of Royal Marines aboard, lies off our shores. One imagines that the least civil disturbance on Anguilla would serve as a pretext for landing these imposing troops. There is small likelihood of an *internally* induced incident of any kind.

To resume, the Barbados Agreement was immediately declared invalid by the Island Council and by the people themselves in mass meeting. A provisional head of state, Mr. Ronald Webster, was immediately acclaimed pending regular election.

One last insight into why the unfortunate and unauthorized Barbados Agreement calling for Anguilla's return to the St. Kitts-Nevis Federation was signed at all: We do not mean to suggest that melancholy measures were applied to gain assent, but the might and authority of Great Britain—especially when embodied in one who is a high British official *and* a Lord—is not easily ignored after centuries of respect.

WHY WANT US NOW?

It occurs to us that one question may remain in American minds. If Anguilla is as we say it is, why would St. Kitts-Nevis, or the British for that matter, wish to bother with us now? Well, we *are* somewhat of an affront to what they would regard as fitting and proper; and we are a maddening challenge to Prime Minister Bradshaw's authority over his own troubled domain. The fact that unreachable Anguilla is not troubled by St. Kitts's inherited economic and political ills likely does nothing to allay his discontent; that is only human nature.

But there is another reason, quite new, for finding Anguilla desirable. Anguilla, though unassuming, does have an extremely pleasant climate, cool and dry...and magnificent, untouched beaches. We are "developable."

We could settle our financial distress today were we willing to sign any of the numerous offers we have received from land and resort developers. One company dangled $1,000,000 cash for gambling concessions. We turned it down flatly, despite the anguished realization that this amount of money would underwrite our development for years.

EVEN ONE GREAT HOTEL

Why did we turn these offers down? Because even one magnificent, Hiltonesque hotel on an island of 6000 people, *4000 of whom are youngsters,* would turn us into a nation of bus boys, waiters, and servants.

There is nothing wrong with service or hard physical work, you understand, but a whole *nation* of servants is unthinkable. In five years—or perhaps less—Anguillians would become as sullen, malcontent, and rootless as the rest of the Caribbean; or Harlem, as far as that goes.

Though we haven't mentioned it before, we are a nation of what you would call "Negroes." To us, we are simply Anguillians, because nobody has ever brought the subject up, and that's the way we intend to keep it. But you do see what we mean, don't you? Even one fine hotel and we would become "natives."

HOW LONG CAN WE RESIST?

That brings us up to now. As of this writing the British have not landed troops nor are we given to despair. We still hope for recognition from the United States, from the United Nations, from Great Britain, or from anyone. But if no one chooses to recognize us we shall continue, as we always have, to go it alone.

How long can we hold out? Indefinitely—even without recognition—but we can use temporary financial aid in the meantime.

Our needs are ridiculously small by any standards but our own. For example: our entire island budget—including schools (for those 4000 children)—comes to only $25,000 per month. All our island funds to the amount of $250,000 U.S. are impounded in St. Kitts, yet we have managed.

We have eased the currency shortage somewhat by the issuance of emergency coinage. These "Anguilla Liberty Dollars" are overstamped South American silver dollars, for the most part (see next column).

These coins are being redeemed by friends of Anguilla abroad, and we are putting into circulation the money they fetch.

...TO SURVIVE NOW

It is a little embarrassing for our government to ask you for financial aid on the basis of the unique collateral we have presented here. However, we have no doubt that we will survive this crisis—and do it without selling ourselves out—if we have enough money to survive *now*. We must seek assistance from individuals.

To show our gratitude, we should like to give you something in return, if only to prove that Anguilla is really here and thinking of you even as you think of us.

First off (to disprove the Times's allegation that we don't really have a "representative government"), we had better send you an autographed picture of the Island Council, a facsimile of the original handwritten version of our national anthem, and a small Anguillian flag (a replica of the one now flying over the airstrip). If you wish to help us with as much as $25.00, we'll also send you one of the Anguilla Liberty Dollars.

Those sending $100 or more will become Honorary Citizens of Anguilla. They will receive a document in the form of an Anguillian passport, identical to that which we are issuing to Anguillians, except that it will have an Anguillian Dollar inlaid as shown in the picture. While Americans should not expect to use this passport for foreign travel, it will be good for entering Anguilla. In fact, *only* holders of this passport will be able to visit Anguilla as guests. Why?

In the first place, we have only 30 guest rooms on the entire island at the moment, with no plans to expand. We would not think it either good or polite that so many visitors should be on the island at once that they couldn't at least have lunch with the President. (Besides, since we have such a small population, any more than a very few guests would automatically become "tourists"; we wouldn't want that, and neither would you.)

HOW TO SEND CONTRIBUTIONS TO ANGUILLA

Since we are cut off from direct postal service—and to give you assurance that your money is safe—an account is being established at the Chase Manhattan Bank on nearby St. Thomas, U.S. Virgin Islands. So please make out your check to: THE ANGUILLA TRUST FUND. And address the letter to: The Anguilla Trust Fund, Chase Manhattan Bank, St. Thomas, U.S. Virgin Islands.

Thank you for your kind attention during all these troubled weeks, and for hearing us out now, and for your generosity. We won't forget it, or you.

Ronald Webster
Chairman, The Anguilla Island Council

THE NEW YORK TIMES, MONDAY, AUGUST 14, 196

Things got worse when those who'd sent in their $100 didn't receive their passports or the Liberty Dollars they'd been promised.

Roger - Please return

File

WEST INDIES AND CARIBBEAN DEVELOPMENTS
261 MADISON AVENUE
NEW YORK, N. Y. 10016
———
YUKON 6-8835
CABLE "CARIBWIC"

E. A. PARSONS
RICHARD C. COWELL
MURRAY T. KOVEN
JOHN M. WILLEM
ABE E. ISSA, C.B.E.
C. HARRY RANDALL

November 27, 1967

Mr. Freeman Gossage
451 Pacific Street
San Francisco, California
94133

Dear Mr. Gossage:

Attached is photocopy of letter addressed to you on October 23, 1967, and to which to date I have not yet had the courtesy of a reply.

I also telephoned your office before sending that letter, and was told someone would call me back the following day. That return call was never received.

Your advertisement made a specific offer re: "Passports" containing "Liberty Dollars" in return for $100 contributions to the Anguilla Trust Find - contributions which were made both by my wife and by myself.

The merchandise has not been delivered. It seems to me that you have incurred a liability here which must be discharged.

Your reply will be appreciated.

Yours very truly,

John M. Willem

JMW:rm

Gossage went to Anguilla and in his words; "Blew up. I said that we had financed the whole damned enterprise; we brought their missions to the United States; we paid the bills for their Ambassador-at-Large and sent a man to help him out. And what have they done? Discredited us. After my speech they handed me a bar check to sign, for $32."

"Then one of the men asked me what I was going to do next. So I told him, 'I'm going to get a great big boat and tow your fucking island out to sea and watch it sink'."

Obviously he wasn't happy with the outcome - especially when he was saddled with a personal loss of $11,000. But he persisted with Kohr and was, in retrospect, pleased with the impact he'd had with the *New York Times* ad.

As he said: "I don't think we realise what a powerful weapon we have in advertising and how much you can do with very little money. This ad in the *New York Times* and in the *Herald Tribune* in Europe together cost $10,000. Well, to do that much with just one ad, and really to do it that inexpensively, is something."

Yes, it was "something". But not altogether surprising. Gossage was the consummate adman and brilliant writer. He didn't need Marshall McLuhan or any guru to tell him that print is a hot medium and conducive to involvement and interaction.

That was Gossage's shtick. And he, better than anyone, knew how to use it to maximum effect.

With one ad, he'd hoiked the spotlight onto Anguilla, making its half-hearted fight for freedom fleetingly famous. In so doing he had also enjoyed that spotlight's halo effect, and burnished his own image and celebrity.

Which brings us, finally, to perhaps his finest foray into media manipulation and showbiz razzmatazz.

CREATING A PERSONAL BRAND

Have a look at that photograph. On the mirror's frame was an inscription. Translated from the Spanish, it read: "Do not look into this mirror to see yourself as you are, but as you would like to be, and you will become that desired image."

And what an image Howard Gossage projected.

According to his colleague, art director Dugald Stermer, "His complexion was corpse-like, porcelain. He looked older than his age ... His hair was absolutely white and I don't know how he did it but it always looked flowing but was always in one place. He was a great-looking guy. He was very dramatic-looking. Looked more like an actor than an advertising man."

Alice Lowe agreed: "There is no question that Howard was every bit as much an actor as [his wife] Sally."

Jerry Mander, also saw the actor in the adman. To Mander, Gossage was "a ham. He occupied the room. If he was to walk into a room, all eyes would turn to him."

I think we can be sure, that's what he wanted. To be the centre of attention. To be, yes, famous.

And he set about it using the techniques we've seen him employ when accomplishing the same task for his clients and Marshall McLuhan.

"I'VE ALWAYS BEEN A HAM. A PUBLICITY HOUND"

Howard Gossage was part Jay Gatsby, and part Don Draper. Like both, he was that quintessential American hero: the self-made man.

And, in this case, Self-made.

As with the other two, Gossage's Midwestern origins were inauspicious.

He was born in Chicago on 30th August, 1917 and grew up in New York, Denver, New Orleans and primarily Kansas City.

Howard's mother, who hailed from a family of vaudevillians, was away touring for months on end. His maternal grandmother was a poisonous woman. She split the family and turned the boy against his father - a trauma that took him years of psychoanalysis in the 1950s to deal with.

The craving for attention that characterised his behaviour in later life could well be explained by the neglect he felt back then.

Shy, embarrassed by a heavy stammer and raised as a strict believer in the Church of Scientology, he wasn't the most outgoing of kids. And certainly not the happiest.

In one of a series of revelatory letters he wrote to his sister Jane in 1959, he spoke of the "guilt (possibly we felt, as little kids, that we were responsible for breaking up the family – that sacrifices were made by Mama and Papa in separating for our sake): a sense of shame. I seem to have spent most of my teens, at least, being ashamed of one thing or another; the smell of poverty, inadequacy, social unacceptability."

Latterly, when asked about his early years, there was just one highlight. And it tells us much about the man the boy would become.

One Sunday morning in July 1936, he was reading *Adventures of Huckleberry Finn* in bed and got to the bit where the hero fakes his own death and heads down the Mississippi. Gossage and a friend immediately took off on a 45 day canoe trip to New Orleans. As he explained, "there are lots of clippings about it. I was even on the radio in St Louis. In case you were wondering how anybody knew about it, I've always been a ham. A publicity hound. As soon as we'd stop in a town, I'd go see the newspaper editor."

Think back to the Rainier Ale "Walk to Seattle" on pages 78-81, and here you have the prototype for that media event.

Even at age 17, Gossage sensed that editors were hungry for stories - and he knew how to feed them to his own advantage. It was a realisation reinforced when, as an undergraduate, he became an editor of the Kansas City University newspaper - the portentously titled *Kangaroo*.

FROM "HARD LUCK GOSSAGE" TO WAR HERO

Upon graduation he worked in his father's record shop, *The Groove*, in Houston. Then in 1940, perhaps to relieve the boredom, he enlisted in the US Navy, first as a Seaman 3rd class and then as an Aviator. Early photos show a gauche young

man - barely recognisable as the debonair flaneur of later life. His personality also seems to have been quite different.

Of their first date, his future first wife, Francis Page Fox wrote "Howard was quiet, reflective, apologetically clumsy and almost depressing. He told me people called him "Hard Luck Gossage. He had little else to say."

He must have been a bit more talkative the following evening because he proposed. She accepted, and he went back overseas. They were, as Francis acknowledged "naive" when they married. And, after the stability of life in the Navy, they were also quite rootless once Howard was demobbed.

Once, when they met in the 1960s, Gossage looked back and said, "There is one thing I can't forgive you for. You let me get out of the Navy. I like to drink.In fact, I'm a lush, and I like to think of a Navy career as the best way for me."

You can understand his reasoning.

He'd come through the war with not one but two Purple Hearts, the rank of Lieutenant, a flight of bombers under his command - pictured here from his cockpit - and all the pride and kudos that attended war hero status.

"TO HELL WITH IT, I'VE NEVER BEEN FAMOUS BEFORE"

Back on civvy street, he was a nonentity.

But it wasn't long before he was in the local papers. His first job was as promotions manager at *KLX* radio station in Oakland where he came up with gimmicks and stunts aimed at getting local companies to advertise with the station. As this cutting suggests he was obviously good at it.

RADIO NEWS
Highlights · Sidelights · Personals · Comments

"Awards of Merit" from City College of New York for KLX. Station President J. R. KNOWLAND (seated) shakes hands on the occasion with GLENN SHAW, station manager. HOWARD GOSSAGE, promotion manager, beams with them. The awards came for hourly news promotion and over-all station promotion.

Then there was the bizarre episode when, in 1949, he contacted the *San Francisco Post Enquirer* with a crazy idea about a "Perpendicular Bridge running from Golden Gate Bridge down the Bay to San Jose". Another stunt, perhaps?

Perpendicular Bridge Now
It Grew Out of a Ham Sandwich

By Jerry Fitz-Gerald
(Post-Enquirer Staff Writer)

Howard Luck Gossage, 32, of 28 Domingo avenue, Berkeley, is never a man to let the little things of life bother him. He's heard the arguments for a parallel bay bridge, a Southern crossing, and a butterfly span.

"Hooey," says Gossage, "let's have a perpendicular bridge."

IT'S NOT VERTICAL

What is a perpendicular bridge? Says Gossage: "It would run from the Golden Gate Bridge down the Bay to San Jose. The plan as conceived now, would call for a western terminus at the Marin end of the bridge, thence to Belvedere, Angel Island, Yerba Buena Island and on down the bay intersecting the San Mateo and Dumbarton bridges."

Gossage is a San Francisco advertising man with weary eyes and a crew hair-cut.

"I get tired of people who get perpendicular confused with vertical," he says petulantly. "Perpendicular is at right angles to any given line.

"We have formed a group of interested far-sighted citizens called 'Citizens United for the Perpendicular Crossing.' Everyone is welcome to join.

"I think it is refusing the challenge to American know-how to cross the bay the easy way with a parallel bridge. Let's do it the hard way—the American way.

IDEA AND SANDWICH

"No, I am not an engineer. We need engineers, badly. This idea came to me last Tuesday while I was eating a ham and cheese sandwich. I rushed out and ordered stationery and then I called a meeting. It is really amazing how enthusiastic people are about it.

"You know when you think about the plan for a while it does not seem too preposterous.

BOON TO MILPITAS

"The problem of tolls has come up. Colored tickets collected at the exit toll plazas would solve that.

"Our motto is "Straight down the Bay to San Jose—Eliminate all Waste.

"I think it is a kindness to Milpitas. That place has been the butt of all the jokes around here for years. The bridge will go right through Milpitas—the town will boom.

"This project will solve all provincial rivalries. You can go to any given point in the Bay Area without going through any of the neighboring cities. People who hate San Francisco or Oakland can avoid both completely. All the advantages of aviation without getting off the ground.

"The only alternative to a cobweb of bridges over the Bay is paving over the whole thing.

"Cost? It will possibly be more expensive than the other proposed bridges—but the cost is nothing compared to the advantages offered. I contemplate an 18-lane highway, with housing projects on Angel Island, and pedestrian walks with benches for the weary. Great, isn't it?"

Gossage smiled weakly. "I haven't had a thing to eat all day. Would you care for a cup of tea?"

BRIDGE PLANNER GOSSAGE
''Let's Do It the Hard Way''

—Post-Enquirer photo.

He got in the papers again organising street parties at which attendees donated cans of food for the hungry kids in a still war-ravaged France. The first event was a flop - rescued by Gossage's already well developed ability to manipulate the media.

As he told his boss, "Reality has nothing to do with it, we will make this one of the most successful propaganda events ever. Reality is not what happens but is controlled by what is written and said about it. We control the print and the air. Remember all those starving French kids…."

He was right, and a suggestible public duly turned out for the second event.

Enjoying the limelight, Gossage accepted an invitation to accompany the mercy mission to Paris - even though he knew the station would fire him for taking unauthorised leave.

After that came his first stint as a writer (see his Bank of America ad on page 20), a couple of years doing his PhD in Europe, his return to San Francisco, the job as junior writer at Brisacher, Wheeler & Staff, the ads for Qantas and finally fame.

As Roger Jellinek wrote in a 1969 profile of Gossage for *Esquire* magazine, the Kangaroo campaign made the front pages of the daily tabloids in what was "a personal coup for Gossage … 'You're famous, but don't let it go to your head', warned his elders and betters. 'To hell with it – I've never been famous before!'"

The Gossage show had started in earnest.

PUTTING THE WRITER FIRST

Thereafter, he seemed incapable of doing a conventional ad. He explained why in a talk he gave while at Brisacher: "I think you have to really throw the bull over the fence every now and then or it's not much fun being a copywriter."

As we saw in Part 1, he had fun doing the bizarre Qantasylvannia competition … the quirky Aalborg ads … the groundbreaking radio spots with Freberg.

Not only did this work grab the audience's attention, it also attracted John Cunningham whose agency Cunningham & Walsh duly bought Brisacher.

Gossage maintained that his ads were the reason for the acquisition.   And it is true that, like Gossage, Cunningham was a fan and exponent of the soft sell. Cunningham was, as Gossage would become, also an outspoken critic of the bombastic hard sell. But, as a *TIME* magazine profile explained, "this debonaire Don Quixote of advertising ... gets away with such blunt talk because admen admire him as one of the great copywriters of all time."

"Debonaire Don Quixote ... blunt talk ... one of the great copywriters of all time" Could it be that Gossage found a role model in his new boss? If so, he wasn't about to play understudy for long. And by 1957 had founded Weiner & Gossage, where the spotlight was well and truly on him.

The aim was to do ads that made not just the client but also the copywriter famous. And he was always adamant about the latter part of that equation.

In 1963, during *KCBS* radio's "Spectrum" phone-in show, one caller asked "if Mr Gossage would agree that his most successful promotion is himself?"

His reply?

"From a personal point of view, I'd like to think so, yes, since I'm a person. But I take responsibility for any advertisement that I put out, much the same way as an actor would for any role that he plays."

In his own, regrettably unpublished, book on advertising he elaborated on this:

"I have been criticized, as you might gather, for trying to build up myself in my ads, I have never denied it, though I put it a different way that is possibly stronger than they would dare.

"The first thing a creator of an ad should do is make himself look good. Because if he does, then he is sticking his neck out; he is responsible and identifiable. If it lays an egg he is the culprit, no one else. And the chances are that if it makes him look good it will make the client look good, too".

In the last chapter, we likened Gossage's antics to those of the ultimate showman, P.T. Barnum. Apparently, his favourite word for his own extrovert behaviour was "humbug".

In *The Anatomy of Humbug,* Paul Feldwick gives this definition: it is "about shamelessly rigging the odds in your favour. It's going with your gut feeling. It's sticking your neck out and not worrying too much what others think. It believes there's no such thing as bad publicity. It's not ashamed to be popular, vulgar, even crass. It doesn't take itself too seriously but it also knows that if it doesn't get enough people in the tent, it won't eat. It's confident and has a brass neck."

Sounds like someone we know?

It demanded equal measures of chutzpah and skill for Gossage to carry off his personal brand of humbug. And we've seen the toll that "sticking his neck out" took on the man. The pressure to maintain his high standards and the risk of personal failure eventually made him avoid writing.

But from 1957- 65 Gossage's audacious ideas made his tiny San Francisco agency the talk of the industry. And it wasn't just the brilliant work that came out of the Firehouse that grabbed attention. So, too, did the building itself.

REPURPOSING THE SELF

Back then, no one was renovating old industrial/institutional buildings. They were tearing them down.

W&G bought the San Francisco Firehouse #1 in 1959 and tasked Marget Larsen with restructuring, designing and decorating what became the most flamboyant offices in the business.

Thereafter, as Alan W. Cundall wrote in *Western Advertising,* "I am convinced that Howard Gossage's fire-house has been publicised more than any other building in the world, with the possible exception of the Sistine Chapel."

That was certainly Gossage's intention, as Roger Jellinek explained in *Esquire* magazine: "The firehouse is more than an exotic place of business for Gossage. It is a statement of his style, a stage for his soliloquies, and the nexus of his constellation of cronies."

The "style" that Jellinek referred to was as carefully cultivated as Marget Larsen's interior designs.

Indeed, you could say that Gossage had himself been repurposed.

The hick from the Midwestern sticks had become the cultured, urbane, intellectual. And all his accessories and accoutrements spoke to that persona.

He smoked only Gauloise Bleu. His signature brand of Champagne was Veuve Clicquot. As for whiskey, it had to be Irish, and then only Paddy.

When travelling, it was always First Class, preferring the best smaller hotels: The Lombardy or Carlisle in New York, The Connaught in London and The Lancaster in Paris. For trips to Europe, it had to be the *SS France*.

Sartorially, he was conservative. Well, his elegantly tailored suits were.
But, for an idiosyncratic flourish, he'd occasionally sport a floppy bow tie and, yes, even a monocle!

Even the hair was a statement. At a time when buzz cuts and short back and sides were the norm, Gossage wore his long, drawing the comparison from journalist James Lincoln Collier as "a cross between Leonard Bernstein and The Joker."

If Bernstein was one of a new breed of celebrity classical musicians then, along with Ogilvy, Gossage was the celebrity adman. And there were no shortage of photo-opportunities at the Firehouse. Especially with highly accomplished photographer, George Dippel, on staff - camera at the ready.

What Dippel was expertly capturing was a masterclass in impeccable personal branding - and another example of just how far Gossage was ahead of his time.

PERSONAL BRANDING TODAY…

Because, oh dear, if you type "Personal Branding" into your search engine today you'll get 4,920,000,000 results.

There seem to be almost that many self-help gurus making their hyperbolic claims about the success you'll enjoy by creating your persona, raising your profile and presenting the very best version of yourself to the world.

Follow their advice and, in pursuit of likes, shares and followers, attention becomes your currency, and an audience, the primary measure of your self-worth.

Which is why, from the performative outrage of X's keyboard warriors to Tik Tok's micro-celebrities, much of social media is now showbusiness for the untalented.

In corporate life, the development of a core competence based on training and tutelage is being replaced by a reliance on manoeuvring and manipulation.

Increasingly, it's an arena in which optics trump aptitude and success is decoupled from any proven talent or skill.

The *reductio ad absurdum* of this self-promotional charade can, of course, be seen in the delusional exhibitionists who compete in TV's *The Apprentice*.

Gossage's first and foremost guru, Marshal McLuhan, saw all this coming. In the late '60s he told a group of bemused advertising men that they no longer needed products, images were enough. Indeed in the electronically mediated world, the image would be everything; a point of view propounded not only Daniel J. Boorstin but also that other great seer of the 'sixties, Andy Warhol.

The production and projection of that image on an industrial scale would, however, have to wait 30 years for the coming of digital's dopamine-driven feedback loops - and the solipsistic hall of mirrors that is social media.

The man who popularised the personal brand was himself a celebrity. Tom Peters was the king of the conference circuit on the strength of his massive best sellers: *In Search of Excellence* and *Thriving on Chaos*. His introduction of the personal brand first appeared in a 1997 article for that, now quaintly analogue organ, *Fast Company* magazine.

… AND DONE EXPERTLY SIXTY YEARS AGO

Peters began: "We are CEOs of our own companies: Me Inc. To be in business today, our most important job is to be head marketer for the brand called You." He went on to give guidance on how to build that brand. Have a look and compare it to what Gossage was doing in the 1950s and '60s.

• "Sign up for an extra project inside your organization, just to introduce yourself to new colleagues and showcase your skills - or work on new ones."

Remember how Gossage went to his Creative Director at Brisacher, Wheeler &

Staff and volunteered to work on "some account that's a real dog … that no one wants and that doesn't amount to a damn?" That account was Qantas.

• "Try teaching a class at a community college, in an adult education program."

In 1963 Gossage signed up as Distinguished Visiting Professor at Penn State University teaching a course in "The Nature of Paid Propaganda."

• "If you're a better writer than you are a teacher, try contributing a column or an opinion piece to your local newspaper."

Gossage had not one but two such writing gigs: "The Easy Chair" in *Harpers* and a weekly column in the *San Francisco Examiner*. He was also a regular contributor to the trade and business press. Moreover, he combined with Barrows and Dagmar Mussey to produce a compilation of his writings and speeches: *Is There Any Hope for Advertising?* There was no US publisher for this until 1988, but a German edition came out as *Ist die Werbung noch zu retten* in 1967.

• "And if you're a better talker than you are teacher or writer, try to get yourself on a panel discussion at a conference or sign up to make a presentation at a workshop."

Gossage was so busy on the speaker circuit, you wonder how he found time to do any work. In the first three months of 1969 when incapacitated by illness, he managed to speak at such diverse gatherings as the National Council for Fine Arts Deans, The California Association of School Psychologists and the Sociology Department of the University of Houston.

• "A project-based world is ideal for growing your brand: projects exist around deliverables, they create measurables, and they leave you with braggables".

From day 1, that was W&G's business plan. Getting bogged down in conventional, open ended campaigns was to be avoided.

As Gossage told *Newsweek* in January 1962, "A client must be able to pose a problem. We continue with them until we solve the problem and renew if they come up with another problem. If not we help them get another agency to do the treadmill type of thing." Hence, for example, Turning Times Square Green …

Shirtkerchief... Pink Air ... Repealing the 18th Amendment ... Dudley and NUCOA ... The Paper Airplane Competition ... the Coffeholics ... and the Salada gypsy strike. There was no fun or glory in doing the "treadmill" work on trade, dealer and product ads. Gossage went for big ideas that delivered quick results, lots of publicity and, of course, his "braggables".

And finally, here's another of Peters's suggestions: networking. That concept was, of course, unknown in the 1960s. But it already had a brilliant exponent.

NETWORKING

As Roger Jellinek observed: "Herb Caen, the man who coined the word beatnik, is an important friend. His daily three dot gossip column in the *San Francisco Chronicle* fans the Gossage legend with frequent stories and bon mots of 'adman Howard Gossage.'"

Apparently he would call Caen every morning at 11.10 to suggest ideas for the column - and not surprisingly quite a few featured you know who.

Often the stories would revolve around the parties held at the Firehouse.

These extravaganzas did much to cultivate the Gossage legend and extend his network.

Amongst the attendees might be Oscar winning film director John Huston or Nobel Prize winning novelist (and Rover car driver), John Steinbeck. There were also the likes of Jessica Mitford, Dr Benjamin Spock, Buckminster Fuller, and young gunslinger journalists Warren Hinckle and Tom Wolfe.

Hollywood was also present. It might be the English comedian, Terry-Thomas, the great character actor, Sterling Hayden or up-and-coming star, Candice Bergen.

Gossage was also a big friend of Enrico and Suzy Banducci. They owned the happening *Hungry i* cabaret club and would bring their performers with them. On one occasion, for example, a young and shy Joan Rivers.

Of course, showbusiness was best represented by Gossage's third wife, actress Sally Kemp - seen with Howard and Alice, right. As glamorous as she was gregarious, the Broadway star was the perfect partner for the flamboyant adman. Indeed so extrovert were they that, as we've seen, they frequently featured in the agency's ads.

Which is something Mr and Mr Bernbach or Mr and Mrs Reeves never did.

Speaking of whom, while there were theologians and philosophers, architects and activists at Gossage's famous gatherings there's no record of anyone from advertising being invited (those other self-publicists, David Ogilvy and Carl Ally were the only two Gossage seems to have got on with).

True to the dictum that to be famous you must be known by those outside your natural constituency, he aimed for a different kind of renown to that enjoyed by the kings of Madison Avenue.

As part of that positioning, he went out of his way to not only distance himself from but also antagonise them.

ZIGGING WHILE OTHERS ZAGGED

In his articles and speeches, he railed against advertising's flaws and failings.

"Is advertising worth saving? From an economic point of view I don't think that most of it is. From an aesthetic point of view I'm damn sure it's not."

"It is a multibillion dollar sledgehammer driving an economy-size thumb tack."

"I don't know a first class brain in the business who has any respect for it."

"I cannot recall the time when our industry has taken a public stand on anything that anybody gave two whoops about."

"I long for the day when it will become a business for a grown man."

"The bulk of intelligence-insulting, banal, tasteless advertising is done by the biggest agencies for the biggest clients."

The people in this "gutless, formless industry" were understandably none-too-happy to be publicly derided - and by one of their own. *Business Week* reported that "he is looked upon as an iconoclast by some peers and as a scoundrel by others".

But in violently zigging while others zagged, he was doing for himself exactly what he'd been doing for his clients: Manipulating the media. Getting noticed. Being different. And saying something interesting that sparked a response.

THE FALL OF THE CURTAIN

Dan Wieden has spoken of Gossage's "searing honesty". And it seems that nothing was off limits. Even if that meant writing about the leukaemia that was killing him.

Nowadays, in the age of the curated self where every experience can be merchandised and monetised, stars and celebrities are swift to share news of their potentially fatal illnesses. For them the "C" in C-word stands for clicks.

But in 1969 death was taboo. Ever the contrarian, Gossage took to *Advertising Age* to discuss his condition and how it was "fatal but not serious". He followed this with "Tell Me, Doctor, Will I be Active to the Last", which actually appeared in *The Atlantic* magazine after he died in July 1969.

In that article, the actor Gossage cheerfully conceded that his response to the news of his illness was lifted directly from the daytime soaps. "It was uncanny, I knew exactly the words they were going to say, and I made the responses automatically. Then it dawned on me why. They had picked it up the same place I had."

As you can see from the photo taken at his 50th birthday party below, the leukaemia had already taken its toll.

Yet, by all accounts, for the next 20 months he gave the most heroic last hurrah. His friend, journalist Warren Hinckle, said it was 'beyond bravery, a final act played with great style but without bravado'.

According to Hinckle, Gossage seemed to enjoy his new role: "Howard made great sport of telling his friends, a performance that was part Shinto ceremony, part Miracle Play, part barroom hijinks. 'Hey, no shit, I'm really going to die', he would insist, somewhat impatiently, to those who failed or refused to accept the technicolor announcement of his own doom."

Looking back Alice Lowe, who was with him "to the last", marvelled at how a man could contemplate his own death with such objectivity.

It seemed he was able to detach himself from The Howard Gossage Show and observe and comment on his own exit from the stage.

In the past he'd been quite capable of putting on a performance just to keep himself alert and amused.

William Walsh, who hired Gossage to write the Whiskey Distillers campaign, told Alice of a lunch meeting they'd had: "I was preoccupied and inattentive and conversation lagged. Then for no apparent reason Gossage brightened and resumed whatever he had been saying with all his usual sparkle. He had caught sight of his own reflection in a wall mirror and was being his own audience ... that day it occurred to me what Gossage really was; a great actor, an actor of genius, who because of some curious quirk was using print instead of a stage. Perhaps it's because in print he could reach the whole world instead of just a theatre full of people."

And that point about using print as his theatre shines the spotlight on why Gossage so remarkable.

Being a great actor made him an ad man of genius. It gave him an acute awareness of the audience's presence. And the need to engage and involve that audience in the show.

He said of other advertising that "it wants to speak to me but is apparently talking to someone over my shoulder. Its gaze is slightly disconcerting, like that of a man with a badly fitting glass eye. Or a politician using a teleprompter."

The latter day equivalent of Paul Feldwick's pedlar, Gossage used every trick at his disposal to catch the audience's eye. The challenging headlines ... the weird layouts ... the wacky promotions ... the eccentric prizes. Having gained their attention he broke down the fourth wall which exists even more in advertising than it does the theatre. And then spoke directly with the people out there.

Thereafter, their response was his applause. Despite his apparent disdain for advertising, the coupons that came back were very important to him. He was proud of the fact that he held the record for the most responsive ads ever to run in the *New Yorker*. And he delighted in reading those responses.

Alice Lowe recalls him "Eagerly rifling through hundreds, sometimes thousands of readers' responses, the campaign creator could not resist snatching one out occasionally to read out loud. 'Listen to this', he would cry happily ... his normally pale face flushed with unaccustomed pink, he interrupted himself with a great burst of uproarious laughter".

Alice could have been describing an actor reading their glowing first night reviews.

HIS LAST AD

Just a few weeks before he died, he took his final bow.

The client was publishing house Harpers & Row, which was promoting: *ABM: An Evaluation of the Decision to Deploy an Anti-Ballistic Missile System.*

It was a deadly serious book, with a serious budget. The client was spending $40,000 on space in the *New York Times*, *Boston Globe*, *Chicago Tribune*, *Washington Post*, *Minneapolis Tribune*, and *Los Angeles Times*, and they'd also shifted the brief to Gossage from their agency of record, Denhard & Stewart.

Once again, Gossage was under pressure. But extremely so this time because his leukaemia was now fatal, and very serious.

However, although exhausted by cancer and crippled by the cortisone he was taking to alleviate his pain, he created an advertisement of epic ambition, with a layout the likes of which no one had seen before, a headline in direct proportion to the issue under discussion and a "call to action" that once more spoke directly to the reader and put "the heat" on the people in power.

Whatever became of back yard fallout shelters? Remember? They were *the* topic for years. It was big business, remember the ads? Banks offered E-Z credit. IBM gave employees interest-free loans. Companies were formed with names like Surviv-All. Clergymen argued the morality of shooting your neighbor if he tried to get in, and TV was filled with dramas on the theme. Remember them? "Life" published details on How to Build Your Own Survival Shelter. And every one of us, for at least a moment, thought maybe it *was* a good idea. Remember? What happened? It was only seven years ago. How many of those back yard shelters still exist, stocked with condensed milk, stale water, and army cots? Are they playrooms now? When did we stop believing we could ever be "safe" in fallout shelters? We were all taken in, for an

instant anyway. It was a mass delusion, but we wanted to believe we could still do *something*. Remember? Well, now, what do you think about the ABM?

Please fill in and mail to Cass Canfield, Harper & Row, Publishers, 49 East 33d Street, N.Y., N.Y. 10016. We will tally the results and forward them to Congress.

I REALLY BELIEVE MY FAMILY AND I WILL BE SAFE ONCE WE PROCEED WITH THE "SAFEGUARD" ABM

YES ☐   NO ☐

Just published, and in your bookstore now:

"ABM: An Evaluation of the Decision to Deploy an Anti-Ballistic Missile System"

BACK IN THE DAYS of back yard fallout shelters, seven years ago, there remained the delusion that each one of us could do something individually to protect our families and ourselves.

Never mind that most of us didn't actually build a shelter, we *considered* it. That showed our vulnerability to "security" appeals right there. And ever since then, whenever the Pentagon announced some new multi-billion dollar "safety" system we tended to go for the "experts' " word that it was just the thing.

It is certainly understandable. A man has got to believe in something. And in this, the nuclear-computer age, the forces that control a man's life or death have been pretty much removed from his *own* decision-making power. The data is *so* complicated and so much of it is classified, how are we to know what to think about it, one way or the other? Most of us laymen haven't yet figured out if it's a good idea to get into airplanes, or how they ever manage to stay up in the air.

With no way even to start thinking intelligently about today's "security" problems, we tend simply not to think about them at all. The result is that our safety is truly in the lap of the gods, or, to put it more accurately, in the lap of the Pentagon.

Experts in high places "with greater access to information" tell us that for our safety we need this or that. And we implicitly give our go-ahead and wind up paying for it besides. Like putting quarters into the insurance machine before getting onto an airplane. It won't keep the plane up, but at least it's doing something.

Which brings us to ABM.

"An anti-missile defense is foolproof. It will give us a seamless garment of security in an age of acute danger."

—AP quote from pro-ABM presentation, May 7, 1969

The ABM (Sentinel-Safeguard) is probably the most complicated electronic system ever attempted.

Each of its elements—missiles, computers, radars—is at the extreme of sophistication for its type. The computer programming alone, for example, presents problems not yet solved even on the theoretical level.

The computers will be asked simultaneously to steer the radars, identify potential targets, predict trajectories, distinguish between warheads and the thousands of possible decoys, eliminate false targets, reject signals from earlier explosions (some of which may be deliberately diversionary), correct for blackout effects, allocate and guide interceptor missiles, and *automatically arm and fire them* if an enemy missile is interpreted as being in range.

All of this must be done continuously and with 100% precision between the time attacking missiles first appear and their moment of impact. That time may be as little as 10 minutes.

The whole operation, in other words, is just too rapid and complex even to allow for human checking or more than a last second okay by the President.

The computer will do the checking itself.

Well. If everyone knew for sure that Safeguard would work, then there might be some (shaky) confidence about turning our lives over to it. But a look at the chart shows the gap between expected performance and actual performance in the case of systems many times less complex than this one. Performance is nearly always below promise, even when there is plenty of time and the possibility for testing.

There is no such margin of error with Safeguard. It must work first time out. There is no reason to believe it will.

The possible consequences of its not working just so may be illustrated by this Newsweek note, December 19, 1960, concerning the Pentagon's previous "security" creation, Ballistic Missile Early Warning System:

"The Air Force disclosed last week that the giant radar picked up a [hostile] *signal, and the 'missile's' position* [30 minutes from a U.S. target] *was instantly flashed on a screen at the underground SAC headquarters in Omaha."*

Fortunately for the world, the reflex to counterstrike, which was supposed to be nearly instantaneous upon sighting of such an enemy missile heading our way, did not operate on this day, simply because the scientists who worked on BMEWS radar, and who supervised and knew its real capabilities had in their hearts no confidence that it had yet been made to work with any reliability. They realized the much too frequent fallibilities of such inventions as these. It is a good thing they did. For as Newsweek concluded:

"The 'missile' that had reflected the radar signal turned out to be the moon."

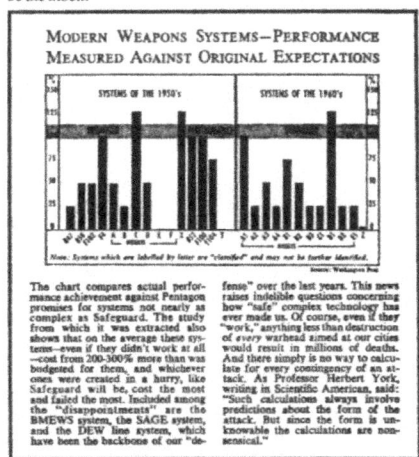

MODERN WEAPONS SYSTEMS—PERFORMANCE MEASURED AGAINST ORIGINAL EXPECTATIONS

The chart compares actual performance achievement against Pentagon promises for systems not nearly as complex as Safeguard. The study from which it was extracted also shows that on the average these systems—even if they didn't work at all—cost from 200-300% more than was budgeted for them, and whichever ones were created in a hurry, like Safeguard will be, cost the most and failed the most. Included among the "disappointments" are the BMEWS system, the SAGE system, and the DEW line system, which have been the backbone of our "defense" over the last years. This news raises indelible questions concerning how "safe" complex technology has ever made us. Of course, even if they "work," anything less than destruction of *every* warhead aimed at our cities would result in millions of deaths. And there simply is no way to calculate for every contingency of an attack. As Professor Herbert York, writing in Scientific American, said: "Such calculations always involve predictions about the form of the attack. But since the form is unknowable the calculations are nonsensical."

Malfunction of such new equipment as BMEWS is more the rule than the exception. And yet now, some scientists at the Pentagon say we should proceed with a far more difficult project, and, what's worse, one that does not allow for ultimate human analysis and control.

Abridged Table of Contents from

"ABM: AN EVALUATION OF THE DECISION TO DEPLOY AN ANTIBALLISTIC MISSILE SYSTEM"

INTRODUCTION
U.S. Senator Edward M. Kennedy

ABM DEPLOYMENT: WHAT'S WRONG WITH IT?
Abram Chayes: *Former Legal Advisor to Department of State, 1961-1964*
Jerome B. Wiesner: *Former Science Advisor to the President, 1961-1964*
George W. Rathjens: *Visiting Professor of Political Science, MIT*
Steven Weinberg: *Professor of Physics, MIT*

MINUTEMAN DEFENSE: WILL IT HELP?
Carl Kaysen: *Director, Institute for Advanced Study*
Bill Moyers: *Former Special Assistant to the President, 1963-1967*

SAFEGUARD SYSTEM: WILL IT WORK?
Leonard S. Rodberg: *Associate Professor of Physics, University of Maryland*
J. C. R. Licklider: *Professor of Electrical Engineering, MIT*
Hans A. Bethe: *Professor of Physics, Cornell University*
Adam Yarmolinsky: *Former Special Assistant to Secretary of Defense, 1961-1964*

STRATEGIC BALANCE: WILL IT BE UPSET?
Marshall D. Shulman: *Director of Russian Institute, Columbia University*
Allen S. Whiting: *Former Chief of Intelligence and Research, Far East, Department of State*
Theodore C. Sorensen: *Former Special Counsel to the President, 1961-1964*

ARMS CONTROL: WILL IT BE SET BACK?
Bernard T. Feld: *Professor of Physics, MIT*
Jeremy J. Stone: *Council of the Federation of American Studies*
Mason Willrich: *Professor of Law, University of Virginia*
Arthur J. Goldberg: *Former Ambassador to United Nations, 1965-1968*

The book also contains extensive notes, a glossary, basic documents, and a summary of the full case against ABM deployment at this time.

At a certain point it is necessary for the people in whose names these creations are introduced to remind government that we do not wish to abdicate our rights of control and approval merely because we don't understand the technology right off. We do understand the consequences.

And simply taking the experts' word, while it may relieve the anxiety (as with back yard fallout shelters), all too often leaves us with the feeling that we've just had one more turn around the track after the rabbit we can never catch.

It is the ultimate conclusion of the authors of "ABM: An Evaluation of the Decision to Deploy an Antiballistic Missile System" that Safeguard, for all its tens of billions of dollars, will produce at best a *false* sense of security, and at worst, an increased prospect for nuclear war.

They explain why, point by point, cutting through the technological rhetoric, demonstrating the distinctions between Pentagon fantasy and simple fact.

The book is, therefore, the first full scale attempt to provide, in lay terms, and while the Congressional debate still rages, the non-Pentagon side of this issue.

You will find it in bookstores now. (Harper & Row clothbound edition, $5.95; New American Library paperback, $.95.)

191

Four weeks after that ad appeared, Alice Lowe got a call from her boss.

"I remember distinctly what he said: 'For the first time in my life Alice, I feel completely free. I've gotten completely out of the advertising business - Jerry Mander's going to be taking care of that - I'll be able to do anything I want from now on.' He was so weak, he could barely whisper."

He died two days later.

The memorial service at the Firehouse was, as you'd imagine, a very theatrical affair. There were prayers from Rabbi Joseph Karasick and Father John Culkin. Then, to reflect Gossage's love of music from both the concert hall and the carnival, a string quartet from the San Francisco Symphony Orchestra and Salvador Padilla's Mariachi Band.

In between were reminicensces from Howard's closest associates: Tom Wolfe, Warren Hinckle, Herb Caen, Gerry Feigen and Father John.

The last word was left to his great friend and collaborator, Stan Freberg.

He said that while Howard's passing would surely be marked by the advertising press it should also have been covered by *Daily Variety*, the entertainment industry trade paper, because, "Inside that pundit suit, Howard was a minimum of 75% showbusiness ham".

The ham would have loved the final flourish.

In the far distance could be heard the approaching strains of a band of Scots pipers. They processed down Osgood Alley, crossed Pacific Avenue and entered the Firehouse, circling slowly and ponderously as they played their lament.

Then, as Alice Lowe remembered, they left as they'd entered, "the sound of their mournful music fading gradually to a whimper. It was a fittingly dramatic close to the afternoon."

And to the life of the great showman, Howard Gossage.

Howard Gossage is dead

Howard Gossage, one of the country's most renowned ad men, died in SF of leukemia. He was 52. He began in radio and went on to start his own agency, Freeman, Mander & Gossage. He was well-known for his successful, innovative campaigns including Qantas ("Win a real live kangaroo") and Eagle Shirts. His recent copy for the latter inspired an article in A/D last month by Dick Feleppa. He also launched the Beethoven sweat-shirt fad. His soft-sell concepts were marked by a penchant for audience participation as in a recent ABM book ad for Harper & Row.

INDEX

ABOUT The AUTHORS

Steve Harrison had his own agency, HTW, which, before he left in 2007, won more Cannes Lions in its discipline than any other in the world. He then wrote "How to do Better Creative Work" which became the most expensive advertising book of all time when trading on amazon at £3,000 a copy. His last book, "Can't Sell, Won't Sell: Advertising, Politics and Culture Wars" was decribed by the IPA as the "most provocative advertising book in years". Steve has already written a biography of Howard Gossage. If you've any thoughts about that book or this one, email him: harrisosteve@googlemail.com

Dave Dye has worked at a lot of agencies, starting in the bad ones back in the 80s, before graduating to the best ones, like Mother, AMV/BBDO and BMP/DDB. He's also founded a few of his own - the Omnicom backed Campbell Doyle Dye, the 'savings' backed DHM and the COVID victim; LOVE or FEAR. Now, he runs the advertising/design boutique TH?NGY. He's won every major global award, several times over. For the last 10 years, he's also run the blog/podcast Stuff From The Loft (davedye.com). He also teaches at ArtCentre in California. You can email him on dave@davedye.com

→ I designed it and found the thoods.
— Dave.

www.ingramcontent.com/pod-product-compliance
Lightning Source LLC
Chambersburg PA
CBHW061305270326
41932CB00029B/3480